MURDER IN THE
NAME OF HONOUR

The True Story of
One Woman's Heroic Fight Against
an Unbelievable Crime

Rana Husseini

ONEWORLD

OXFORD

MURDER IN THE NAME OF HONOUR

First published by Oneworld Publications 2009

A CIP record for this title is available
from the British Library

ISBN-978–1–85168–524–0

Typeset by Jayvee, Trivandrum, India
Cover design by James Nunn
Printed and bound in Great Britain
by Bell & Bain, Glasgow

Oneworld Publications
185 Banbury Road
Oxford OX2 7AR
England
www.oneworld-publications.com

CONTENTS

Foreword by Jane Fonda ix
Introduction xi

1. Murder in Amman   1
2. Interview with a Killer   8
3. Honour as an Excuse   19
4. Bound by Honour   31
5. Excusing Murder   45
6. We Fought the Law ...   51
7. The Royal March for Justice   60
8. Opening the Floodgates   68
9. Changing Attitudes   81
10. Two Steps Back   89
11. A World of Honour   101
12. Love, Honour and Obey   157
13. Chaos in Europe   183
14. Honour in the USA   203
15. The Road to Real Honour   214

Notes 223
Acknowledgements 231
Index 239

FOREWORD
Jane Fonda

As I write this foreword, CNN is broadcasting the footage of a young woman being publicly stoned to death by a lynch mob, while the police just stand by watching. It pains me deeply to live in a world where a Kurdish woman has been killed for falling in love with a man from a different faith. Murders like this, which happen around the world, destroy the honour they are intended to restore. Honour is respect for life. Honour is respect for love. There is no honour in murder.

I first met Rana Husseini in 2005, at an international meeting of women in the media organized by Equality Now with journalists from Algeria, India, Jordan, Kenya, Palestine, Peru and Saudi Arabia. Rana Husseini was being honoured for her groundbreaking work as an investigative reporter for *The Jordan Times*. She had broken the silence on so-called 'honour' killings in Jordan. The stories were devastating, but Rana was utterly inspiring. She is a young woman of courage, committed to the principles of truth and justice, and her writing has sparked a national campaign in Jordan to stop this violence and to hold those responsible for it accountable under the law.

Rana's work is a testament to the power of the pen over the sword, and this book will no doubt be an invaluable contribution to advocacy efforts around the world to end gender-based violence. No country is free from violence against women, and the UN has estimated that one in three women around the world will be beaten or raped in her lifetime. Domestic violence and rape are universal, while other forms of violence take culturally specific forms. Rana's clear, strong voice cuts through the north/south, us/them divides that are so often used to marginalize violence against women in its varied forms.

Breaking the silence is only the first step towards social change. Rana's work has provoked much discussion in Jordan, and it is heartening to know that over time attitudes have started to change and the legal system is beginning to take these 'honour' killings more seriously. In this heated debate, prejudice is plainly exposed and the way in which women are spoken of is all too familiar. Women as property and the sanctity of the hymen, dubbed by Rana as 'the small piece of quasi-mythical flesh' by which women's value is measured, are all too familiar themes that reinforce discrimination against women around the world.

The Universal Declaration of Human Rights starts with the principle that 'all human beings are born free and equal in dignity and rights', a principle universally challenged by violence against women. From the time she came across her first case of 'honour' killing, the murder of a girl by her brother for having been raped by her other brother, Rana Husseini has followed her instinct, guided by her heart and conscience. If enough people read this book, maybe the next time a young woman is being stoned to death for having fallen in love, someone will intervene to save her life.

INTRODUCTION

Imagine your sister or daughter being killed for chewing gum, for laughing at a joke in the street, for wearing make-up or a short skirt, for choosing her own boyfriend/husband or becoming pregnant.

This is what happens to *five thousand women* who are murdered each year in the name of honour; *that's thirteen women every single day*. It is very likely that this figure, calculated by the UN in 2000, is a gross underestimate. Many cases are never reported and many more so-called honour killings are disguised as suicides and disappearances. This is something I know to be true in my home country of Jordan where, according to police and medical officials, there is an average of twenty-five so-called honour killings annually.

A so-called honour killing occurs when a family feels that their female relative has tarnished their reputation by what they loosely term 'immoral behaviour'.[1] The person chosen by the family to carry out the murder (usually male: a brother, father, cousin, paternal uncle or husband) brutally ends their female relative's life to cleanse the family of the 'shame' she brought upon them. The title 'honour killing' is ironic in the extreme because these murders, and the manner in which they are carried out, lack any honour whatsoever.

It was in my capacity as a journalist writing for *The Jordan Times*, Jordan's only English-language daily newspaper, that I had an eye-opening encounter with one such murder that changed my life forever. Thankfully, despite strict state censorship of the media when I started reporting in the mid-1990s, my courageous editors agreed that the story should be published. The resulting article, published on 6 October 1994, appeared under the headline 'Murder in the name of honour'.

I did not know it then, but I had begun a quest that has since become all-consuming and has taken me all over the world. Thanks to the continued support of my editors, I was able to investigate and report on honour killings in depth. As time went on, I gradually realized that while reporting these crimes was a step in the right direction, it was never going to be enough – I had to do something else to end these senseless murders. So I began a sensational campaign to change the law and attitudes in Jordan, a campaign that I, along with many others, have since taken across the world.

This book tells my story so far, from my humble beginnings as a naïve but enthusiastic and stubborn journalist to the campaigns to change Jordanian law, as well as my experiences in other countries in the Middle East, and investigations into so-called honour killings across Europe (especially the UK) as well as the USA. This book is also an evaluation of the current situation around the world in terms of the numbers of honour killings and the laws available to murderers to escape justice. I am sure that many readers will be truly shocked to see just how widespread and out of control this phenomenon is across the world, from the Third World to the First.

Fighting so-called crimes of honour has proved to be a perilous and traumatic journey. My life has been regularly threatened and my reputation is under constant attack. I find myself frequently slandered and libelled. Examples include accusations that I am a 'radical feminist seeking fame' or that I'm a 'western-collaborator intent on tarnishing the delicate fabric of the pure [Jordanian] society'.

Unfortunately, some influential and powerful people, such as MPs, judges, lawyers and policemen, have opposed me and, as extraordinary as it seems, believe that those who claim to have killed in the name of honour deserve lenient punishments, because everyone has the right to protect their family's honour. In my own country, Jordanian law states that those who murder in a passionate frenzy (for example, men who have caught their wives in the embrace of another) deserve mercy. As we shall see, such laws and leniency are by no means unique to Jordan (for example, a similar law is still in place in the UK). Perpetrators are well aware of the sympathy shown by their country's legal system, and abuse it to their advantage. Thus, in many cases, the crimes often have serious hidden intentions far removed from honour – such as the murder of female siblings in order to claim sole inheritance of the family estate. Murders are often meticulously planned by several family members but are then claimed as 'crimes of honour', again far removed from the state of blind anger associated with this crime.

Sometimes all that is needed to incite murder is a deliberate and malicious campaign of gossip. In fact, the majority of so-called honour killings I reported on were based on mere suspicion, something I have since seen repeated in countries across the world. The problem is not restricted to adultery. Generational conflict, teen culture, urbanization and adolescent rebellion are common trigger factors in immigrant communities in European countries as well as the USA.

As I have already mentioned, honour killing is a global phenomenon and takes place in many more countries than most people realize. Besides Afghanistan, Bangladesh, Brazil, Ecuador, Egypt, Palestine, India, Israel, Iraq, Pakistan, Morocco, Turkey, Yemen and Uganda, honour killings occur throughout Europe and the USA. The number of honour killings has been rising in recent years among immigrant communities in Europe, particularly Germany, France, Scandinavia and the UK – and the authorities have been caught napping. For example, British police are currently reviewing more than one hundred murder cases in the belated realization that they may in fact have been so-called honour killings.

Until recently, so-called honour killings have received little attention because they are all too often disguised as a traditional or cultural practice which has to be respected and accepted by everyone. Many people associate them exclusively with Islamic communities, but while some Muslims do murder in the name of honour – and sometimes claim justification through the teachings of Islam – Christians, Hindus, Sikhs and others also maintain traditions and religious justifications that attempt to legitimize honour killings.[2] But crimes of honour are just that: crimes, pure and simple. For me, wherever their roots are supposed to lie, they are nothing to do with tradition, culture or religion. They are all about control – an effective method of regulating the freedom of movement, freedom of expression and sexuality of women. They violate rights to life, liberty and bodily integrity; they violate prohibition of torture or other cruel, inhuman or degrading punishment; the prohibition on slavery; the right to freedom from gender-based discrimination and sexual abuse and exploitation; the right to privacy and to marry and start a family.

I am not a legal, religious, cultural, historical, tribal, social or moral expert, but I am an Arab Muslim woman intent upon living in a sound society where all members benefit from justice, regardless of rank, religion, race or gender. I, like any other citizen of this world, seek to feel safe. I want to live as part of a system in which crimes are seen for what they are, freed of the double standards that mask their heinous nature, and punished with a severity that matches the crime.

CHAPTER 1

Murder in Amman

In summer the temperature in Jordan soars to the unpleasantly high thirties. Across the sweltering capital, those of Amman's citizens who were fortunate enough not to have to make their living on the teeming streets hid away from the sun in the city's many coffee shops.

It was 31 May 1994, the day that Kifaya's mother, uncles and brothers had decided she would die.

In the built-up part of the conservative old city, Kifaya sat, tied to a chair in the kitchen of her family home. The sweets that her older brother, Khalid, had bought earlier to persuade her that everything was all right lay untouched on the counter.

Kifaya's crime was to have allowed herself to be raped by her other brother, Mohammad. She had then been forced by her family secretly to abort his child and had been made to marry a man thirty-four years her senior, whom she had divorced after six miserable months.

She had shamed her family. There was only one solution.

Khalid held a glass to Kifaya's lips, and told her to drink some water. He asked her to recite verses from the Quran and picked up a knife. Kifaya begged for mercy. Outside, the neighbours listened but did nothing as she started to scream.

* * *

'You're a professional,' I muttered to myself. 'Don't worry, you'll know what to say when you get there. Just stay focused, stay focused.'

It was 1 June 1994. I turned off Amman's busy commuter high-way and drove upwards with mounting apprehension towards one of the most impoverished areas of the city.

Jordan's capital, home to two million souls, is always congested, but nowhere more so than in the poorest parts of the city. There's no rail or metro system, and in old Amman, the narrow streets cannot hope to cope with freight trucks, buses and cars.

As I sat behind an ancient truck that coughed exhaust fumes at my battered rust-bucket of a car, I recited the words I'd read in the paper for the umpteenth time that morning. 'Thirty-two-year-old man kills sixteen-year-old sister in Hashemi Shamali. Surrenders to police. Investigations underway.'

I don't know how many times I saw similar four-line stories spread all over the Arabic press. Something told me that I needed to investigate these stories. As a twenty-six-year-old crime journal-ist, I was still somewhat uncertain of myself. I had been working for *The Jordan Times*, the only English-language daily in Jordan, for just nine months.

Journalism had become a career choice almost by accident. My father, a civil engineer, and my mother, a librarian, both supported my dreams of studying Public Relations and Advertising at a US university and so when I won a place at Oklahoma City University in 1987 they were only too happy for me to go.

This was around the time of the first Palestinian uprising, and a reporter called Corky Huffin asked me to write about the intifada (although I hold Jordanian nationality, I am originally Palestinian). I wrote the article and it was published. Corky then asked me to join the university's newspaper since they always needed reporters, so I did and loved it. I wrote about women's sports as I was an athlete myself (I played basketball for Jordan's national team) and then switched majors, focusing on journalism.

During the final semester I worked for the weekly *Oklahoma Gazette*, where I wrote about social issues; I learned how people can make a difference and help each other and how journalism helps them to do this. By the time I returned to Jordan, I knew I wanted to focus on women's issues but had no idea what I was about to get into.

As I drove deeper into the poor neighbourhood, the buildings became shabbier; the road narrowed and the streets soon became jammed with cars forced to a honking crawl as pedestrians spilled from the crowded pavements.

I stopped the car and rolled down the window. A young man was striding purposefully down the road towards me. I called out to him: 'Have you heard about a young girl who's been murdered?'

'Who hasn't?' he replied, pointing back in the direction he'd come. 'Round the corner, close to Omar's barbershop, you'll find her family's house; she was killed there.'

It seemed as though everyone knew. This was, after all, a very crowded neighbourhood where everybody knew everyone else's business. A real-life murder was a sure attention-getter in the absence of other distractions like movie theatres, parks or libraries.

'Do you know why they killed her?' I asked.

He was already walking away. 'Because her brother raped her,' he said casually.

Assuming I'd misheard him (who kills rape victims?), I soon found Omar's barbershop and parked my car. As I got out, a loose paving slab wobbled under the sneakers I'd decided to wear in case I had to run away – I was about to stick my nose in some very private business. My non-traditional baggy T-shirt and loose-fitting jeans also helped me feel more comfortable, although I stuck out like a sore thumb in this conservative part of town.

I pushed the front door halfway open; the smell of stale cigarettes and hair grease overwhelmed me. Through the haze, I saw there were two empty chairs to my left. A fat man, who I assumed was the proprietor from the way he straddled the chair, faced me. Two skinny middle-aged men were slouched on a brown hole-ridden sofa to his left. They were all smoking.

'Assalamu Alaikum,' I said.

'Wa Alaikum Assalam,' they chorused.

'A young girl was murdered around here, have you heard about this?'

At this the two men looked at each other and both sat up. 'Yes,' one of the skinnier ones said. 'Who told you?' he asked, suspiciously.

'It was in the paper this morning.' I pulled out the page I had torn from the newspaper and showed it to them while I remained on the doorstep.

'It's *already* made the papers?' This development was apparently unwelcome. The barber took a drag of his cigarette and asked, 'Who are you and why do you want to know?'

I declared confidently that I was a crime reporter working for *The Jordan Times*. Inside I was a bag of nerves. Media coverage only serves to keep any 'scandal' committed by the victim of the so-called honour crime alive, which is why so few reporters – in fact, no reporters whatsoever – investigated honour killings.

They didn't respond, so I stepped through the door and sat on the sofa next to the two men. Hoping to win their confidence and encourage them to speak to me about the murder, I chatted with them casually about my job, my education in the USA, journalism, the country and politics.

Our chat revealed that the two men on the couch were her uncles. 'Kifaya was not a good girl,' one of them said, as if killing a 'bad girl' was acceptable.

Kifaya. Suddenly, my story had a name.

I stayed and we talked some more. Every now and again I asked why Kifaya had been killed, until one of the uncles said, 'She was raped by Mohammad, her brother. That's why she was killed.'

I straightened my back, and placed my notebook on my lap, not sure what to say next.

Eventually I said, 'Why was she punished and not her brother? Why didn't Kifaya's family discipline him instead?'

One of the uncles looked worried. 'Do you think we killed the wrong person?'

Her other uncle answered quickly, 'Relax. We did the right thing.'

I struggled to contain my fury. It was as if they were speaking about a sheep. These men were part of the conspiracy. Her body not yet cold, yet here they were – on a sofa in a barbershop chatting with the owner and smoking cigarettes.

'She seduced her brother. She tarnished the family's honour and deserved to die,' the skinnier uncle declared.

I sighed at his stupidity. Jordanian society blames women for everything: for being raped, for being harassed on the streets, for philandering husbands, for husbands who divorce them, for bearing a child of the wrong gender – the list is endless.

'But why would she choose to sleep with her brother? If she wanted to sleep with a man, surely, she would not choose to sleep with her brother.'

Instead of answering my question, the barber stood up and said, 'Why do you care for such a story?'

'Why are you dressed like this?' one of the uncles asked, pulling an expression of disgust at my jeans and T-shirt.

'Why are you in our neighbourhood?' the other continued. 'You do not belong here. You have become westernized in America. You forget where you are now.'

I was clearly 'not a good girl'. I thanked them and quickly left.

Outside, I looked at the houses stacked haphazardly on top of and overlapping each other. Kifaya's wasn't hard to find. Even the kids playing in the street could point me to the three-storey house situated at the end of the road. I looked at it with pain in my heart.

'Why did they kill you?' I asked myself. 'You were only sixteen.'

I headed towards her neighbours; a shabby house where a newly-wed couple lived. They offered me tea and told me what they saw.

They had heard Kifaya scream and beg for mercy. They had seen her brother Khalid standing outside his house holding the blood-stained knife and shouting, 'I have cleansed my family's honour.'

His family was waiting to congratulate him.

Khalid then went to the nearest police station and turned himself in, claiming to have killed Kifaya to cleanse the honour of his family.

I arrived back at the newspaper offices frustrated and exhausted. I needed to exorcize this experience from my system by telling my story to my editor, Jennifer Hamarneh. Jennifer had arrived at *The Jordan Times* a couple of years before me. She was a tough editor and would often get mad when I made mistakes. But she taught me so much; though at times it was tough, I took on board what she was telling me in a positive way; I certainly didn't make the same mistake twice.

'I don't want Kifaya's murder to be just another crime story; I want so-called honour killings to become a national issue.'

Jennifer looked at me like she was weighing me up. 'Tell the story, we'll make space for it.'

I think Jennifer knew then that Kifaya's story was going to change my life for good. In order to maintain objectivity, I had to suppress my great anger and sadness as I wrote, hoping that someone important, that any of our readers, would read it and would feel inspired to take action.

The following day my story appeared on page three with a headline that read: 'Victim of incestuous rape killed by second brother'.

The next morning George Hawatmeh, my former editor-in-chief, took a call from a Jordanian woman, who described herself as an intellectual who worked in an official position. George was also a strong believer in the fight against so-called honour crimes and was immediately thrilled at the thought that the caller was also outraged at this appalling murder and wanted to voice her objection. Perhaps she wanted to use her influential post to exert some pressure on the government to help prosecute all those involved in Kifaya's murder.

But his hopes were immediately dashed. She shouted down the phone at George: 'You should stop Rana Husseini from reporting these crimes because they do not exist in Jordan! This does not happen in our society!'

Luckily, George and Jennifer disagreed and supported me when I told them I wanted to become the voice of these women whose lives have been wiped out and every record of their existence destroyed by their family. I would expose each and every murder I heard about.

I didn't realize then quite how busy I was going to be.

CHAPTER 2

Interview with a Killer

As I began to write more and more about honour killings, with the support of opinion writers and my editors, so our postbags began to swell. The readers of *The Jordan Times* are mostly the affluent English-speaking minority, many of whom were already aware of violence against women, but remained apathetic until we started reporting the cases in depth.

At the start of each week I'd arrive at work to find my own in-box filled with threatening letters. A typical one said, 'If you don't stop reporting these murders, I will send someone to visit you at your home or workplace.'

Another memorable warning read: 'I'm going to clean my hunting rifle; it's the season for hunting coloured birds.' Oddly enough, far from deterring me, threats like these made me all the more determined to carry on. I had found my life's mission.

As well as the threats, our postbags also began to fill with letters of support from readers, expressing their anger and outrage about the killing of innocent women and the leniency shown to killers for murder in the first degree.

But even some supporters, friends and colleagues were discouraging, and argued that we were wasting our time with a lost cause. 'No one will listen to you,' one friend told me. 'Nothing ever changes in this country.' Many urged me instead to write about politics because it was 'more rewarding' and because achieving social change was next to impossible.

I listened, but simply followed my heart and my conscience. These women needed a voice. They were lost souls, buried without ceremony in unmarked graves; it was as if they'd never existed. People needed to know that they had lived, loved and died in the cruellest manner possible. They needed to know who had murdered them and why their killers had gone unpunished.

I first met Sarhan in 1999, when CNN decided to film a documentary about so-called honour crimes in Jordan and approached me to be part of it. The programme makers wanted to interview prisoners who had killed their female relatives to cleanse their family honour, or who were in prison awaiting a court verdict.

I agreed immediately. Back then it was almost impossible for a Jordanian reporter to be allowed to interview prisoners at all. This restriction, however, did not apply to the majority of foreign media representatives who were welcome to film inside prisons and interview any inmate they wanted. The double standards towards the two different media bodies still apply on occasion in other bureaucratic institutions around the country.

It was decided that the shoot was to take place at the Jweideh Correctional and Rehabilitation Centre, home to over a thousand men waiting to be tried for crimes ranging from robbery to first-degree murder.

After going through several security checks, the CNN crew and I were ushered into a small, windowless room filled with half-a-dozen prison guards and officials in civilian clothes. The crew began setting up their equipment and adjusting their cameras. I was directed to sit on a chair. The guards kept eyeing me, wondering what was so special about me that CNN wanted me on their programme.

A few minutes later, a well-built man in his late twenties entered the room, accompanied by several guards who seated him opposite me.

One of the prison officials said, 'This is Sarhan, he killed his sister to cleanse his honour.'

Oddly, Sarhan had a wide smile on his face, apparently welcoming the attention.

His sister, Yasmin, had been raped by her brother-in-law. Knowing full well the consequences of such a crime, she had turned herself in to the police, rather than risk the wrath of her family.

Sarhan headed to the police station the following day and tried to bail out his sister. His request was refused; the police thought he might kill her because she had lost her virginity.

Sarhan went to a friend's house and stayed there for a couple of days. When he returned home, he found his sister in the living room. Without uttering a word he shot her four times with an unlicensed gun and turned himself in.

The minute we made eye contact, I felt rage beginning to boil inside me. I tried hard to suppress it; I wanted to remain professional. I didn't want to get emotionally involved, not now.

'I killed her because she was no longer a virgin,' he told me. 'She made a mistake, willingly or not. It is better that one person dies than the whole family of shame and disgrace. It is like a box of apples. If you have one rotten apple would you keep it or get rid of it? I just got rid of it.'

When I challenged Sarhan by pointing out that his act contradicted the teachings of Islam and was punishable by God, he said, 'I know that killing my sister is against Islam and it angered God, but I had to do what I had to do and I will answer to God when the time comes.'

He added: 'People refused to talk with us. They told us to go cleanse our honour; then we were allowed to talk with them. Death is the only solution to end disgrace ... Even if we had wed my sister society would not stop talking. They only stopped talking when she is dead.'

The story didn't end there. A few weeks later I was covering a high-profile case of a Jordanian teenager who killed his entire family because, he said, of the pressure they were putting on him to pass his school exams.

I was at court when I noticed a familiar face among the crowd. It was Sarhan! I could not even guess why he was a free man after such a short time in prison.

I found a seat next to him on the bench. He flashed the same smile he gave me during our interview. When the court adjourned for a ten-minute break, I was able to exchange a few words with him.

'What are you doing here? Who wants to be back in the court-room where he was tried?' I asked him. He told me proudly that he had returned to offer support to a defendant with whom he had struck up a friendship during his incarceration.

I asked him how he ended up receiving such a lenient penalty when the facts of his sister's case were clear; it was a premeditated murder. Sarhan explained he took the advice of one of the officials who questioned him after he had turned himself in. Sarhan told the investigator in his initial testimony that he decided to kill his sister after learning that she was no longer a virgin. He said he asked his family to bail her out and that he waited for them to bring her home, which they did. The minute she walked in, he shot her to death.

The investigator informed him that if he insisted on this version then he might face life imprisonment and advised him to change his story to say he was taken by surprise by his sister's rape and the loss of her virginity, in order to get the lightest sentence possible. His lawyer gave him the same advice when the case was about to be heard in court.

Sarhan's confession meant that his father was an accomplice – a fact that was nowhere to be found in the verdict or in the charge sheet.

'I took the stand and told the judges that I had to kill my sister, because if I did not kill her, it would have been like killing more than a thousand men from my tribe.'

I told him this was impossible. How could a court accept such an argument?

After the court session had finished, I followed Sarhan outside. Again, I asked him why he killed her. Again, I pointed out that she had been raped. She was not at fault. He repeated what he had already told me; that she had to die because she had lost her virginity.

He said that he sat with his father, his mother, his uncles and around eight hundred men of his tribe and they had reached this consensus together. 'If I hadn't killed her, people would look down on me. Once she was raped, she was no longer a girl. My only alternative was to kill her. Death is the only way to erase shame.'

He also told me that his family and relatives visited him in prison to congratulate him on the act. Nevertheless, he did indicate that he was not entirely comfortable with what he'd done and told me he'd been 'forced' to kill his sister, whom he grew up with and loved deeply.

'I know my sister was killed unjustly but what can I do? This is how society thinks. Nobody really wants to kill his own sister,' he said.

I asked him why Yasmin's rapist was neither similarly punished nor questioned by his family. Sarhan said his brother-in-law had vanished. He insisted that if he found him he would kill him as well.

During the course of our conversation, I asked Sarhan how long his sentence was.

'One month for possession of an unregistered firearm and six months for the misdemeanour.'

I sat in shock. Misdemeanour?!

Sarhan had pleaded guilty to manslaughter and possessing an unlicensed gun during the trial, but the court decided that he did in fact 'benefit from a reduction in penalty because he committed his crime in a fit of fury.'

'Sarhan lost his temper and killed his sister in a moment of extreme rage after learning she was no longer a virgin. This was proven by the medical report,' the court verdict said. The court considered the girl's loss of her virginity a crime – even though it was clearly recorded by the court that she was raped. This lenience was made possible by Article 98 of the Penal Code which permits those acting in a 'fit of fury' to benefit from reduced penalties.

I couldn't understand the verdict. I immediately sought out one of the tribunal's three judges. Many judges had already heard of me and I had managed to build up relationships with some of them, and so one of them agreed to an interview. I had to be extremely careful about how I discussed any issue with the members of the judiciary; as a rule, no doubting, blaming or questioning was allowed. Judges were and still are considered to be among the most respected authorities in the kingdom. It was going to be extremely difficult for me to hold my tongue.

The judge was welcoming, and ordered us some mint tea. As soon as it had been poured I took a deep breath and started the interview. 'How do you explain that Sarhan received only six months when the case clearly does not qualify under the fit of fury clause as stipulated in Article 98 of the Penal Code? The girl was raped and it was not her fault,' I said. Yasmin had turned herself in to the police for protection. Before the authorities released her, her father signed a guarantee that she would not be harmed. Obviously – to me, at least – the 'fit of fury' argument should not apply in the court's consideration of the case, since, plainly, the murder was planned and coldly executed.

The judge took a sip of mint tea. 'The rape happened within the family, so it was clearly a family affair. Sarhan killed his sister after family encouragement, so this murder was a product of our culture.'

'But what about Yasmin? Who should then defend her? She was also a victim. Was her life worth nothing?'

The judge looked at me and said nothing. For a fleeting second, I felt that my argument had had an impact on him. But it was time for me to leave; the judge told me he was a busy man. I had pushed too hard.

Inam Asha, a social worker and activist who had seen Yasmin at the police station, offered me further details. The head of the station told her about the interrogation that took place. Yasmin had arrived at the station with her brother-in-law, the rapist, and he had asked her to claim that someone else raped her to cover up his crime. Yasmin tried to obey but because she was scared she kept getting the story wrong. Finally, after one of the interrogators slapped her across the face, she collapsed and told the truth.

My courtroom encounter with Sarhan was not the last. He was repeatedly interviewed by many local and international media agencies, some of which I worked for as a mediator. On one occasion, after Sarhan had finished an interview, I asked him if he regretted what he had done. He said that the murder had ruined his life. Today, he said, no woman wants to marry him. He had tried to seek the hand of eleven women in marriage, but they all refused, including a cousin whose father had encouraged him to kill his sister.

'They all refused for fear that I might kill them or my daughters one day. But if I were put in the same situation again I would kill my sister and any other sister who goes through the same thing. This is our society, this is how we are brought up and it will never change.'

He nostalgically told me he was treated as a hero in prison. 'All the men who were with me for the same reason in prison were treated as heroes by everybody.' Once he was back in the real world, he was ignored and felt worthless.

Sarhan kept telling me how much he loved his sister, even though he ended her life. 'She was so close to me. She was the one who resembled me the most. I had to kill her, I had no other choice.

This is what our society wants. It is better to sacrifice one soul than to sacrifice my whole family.'

But he insisted his sibling died unjustly. 'I am sure of that fact. No one wants to be the one to kill his sister, but traditions and society inflict things on us that we really do not want to do. If society would not have shunned us after her rape, we would not have killed her and instead locked her inside the house until she died or someone married her.'

Sarhan's family's promises of rewarding him and helping him out for killing his sister were never fulfilled. He has been unable to find regular work and instead does odd jobs every now and then.

In one of our most recent interviews, he told me, 'To be honest with you, Rana, I am scared to have female children because society is harsh and I have a feeling that I might want to bury my female daughter because this is what I would feel is right… I wish my other sister would get married quickly because women are a source of concern. If something goes wrong, they do not pay the price; we do.'

He also acknowledged that his lenient punishment would encourage him and other males to murder again in the name of honour.

'If the state amends the law to execute men who kill their female relatives or lock us behind bars for good, I do not think that any family would venture and push her male relative to kill. No family wants to see its male relative executed or locked up for good.'

His final comment to me was, 'I hope that the situation will change because I alone cannot change or fix things in my society. My whole society has to change.'

Even Khalid, who admitted to murdering Kifaya, received a lenient sentence of seven-and-a-half years and was released for good behaviour two years early. I only found out by accident when I returned to the scene of the crime to try and speak to Kifaya's father. They weren't there but the neighbours told me that Khalid was living on the first floor of their three-storey building. Feelings of anger and excitement flowed through my veins as I climbed the stairs and knocked on his door.

The door opened slowly and a short, tired-looking man in his mid-thirties asked me who I was. He invited me into the tiny one-room flat. Inside, he had mattresses spread out on the floor and so I chose a small one and sat on it. Khalid called his wife and asked her to make us some tea.

I started by asking him about his days in prison. 'All my cell-mates sympathized with me and treated me as a champion. All the men who were in the prison for killing their sisters or female relatives were treated as champions.'

He told me he realized that what he did was against the Sharia (Islamic law), 'but society is stronger than me or religion. I had to kill her to preserve the family's honour. Society imposes rules on us and I did it to please society. No one was talking to me in the street. We live in a backward society that imposes backward ideas on our lives.'

He also told me bitterly that he suffered even though he was treated as a hero in prison. 'It was a tough experience that I had to go through. I have four children that I have been deprived of being with for over five years and now I am trying to compensate for these lost years.'

'Do you regret killing your sister and if you were put in the same situation again would you kill her?'

His answer was similar to many I would hear from killers I inter-viewed over the coming years.

'No, I do not regret killing Kifaya. But if I went back in time, I would not kill my sister. I would tie her up like a sheep in the house until she either died or someone married her. I have wasted enough of my life in prison and I would not repeat the same mistake.'

His words made me realize that Khalid was, like his sister, but to a lesser extent, a victim of his own society; a victim of ancient and unfair traditions that turned a normal human being into a killer.

Three years after Kifaya's murder, I found her father. I had been planning to do a follow-up story on her family but hadn't held out much hope of finding them in the same area. I knocked on the door and it was opened slowly, revealing a white-haired and sad-faced man in his mid-fifties. He invited us in, confirming in a sorrowful voice, 'Yes, I am her father'.

He ushered us into the sparsely furnished living room. A small coffee table was surrounded by mattresses where we sat. Kifaya's father called one of his daughters and asked her to make us tea.

'I am against what they did,' he told me. 'I would never have allowed anyone to kill my daughter, no matter what. Damn them for taking such a decision.'

At the time of the murder, he was working in the USA. 'I immediately returned to Jordan when I heard that my daughter had been killed. I could not believe it. I did not expect them to kill her. They did it because they were jealous of me living and working in the US.' He laughed bitterly and told me, 'You should see the kind of life I had in the US they were so envious of. I worked the dirty jobs that most immigrants take – as a garbage collector, a mechanic, a grass-cutter.'

I felt his bitterness as he talked. He told me that his wife, Kifaya's mother, died of cancer six months after her daughter's murder.

'Kifaya's mother had a hand in her death,' he added.

I was startled. 'What do you mean?' I asked him quickly.

'Her mother helped plot her murder along with her uncles,' he explained.

I screamed, 'But why?' He couldn't give me an answer. I thought that maybe she had no choice because they might have killed her as well had she not helped.

One of Kifaya's sisters offered me a small glass of tea. Her two siblings sat quietly next to their father. I asked him about Mohammad, the brother who raped Kifaya. 'Let him rot in prison.

I have no sympathy for him. I do not want to see him ever again in my life.'

I then asked for his permission to discuss Kifaya's murder with his three daughters. The eldest sister, who was fifteen at the time of the murder, said Kifaya did not deserve to be killed and Mohammad was to blame for all the misery they had endured since her death.

The middle-aged sister, who was thirteen at the time, was undecided; she did not know what to think. The youngest sister, twelve at the time of the murder, was the most critical of her sister's actions. She blamed Kifaya for everything that had since gone wrong and accused her of destroying the stability of their family. She told me Kifaya had ruined her father and that both brothers were in jail because of her.

I asked the older sister if they had a photo of Kifaya. I just wanted to see her face and see what she looked like. I wanted to read her features, to try and get to know her, to establish her identity.

'We don't have any photos of Kifaya. Her uncles burned them all.'

It was as if she had never existed.

CHAPTER 3

Honour as an Excuse

Zarqa, about thirty kilometres north of Amman, is Jordan's industrial capital. It sits on the edge of the great eastern desert that stretches all the way to Iraq and Saudi Arabia. Founded in the 1920s, the large town is home to Jordan's main oil refinery as well as several military bases. Together, they have turned the river black.

In the autumn of 1995, Zarqa's market square was packed with people, vehicles and goods as usual. Traders competed with the old trucks to be heard and shoppers shouted to each other as they discussed the wares, competing in the din.

Suddenly, a window in a residential house above the square shattered. Stunned shoppers screamed as they saw a young woman plunge twenty feet through a shop awning, landing headfirst on the pavement. Still conscious, she fought to stand, but, badly concussed, she swayed and half-collapsed, half-sat down in the street.

A horrified shopkeeper who had rushed outside recognized the young woman. Her name was Kifaya and she was twenty-three years old. He looked up at the window and saw her brother Mohammad, shouting at the fallen woman. He knew Mohammad well; everyone knew him to be a troublemaker who had been in and out of prison for various petty crimes. He held a pistol in his hand. People thronging in the busy street screamed and ran for cover as he fired; the first three bullets missed their target, ricocheting off the road.

The shopkeeper started to run to help Kifaya, but he was too late. The fourth bullet was deadly. It struck her in the head.

*   *   *

On 30 December 1995, I went to the Criminal Court as part of my routine tour looking for new verdicts. Most verdicts were usually published at the end of each month. I knocked and entered the office of one of the judges with whom I had become friendly.

'Anything interesting coming up?' I asked.

He told me there was a much bigger story than anything happening in his court that day. 'I just heard from one of our criminal prosecutors that a thirty-eight-year-old man shot and killed his two sisters in Zarqa and then fled before turning himself in the following day.'

'Is it related to family honour?'

The judge nodded. There was something about this case that was unusual. Killers who struck in the name of honour normally turned themselves in immediately, proud of what they had done. I asked the judge why he thought this man had waited a day.

He said he was told that the killer sounded confused and scared and had run to a friend's house to hide. He had spent the night there before his friend persuaded the murderer to turn himself in.

The next day the killer handed investigators the gun he'd used and re-enacted the crime in front of the prosecutor and other officials. The only other thing the judge knew was that the murderer had claimed he'd found a 'strange man' in his sister's house.

I thanked him and said I would head to Zarqa to check out the story. Next I called Widad Adas, my close friend who is a researcher, hoping she'd want to join me. I was very happy to hear that she did.

Zarqa is less westernized and more conservative than many places in Jordan. My T-shirt would have attracted angry responses there, so this time I wore long sleeves, which made the midday heat all the more intense. I was directed to the crime scene almost immediately with no question.

I spoke to a man in his fifties who owned a vegetable shop and who knew the murder victims, Kifaya and her older sister Nadia, who was thirty-two. 'Sure, they were killed by their brother, Mohammad, a real troublemaker that one,' he told me as he heaved crates of vegetables round his store. 'I saw it happen with my own eyes.' He pointed to a building exactly opposite his shop. 'Kifaya fell from that window.'

'Was it an honour killing?' I asked.

'It had nothing to do with "honour". Nadia and Kifaya were regular customers of mine. They were killed for their inheritance. Those poor women were totally innocent. Everyone here knows this is the truth.'

I asked him if the police and the investigators knew this. He said he had no idea but insisted everyone in the neighbourhood knew that these two women were 'innocent of any wrong doing'.

'Kifaya's brother was a good shooter, he used to be a security officer.' He looked down at the ground, his eyes wet. 'It was only later that I found out he'd killed Nadia too.'

I thanked him and we headed to the shop next door where we spoke to a thirty-year-old woman. 'I fainted when the bullet hit Kifaya in the head,' she told me.

She also stressed that Kifaya and Nadia had good reputations in the neighbourhood, while their brother, Mohammad, had a criminal record. 'He was known to be a troublemaker and had been in jail.'

She told me she heard that Mohammad killed his sisters because 'Nadia was married to a man without the knowledge of her brother, and when he learned about it, he killed them.'

'But everyone knew that Mohammad often quarrelled with his two sisters over their share of the inheritance. He wanted them to give their share up to him.'

Several other shopkeepers repeated a similar story as we walked from one side of the square to the other.

The following day I went to the chief prosecutor's office; he was a man I knew and got on with quite well. When I asked him about the murder of the two sisters, he confidently said, 'It is a crime of honour. The suspect killed his two sisters because he found a strange man in the house.'

He made no mention of the inheritance issue or the alleged 'secret marriage'. I was surprised that while the inheritance story was the talk of the community, the chief prosecutor had no knowledge of it.

I excitedly told him about my own investigation, believing that he would instruct his investigators to act on this new and important information. Instead, he looked at me benignly and, with a calm smile, he asked, 'Why do you care for such small and minor cases? Forget about this story. It is not important; you're wasting your time.'

I couldn't believe it. My information should have transformed the investigation.

Instead, Mohammad was charged with the manslaughter of his sisters after finding a strange man in the house. As expected, the court said the defendant benefited from a reduction in penalty as stipulated in Article 98 of the Penal Code because he 'committed his crime in a fit of fury to cleanse his family's honour'. He was also entitled to a reduction because his family dropped the charges against him.

Mohammad claimed that on the morning of the incident he stopped by the house to pick up his mother. After she came down, she realized she had forgotten to bring something from the house. Mohammad offered to get it for her. He climbed the stairs to the apartment and knocked on the door. His sisters took a while to answer. When they did answer, they looked scared and confused. He became suspicious, searched the house and found a strange man inside. The man pushed him aside and fled, Mohammad said. He claimed he tried to catch up with him, but failed. Instead, he returned to the apartment to face his two sisters.

He claimed in court that Kifaya told him 'this man is not mine'. Mohammad drew a gun he was carrying, shot his sister Nadia in the head and chest and then went after his other sister, Kifaya. Kifaya jumped out of the window through the glass. Mohammad confirmed that he fired at her from the window.

The court said it relied in its ruling on Mohammad's testimony (there were no witnesses who spoke against him) and the testimony of a neighbour who told the authorities he overheard the argument. He said he heard the footsteps of a man descending the stairs quickly, although he did not see anyone.

There was no testimony from a witness or family member mentioning the inheritance. There was no mention of any stranger leaving the apartment building on the day of the incident either, apart from the neighbour who only claimed to have heard footsteps.

The prosecution didn't question the defendant on why he chose to kill his two sisters instead of going after the man allegedly found in their room. It would have been much easier for Mohammad to run to the door and ask people in the busy market to help him capture the man. The court didn't even ask Mohammad if the stranger could have been an intruder who broke in to the house.

Mohammad was sentenced to one year in prison.

I was so frustrated by the verdict; people are given the same sentence for trying to cash a bad cheque, and a longer sentence for robbery. I could not sleep; I became obsessed. I told Kifaya's and Nadia's story to everyone I knew and made it the topic of every conversation. An influential official from the same tribe as the killer confirmed the story about the inheritance, adding that Mohammad had good connections that helped get him off the hook.

*   *   *

A few weeks later, I travelled to the scene of yet another murder, this time where a man had shot his twenty-nine-year-old sister dead. He said she was a Christian and had planned to marry a Muslim man. The real reason was that he wanted to take over the flat her fiancé had given to her and move into it with his mother.

This time, because the woman's fiancé was influential, the killer ended up receiving a fifteen-year prison term but this was reduced by half after his mother dropped the charges against him.

A police officer who visited the crime scene told me the victim was sitting on the couch talking to her brother and brushing her hair when he shot her five times in the head from behind. 'I'll never forget. When we arrived she was still sitting on the couch, and the brush was still hanging in her hair.'

*   *   *

All her life, twenty-three-year-old Rania had been told by her parents that she would grow up to marry her cousin. But when she went to university, she met an Iraqi student named Khaled and they fell in love.

In June 1997, unable to face marriage to her cousin, for whom she felt nothing except a normal familial bond, she ran away from home just a few days before their wedding and moved in with Khaled.

A couple of months after fleeing her home, Jordanian Television broadcast a live programme about honour crimes. The presenter read out a heartbreaking letter Rania had sent to the station in which she asked for her family's forgiveness and understanding.

In the letter, Rania assured her family the man she fled with was not the reason why she did not want to marry her cousin. She did not love her cousin and thought of him as a brother. She wrote that she had tried to convince her uncle and cousin to drop the idea but they refused.

Rania said her cousin told her that she had been meant to be his wife ever since they were children and that 'When you marry me you will learn to love me.'

'I do not love my cousin,' she wrote. 'You, my mother, father, brothers and sisters forced me to run away … you exerted every pressure possible to force me to marry my cousin, knowing that I do not want to be with him.'

She appealed to her mother for help because she felt their bond was especially close:

Dear Mom, I am lost in the dark with no one next to me. Please do not say goodbye. My beloved mother, extend your hand to me and save me from my ordeal … I love and miss you mother … I tell you this with tears in my eyes.

Father, mother, brothers and sisters … you are all dear to me and I need you … I am ready to return home this moment but I want a promise from you that you will not force me to marry my cousin … kill me if you want because I do not care about my life.

Her father called the television station, promising that they would not harm their daughter, that all they wanted was for her to return home, and that the wedding plans had been shelved. Her father spoke on the programme, saying, 'I am urging you from a father's heart that is bleeding tears and blood over your absence, come home and God and I will forgive you. I will do whatever you wish even if it costs me dear.'

One of her aunts also called the programme and asked Rania to return home because 'her parents were worried about her and had forgiven her.'

A joyful Rania agreed to meet her family at a police station, where she was handed over to her father who had signed a JD5,000 (US $7,000) bond that guaranteed he would not harm his daughter. 'Just hand her over to me and I will take good care of her … I will protect her,' her father said.

Two weeks later, Rania's two aunts told her they'd taken pity on her and had arranged a secret meeting with Khaled. As they walked near some railway lines, the aunts suddenly ran off. Instead of finding Khaled, Rania saw her seventeen-year-old brother Rami waiting for her. He pulled out a pistol and shot her four times. After she fell, he fired a fifth bullet point-blank through her forehead.

Medical examinations indicated that Rania was still a virgin. Rania, an innocent child, had been betrayed by the closest members of her family. As Rania's brother was a minor, he was tried at a juvenile court. Her father, who was out of the country, dropped the charges. Rami was sentenced to six months.

I was absolutely outraged by this story. I was also dumbfounded at the amount of criticism I received as a result; newspaper columnists writing for other papers said I was a sensationalist damaging Jordan's reputation in the eyes of the world. I had a growing sense of frustration that I was not helping to change anything at all.

A massive problem for women who felt their lives might be in danger was that they had nowhere safe to run. Once they left the family home they were on their own and were unlikely to receive help from other people, lest they be tarred with the same brush of dishonour. There was, however, (and still is) one extraordinary place I visited that did protect women – but in a way that was deeply and tragically flawed.

In the summer of 1995, twenty-three-year-old Inas eloped with her lover, a talented musician with whom she had been in love for some time. They came from a remote rural area of Jordan, where Inas's strictly conservative family had insisted that she marry her cousin – but she found him repellent.

They decided to escape to Syria where they planned to marry and settle down. Before sunrise on the appointed day, the lovers sneaked quietly from their homes and headed for the border.

Inas's uncle was waiting for them. Levelling his gun, he fired repeatedly at his niece, reloading and firing a total of twenty-two rounds before border guards overpowered him.

Inas was hit in her shoulders, arms, legs and chest; she was rushed to a government hospital where, thanks to her incredibly strong desire to live and the doctors' great surgical skill, she pulled through. Five months later, after a series of lengthy and painful operations, the doctors proclaimed her recovered.

Her lover, who was unharmed, was arrested, tried and imprisoned for two years for the crime of adultery.

Her uncle was also sentenced to two years.

And what of Inas, the would-be murder victim?

After Inas had recovered, she was sent to prison. She would still be there long after her would-be murderer was released.

I first met Inas when I visited Jweideh Correctional and Rehabilitation Centre for Women in 1997, two years after her uncle tried to murder her, when he was already a free man. Located about thirty kilometres south-east of Amman, the white, box-like fortress houses up to eight hundred female inmates.

During this visit I was told that around twenty to twenty-five women were detained, many for indefinite periods and with no official charges, under what the government calls 'protective custody' or 'administrative detention'. These women are kept in prison out of fear their families might kill them for violating their families' honour.

There are no accurate statistics on how many women live in prison in Jordan for their own protection. In July 2003, Hana Afgani, the police major in charge of the Jweideh Centre, told Human Rights Watch that ninety-seven inmates were administrative detainees.

Many of these women have been in prison for over a decade. They have wasted their precious youth in tiny cells, mixing with real criminals, because they might be killed if released.

The prison director told me that some had been involved in 'adulterous and immoral' relations; others became pregnant out of wedlock, failed virginity tests, had run away from home after discovering their families were plotting to kill them; and some had survived attempts on their lives by brothers, fathers and uncles.

Inescapable as Colditz, there remain only two ways out of Jweideh for those women in 'protective custody':

1. An immediate male relative visits the prison and asks for his sister/daughter to be freed. He has to sign a guarantee worth $7,000 that he will not harm her.

2. A male bidder, typically an old man looking for companions, visits the prison and asks to marry any woman prepared to be released into his custody.

To my amazement, I witnessed the second option during this, my first visit to Jweideh. A withered old man in his seventies joined me in the director's office and informed her that he desired to marry any woman in protective custody if she was willing to take care of his children and land.

The director summoned one of the female inmates and informed her of the deal. She agreed and was released.

After this incident, a prison warden directed me to the special section where these women were housed. As we chatted, a typical comment was: 'It does not matter if I am in or out of prison. I am dead either way.' Many had lost all ambition; they no longer desired anything, not even their freedom. 'My family never comes to visit me. They never discuss my affairs with anyone. I am dead to them.'

Inas was different, however. The minute she entered the room dressed in the light blue prison uniform and walked confidently towards me, her eyes gleamed with hope, intelligence and determination. She told me she spent her nights dreaming of what she would do when she won her freedom; she did not and would not accept that she might never be freed. She showed me the pink and white lumpy bullet scars dotted on her arm and leg. I asked her whether her lover was hurt. Inas told me he escaped unharmed because her uncle fired only at her.

Inas was serving an indefinite prison term with no official charge lodged against her. Every day she hoped that her family would forgive her; that it would be her last night in jail. Since the shooting, she had heard nothing. 'They never tried to get in touch with me. To them I no longer existed.' The only time Inas's family visited her in prison was when they tried to convince her to drop the charges against her uncle so that he would get a reduced sentence. Inas agreed in the hope that her family would forgive her.

Nonetheless, despite everything, Inas told me, to my amazement, that she still wanted to be reunited with her family. She had by then written several letters to the governor asking permission to leave the prison. Three of her uncles who had been determined to kill her had died and the remaining two had pledged to leave her alone.

One year later, I returned to Jweideh and, hopeful that her dreams had come true, immediately asked about Inas. She was still there. We sat and chatted together like old friends.

I told her that I would do my best to help her, that I would tell her story to all the journalists I met, that I would always refer journalists to her in the hope that her plight and the plight of other women would be heard and solved.

This would prove to be a great deal harder than I imagined. The Jordanian government was apathetic and unwilling to change. A minister told me, 'We cannot lock up an entire tribe or family. We really do not like or want to imprison women, but what can we do? The concept of [family] honour is socially imbedded in our society.'

The last time I saw Inas was when I accompanied a Human Rights Watch representative to Jordan to write a report on the fate of imprisoned women. Incredibly, Inas was full of optimism. She had studied in prison to become a professional hairdresser. She took us to her 'salon', a corner in a basement room, and demonstrated her skills to us on a fellow prisoner.

Inas's father had recently died and she told me that she had requested again to be freed and reunited with her family. She told me excitedly that her sister and mother had visited her and promised to release her and to send her to the USA.

At least that is what they told her.

My heart sank. Bitter experience told me it was most likely that this would prove to be a ruse by the family to get her released so they could kill her. I had by then reported on almost two dozen cases whereby a father or a brother bailed their female relative only to have her murdered as soon as she got home – in some cases almost as soon as she was outside the prison walls. I told Inas to be wary of this sudden unrealistic development before making a decision that might cost her life, but she still remained optimistic as we said goodbye. She told me she would never give up.

As I reported on Inas and Rania's cases, and many more besides, I became more and more incensed at the injustice and suffering, and frustrated at the amount of criticism I received for reporting these stories that would have previously gone unnoticed. I now knew that reporting these crimes was no longer enough for me. I wasn't changing anything. I *had* to do more.

CHAPTER 4

Bound by Honour

The twenty-first of November 1999 is a day I'll never forget. On that morning I met my friend and colleague at *The Jordan Times*, Dima Hamdan, and together we excitedly headed to Parliament, walking quickly even though we'd left especially early in order to reserve good seats on the terrace. The white building shone in the strong sunlight and, as we passed through the security gates, I wondered whether we were about to make history.

We were, but not in the way we had intended.

Back in 1998 I had achieved some notoriety; I was awarded the Reebok Human Rights Award for my reporting and activism. The award generated a great deal of media coverage, putting what was for many an unwelcome spotlight on so-called honour crimes in Jordan. This fired up a public debate, which became international when ABC and CNN interviewed me for documentaries.

Then, in February 1999, a Jordanian pharmacist named Basil Burgan contacted me and proposed we start a grass roots movement in Jordan, not only to raise local awareness about these brutal murders but to fight to change Jordanian law, and to demand tougher punishments for the perpetrators of these crimes.

Of course, I agreed, and together we emailed all our friends and anyone we could think of who might be prepared to devote some of their time to the cause. I was quite hopeful, as many people had contacted me over the years wanting to take an active role against so-called honour crimes. Twenty people showed up for the first meeting held at Burgan's house.

We decided to name ourselves the Jordanian National Committee to Eliminate So-Called Honour Crimes (I'm the first to admit that it's not a very catchy title, but it was at least un-ambiguous). We continued to meet on a weekly basis to brain-storm on the best means to raise people's awareness of these crimes and to lobby the government to abolish laws that discriminated against women. As we had no headquarters, we took turns meeting in each other's houses. After a couple of months, the group settled at eleven core members: seven women and four men.

In addition to Basil and myself, the committee included Asma Khader, our legal adviser and a lawyer and activist, Muna Darwazeh, a TV production company owner, Maha Abu Ayyash, sculptor and copyrighter, Najwa Ghannoum, an assistant man-ager, Muna Abu Rayyan, a PR and marketing specialist, Sultan Abu Mariam, an agricultural engineer, Khalid Kasih, a food factory owner, Samir Abdul Aziz, an engineer, as well as Ruba Dabis and Nisreen Hannoon, who were both university students at the time.

We decided that one of the best means to fight the status quo was to organize a nation-wide campaign to collect people's signatures and present it to Parliament. The aim was to collect fifty thousand signatures; if we could present this many signatures to Parliament, then the issue would have to be debated. This would be the first petition of its kind in the history of the Kingdom – it was not a popular thing to do. People who had tried collecting signatures for petitions before had found themselves harassed by the security forces.

But we knew if we could show MPs that the people of Jordan wanted change, then maybe, just maybe, they would help to make it happen. We hoped to start a new movement that would bring the government more under control of the people. At least by doing this we would get people involved and interested in how the country was being governed – and it would show people that it was possible to make their voices heard.

We prepared pamphlets that included information and statistics illustrating the problem, and held lectures in public and private institutions to raise people's awareness about the issue and encouraged them to sign our petition. We created an archive that included everything that was written in the press about honour crimes. Several committee members appeared on TV and radio talk shows.

Of course, we had to be very clear about which laws we wanted to change. In March, we met and had an animated discussion with Asma Khader in the chair. Asma suggested that we focus our campaign on the cancellation of Article 340, which dealt specifically with adultery, rather than Article 98, which was generally applied to several types of crime, not just so-called honour crimes, and would be much harder to change.

Article 340 included two clauses of particular interest. One stipulated that 'he who discovers his wife or one of his female relatives committing adultery (with a man) and kills, wounds, or injures one or both of them, is exempted from any penalty.'

The other clause stated: 'He who discovers his wife, or one of his female relatives with another in an adulterous situation, and kills, wounds or injures one or both of them, benefits from a reduction in penalty.'

Article 98 said: 'Any person who commits a crime in a fit of fury caused by an unlawful and dangerous act on the part of the victim benefits from a reduction in penalty.'

I was in favour of targeting Article 98 because I knew, from having witnessed dozens of court cases, that it was the one more commonly used in relation to so-called honour crimes. It was Article 98 that allowed the amending of charges of premeditated murder to misdemeanour.

Khader argued that Article 340, which was a specific article, was the better target because it was so specific. Article 98 was general and it would be difficult to make amendments to it since it was applied in many other criminal matters.

Her opinion was that amending Article 340 would be the first strategic move that would eventually lead to the elimination of all of the laws that discriminated against women in Jordan, including Article 98. When we voted, everyone, with the exception of myself, voted in favour of targeting Article 340. Of course, even though I would have preferred to tackle Article 98 first, I remained a hundred per cent dedicated to our objective.

We called all of our contacts, including several government officials, to try and obtain the necessary approvals for our activities and put together a press conference. One of our first heavyweight supporters was the late Iyad Qatan, the Secretary General of the Ministry of Information. On 21 August 1999, he wrote to the police, stating that we would be gathering signatures in public places, hotels and government institutes and that we had his support. Qatan was a courageous man; he even helped free some of our petition-signature collectors who were held by the police for questioning, despite behaving properly and legally throughout the campaign.

Qatan also sent similar notices to the newspapers and the governor to inform them that the Ministry supported our campaign and gave us approval to hold our first press conference.

Despite this, our first request to hold a press conference in Amman was rejected by the mayor. It took a senior official at the Royal Palace to persuade him otherwise.

Our petition read:

We are a group of Jordanian citizens who have no personal, political, or racial interests, but are gathered with one unifying issue as free individuals, which is our right to a good and safe life, free from violence in a society that protects the rights of all, which abides by the Constitution that assures equality to all in front of the law in rights and duties.

Through the years, our country has witnessed abhorrent crimes that appal every clear-thinking and honest Jordanian. These crimes were committed in the name of honour, and those who have committed them have received soft sentences, which in turn encouraged their belief and that of others that the crime they committed is socially acceptable.

Since the victims no longer have a voice to raise, and since we jealously guard the life and the safety of all Jordanian citizens and the right of each Jordanian to live in peace and harmony based on respect for human dignity, individual rights, justice, security, fair trial and defence and because these crimes contradict Islamic law (Sharia), the Constitution and the International Convention on the Elimination of Discrimination Against Women (CEDAW), we express our support of the decision of the Minister of Justice Hamzeh Haddad and the government, who, in moving to abolish Article 340 of the Jordanian Penal Code, have acted according to the spirit of His Majesty King Abdullah's directives to eliminate all forms of discrimination against women.

Based on these principles, we decided to organize this campaign to practise our civil rights to demand that legislative, judicial and administrative authorities and the various national official sectors take all necessary measures and use all legal, democratic means at their disposal – judicial, legislative, educational and media – to eliminate this ugly phenomenon.

In the name of our sisters, daughters and mothers who do not have any voice, in the name of those who this minute unjustly suffer different forms of violence and injury to protect honour, with no one to protect them and guarantee their human rights, we raise our own voices.

We call for the immediate cancellation of Article 340 in its entirety, which reduces penalties and exempts those who kill or injure in the name of honour.

We stress the need to implement the law so as not to waste any chance to punish killers and to show society that these crimes will not be tolerated. We stress the need to enforce a fair and preventive punishment against anyone who commits crimes against women in the name of honour.

We call on all concerned citizens of this country to share our work to ensure that this initiative is a national effort which will allow Jordanians to express their opinions so that the authorities will take the necessary steps to protect the safety of innocent women who are victims of traditions and social norms that have no basis in Islam, the Jordanian Constitution or basic human rights.

We have prepared numbered petitions [for those who wish to raise their voice against these crimes].

Jordanian citizens who are legally eligible to vote may sign these petitions.

Our aim is to collect thousands of signatures to emphasize the desire of a large percentage of voters to cancel Article 340 of the Jordanian Penal Code and to work intensively with all means available to abolish this inhuman practice.

We launch our campaign by appealing to all citizens to take the initiative and sign this petition.

We also prepared a pamphlet, which was designed for us for free by Ani Orfali. It was simple but eye-catching, with a bold black, white and red design. It included over eighty names of women recently murdered in Jordan in the name of honour, along with murder statistics and information on Article 340 as well as other laws used to discriminate against women.

Whenever we enlisted the support of a respected public personality, we made sure their name was at the top of our petitions – in this way we were able to persuade many more people to join us. Most people were very wary of us and were fearful of what would happen if they signed our petition. Discussions would sometimes last for thirty minutes before someone finally decided to sign. It was a hard, slow process and we often wondered whether we would ever get the fifty thousand names we hoped for. This was a very tall order, considering Jordan was a repressive country, with only four million people back then.

A month before our campaign was due to be officially launched, a special committee at the Ministry of Justice announced that it had decided to abolish Article 340. In its place, it suggested another law to toughen the punishment against adulterers, 'to prevent people from committing adultery', and referred its recommendations to Parliament for voting.

The committee listed four justifications for amending Article 340:

1. The existence of the article violated the constitution since it allowed individuals to take the law into their own hands.
2. It discriminated against women since the leniency in the punishment was only granted to men.
3. It violated the Islamic religion since four witnesses of good reputation are needed to testify to an act of adultery and the state or the ruler are the only ones entitled to inflict punishment on the 'guilty'.

This sounded very promising. We hadn't even officially launched our campaign, and a government committee had already decided to change the law. But, and this was a big but, the committee included a fourth and final justification:

4. The law needed to be changed in response to western human rights organizations' constant criticism of the existence of Article 340.

Conservatives in Jordan have often successfully used the excuse of so-called 'western influence and interference' and 'the west meddling in the internal affairs of Arab countries to destroy the structure of its society' to reject or attack the work of activism, as well as to raise people's doubts as to the motives and intentions of campaigners like those in our group.

This fourth justification gave the conservatives all the ammunition they needed to attack us fiercely. Their anti-western view was widely supported by many ordinary people and I could understand why people might react this way if it were true – but it was not.

On 23 August 1999 we gave our first news conference, appealing to the public to join and support our campaign by signing our petition. Our slogan was 'Right of life and the right for fair trial'.

We announced that around 380 petitions had been distributed in the Kingdom and that we'd managed to collect around three thousand signatures in just two weeks.

'Our aim is to gather a huge number of signatures which we will present to King Abdullah, [then] Prime Minister Abdur-Ra'uf S. Rawabdeh and the Upper and Lower Houses of Parliament to emphasize people's desire to abolish Article 340,' I said.

Basil announced that many royal family members and former Jordanian officials had already signed the petition. Our regal supporters proved to be crucial. They really helped to persuade a great many people to sign our petition. Since ascending to the throne in 1999, His Majesty King Abdullah and Her Majesty Queen Rania have spoken out against so-called crimes of honour several times.

King Abdullah described honour killings as 'a problem not only for Jordan but for all the Third World,' adding, 'Jordan is the first country to actually identify the issue and try to deal with it.' The King also promised the leaders of Jordan's women's movements in August 1999 that they had his full backing.

Queen Rania, a strong advocate of women's and children's issues in Jordan, also spoke publicly, arguing that so-called honour crimes have no basis in religion: 'It was not a practice that was acceptable to the late King Hussein, nor is it to King Abdullah.'

In 2008, Queen Rania addressed the stereotypes facing Arab and Muslim communities on YouTube and spoke out against honour crimes and violence against women, saying it was not exclusive to the Arab world and that it is a 'worldwide shame'.

'It is horrific. It is inexcusable. And there is absolutely no honour in it,' the Queen said in her message, as she acknowledged that while honour crimes do happen, 'It is not a prevalent cultural practice. It has nothing to do with Islam. It is not at all indicative of the status and standing of women in our culture. And it is being challenged.'

Her Majesty Queen Noor has been a determined activist in the fight to end honour crimes and violence against women in Jordan. Ever since the issue began to surface, Queen Noor along with the late King Hussein pushed for a change in the laws that offers leniency to killers in honour crimes.

Her long-standing and outspoken support for my work has been utterly invaluable. One such instance was during an interview with CNN's Christiane Amanpour where Queen Noor spoke of the work done in Jordan to combat these crimes, making positive reference to my work, and providing me with a huge push forward. About these crimes, she said: "this type of violence against women is not consistent with Islam or with [the Jordanian] Constitution ... this [legal] area is being reviewed and amendments are being proposed to make these laws more consistent with Islamic law and the Constitution." She added that she has "very strong personal feelings as a Muslim, as a woman, as a wife and as a mother about this form of violence and every form of violence against women."

Most recently, in her book *Leap of Faith* published in 2003, Queen Noor spoke of the honour crime problem in Jordan and recognised my work again. She wrote: "The Jordanian journalist Rana Husseini almost single-handedly brought this problem to the attention of the public in a series of newspaper articles over a nine-year period. Many criticized her work and motives, and some of her detractors even sent hate mail and threats. But Rana persisted. Her achievements were given special attention when she was awarded the Reebok Human Rights Award in 1998."

King Abdullah's uncle, His Royal Highness Prince Hassan, was one of the first royal family members to address the issue. In August 1996, the sociologist Dr Sari Nasir told me that Prince Hassan was following my work at *The Jordan Times* and wanted me to prepare a paper on so-called honour crimes to be presented at a conference on violence in schools. Prince Hassan addressed the gathering at the opening and spoke about the important role families play in their children's education.

Halfway through his speech, the Prince switched to the issue of so-called honour crimes. 'It must be clear to society and its various institutions that crimes of honour have no religious justification, nor are they sanctioned by Arab patrimony. Should we continue to accept the present state of affairs … if we continue to condone the false concept of "crimes of honour", which can only unravel the fabric of society, we would be abandoning the concept of civilized life.'

In 1997, the late King Hussein made a passionate plea for an end to violence against women in a speech given to the Jordanian Parliament. He said that women in Jordan were still being exposed to inhuman practices that deprived them of their basic essential rights and that 'is why we must pay serious attention to some of the dangerous phenomena that remain a source of women's suffering and which, unfortunately, constitute an inhuman violation of their basic rights … The most serious and dangerous of those is hidden violence … This does not befit our Arab and Islamic society, the society of solidarity.'

Princess Basma, sister of the late King Hussein, has championed women's rights and their empowerment in Jordan, attending and speaking out at many local and international events that addressed the issue of violence against women. The first direct message from Princess Basma on the issue came during a ceremony to launch a regional campaign to eliminate violence against women conducted by the UN Development Fund for Women (UNIFEM) in November 1998. She said that Jordanian society must face issues of violence against women, and 'the issue should no longer be taboo. We should not hide our heads in the sand ... and pretend it does not exist ... the shame is to know that violence against women does exist and allow all forms of suffering to happen against women. The issue should be recognized and solutions need to be discussed, and as long as we do it with dignity and recognize the strengths in our society, the religions and the positive norms, we can make a change and fight it if we work together.'

Despite the royal seal of approval, I never anticipated just how overwhelming the response to our initial press conference was going to be. We were bombarded with supportive phone calls and emails. People were even faxing their signatures to us, asking us to add them to the petition. The most memorable email I received that same day came from a man named Nasri Tarazi who taught at Ahliyyah School for Girls. He wanted to know if his students could sign our petition. This for me was a real breakthrough – discussing the issue in schools would be one of the best ways of changing the mindset of what constituted family honour.

Suddenly the subject was everywhere. Newspaper postbags bulged and columnists only wrote about one thing: Article 340. Of course, not everything was positive – far from it. The opinions of columnists ranged from the sublime to the ridiculous. Abdul Latif Zuhd wrote a column for the daily *Arab Al-Yawm* in August 1999 claiming that women were to blame for the 'fornication' in our society.

He conceded that religion did not allow people to take the law into their own hands, but argued that women were the ones responsible for 'tainting their family's honour and reputation'.

'We are living in a society that does not allow the woman's family to live in a normal manner if a daughter did something wrong. How would a father take care of his daughter after she has tarnished his reputation and tainted his face with mud and brought him disgrace, distress and hardship?'

He put the blame only on women adulterers because by their action of allowing men to sleep with them they violate the religion and defy society's norms and family values. Therefore, women would anger God, cause their family grave catastrophe, and would contribute to spreading fornication.

Many people wrote to *The Jordan Times* claiming that we were exaggerating the seriousness and number of so-called honour crimes. Some even claimed that the problem was small when compared to the number of people killed annually in Jordan in traffic accidents (700–800 compared to about twenty-five honour killings). In support of this figure, Major Bashir Bilbeisi, a Jordanian police officer, analysed 503 murders that took place between 1990 and 1995 and concluded that 150 of them were honour killings.

The writer and feminist Zuleikha Abu Risheh responded sarcastically in her column almost a week later in *Al Rai* newspaper, asking whether we should wait until we're burying women by the thousand before we admit that there's a problem. She argued that we needed to bump the numbers up, and so if women failed to prepare the men decent coffee, or managed to awaken them when doing the housework, then they should be badly beaten and, if they failed to improve, they should be 'given the coup de grace'.

Meanwhile we'd printed three phone numbers on our pamphlet and in the press, including *The Jordan Times*, which ran small daily advertisements for free, urging people to help us by collecting more signatures, an initiative by Amy Henderson, the then local editor. We headed to small villages and towns outside Amman. During our initial canvassing tour in Jerash, a small but busy mountain town popular with tourists and home to a bustling market, a young man approached us, desperate to sign our petition. He was so excited that he tried to sign twice. When I told him he could only sign once, he snatched the petition sheet and raced round the town, collecting signatures himself.

I stepped into a small shop selling cheeses where the old lady running the store said she could not sign the petition because she was illiterate. To make up for this, she made sure everyone around her in the small store signed instead.

Many people were convinced that we were doing the right thing and signed our petitions. Some were afraid to sign since such activities have always been banned in Jordan and many people had been prosecuted or questioned by the security forces. Fortunately, a lawyer voiced her readiness to provide legal representation for anyone who got in trouble for either signing the petition or collecting signatures.

Of course, many people were opposed to what we were doing and many simply told us that women who committed a 'wrongful and immoral act' deserved to die while their killers needed to be legally protected.

We used every method we could think of to collect as many signatures as possible – the internet, faxes, free and paid ads in newspapers, as well as TV and radio interviews. It was tremendously exciting; we carried the petitions with us wherever we went and whatever we did, and we always caused a stir.

Most honour killings occur in poor and uneducated populations where word of mouth spreads fast. They also take place in rural areas, where economic hardship and daily struggles are the rule of the day, so we made sure we targeted these areas as well.

Almost all of the men charged with these crimes come from working- or lower-middle-class backgrounds, including butchers, farmers, soldiers, bus drivers and civil servants as well as the unemployed. Sometimes they say that all they have is their honour, and if they lose that then they have nothing and are worthless. So we made a particular point of targeting these men.

I frequently went with my friends Sultan Abu Mariam and Najwa Ghannoum to restaurants where we approached diners (a captive audience!) and many gladly signed as we chatted. Then we asked the waiters, waitresses, cooks, cleaners and managers. Outside one restaurant I bumped into a garbage collector who asked me what I was doing. Once I explained, he said, 'Of course I will sign. This is against our religion.'

My mother, Randa Saifi-Husseini, played a major role in collecting signatures. As a librarian she asked everyone who came into her building to sign. She had copies with her wherever she went. If she went to an art exhibition, to a restaurant, out with friends or to any public gathering, then the petition, a pen and her determination came with her.

It was around this busy, happy time that I was reminded just what it was we were fighting for when I discovered one of the worst cases of so-called honour killing I had ever encountered.

CHAPTER 5

Excusing Murder

I was waiting in my car, the engine running, waiting for fifty-seven-year-old Um Mohammad and her two young daughters to slip away from her family and neighbours. She had good reason to be fearful. She had decided that she wanted to tell me her story, something that would place her life in danger.

I started my tape recorder and drove off as soon as they'd climbed in. Um Mohammad began her story. 'My daughter Amneh, who was twenty-one, came to me one day complaining that she had stomach pains and was bleeding. I thought it was her appendix so I took her to the doctor.

'Imagine my horror when the doctor told me the last thing I would have expected – my daughter was pregnant! I simply couldn't believe it. I started crying and beat her. She said it was against her will; that the next-door neighbour had raped her.'

Um Mohammad stopped talking as she tried to control her emotions. She looked extremely tired and ill. I'd soon discover that this mother of five had in fact developed cancer. As she told the rest of her story, I felt her sense of helplessness and confusion increase.

'The moment I got back home, I told my eldest son Mohammad the news. He flew into a rage.'

Amneh's sixteen-year-old sister, Sana, interjected, 'I knew he wanted to kill my sister the moment I heard them arguing. I dragged her away and into our room and tried to calm her down. I was still trying to get the full story when Mohammad stormed in. He shouted at Amneh to tell him what had happened.

'I tried to stop him; I said that Amneh should marry the neighbour but he pushed me aside and beat her up, using his fists. I left the room knowing something really bad was about to happen.'

Mohammad was originally going to a wedding and had a gun put by for the occasion. Some Jordanian men liked to celebrate weddings by firing live rounds from shotguns – though the practice is illegal and anyone caught is generally prosecuted.

Mohammad raced back into the room with his gun. While her mother watched, Mohammad shot his younger sister. Um Mohammad fainted.

'When I heard the gunshots I ran back into the room and saw my sister fighting for her life,' Sana continued quietly. 'I could not believe she was shot. She asked my brother and I to take good care of our sick mother. She died in my arms while my brother stood watching, the gun still in his hand.'

Mohammad turned himself in, claiming that he had killed his sister to cleanse his family's honour. He also handed officers the gun he used.

Tears marked Um Mohammad's cheeks as she continued. 'My heart burns every time I think of Amneh's last words. I feel pain whenever I see her photo. I will never forget her. She is always in my mind and my broken heart. I visit her every now and then at the cemetery.'

We sat silently in the car for a few moments. I went over Um Mohammad's story in my mind and then asked her what would seem to most people to be a very strange question – whether she thought that the killing of her daughter had solved a problem.

Amazingly, Um Mohammad started to try to excuse and even justify her daughter's murder. 'She worked every day. She left the house in the morning and came back around 3pm. We did not know anything about her. She was mature enough to know what she was doing.'

She added that there was a chance that the rapist might marry her, adding, 'We should have married her off to the neighbour instead of killing her. It was his mistake and he should have married her immediately and not waited until she was exposed. She is dead and he is alive, enjoying his life.

'If she told us from the beginning what had happened to her we would have reacted differently. But it was a total shock for the entire family. My daughter made a mistake and had to bear the consequences. We live in a society that offers no mercy once a mistake is made,' she said.

Even Amneh's father, who abandoned the family almost fifteen years ago and had taken a second wife, was apparently relieved when he heard the news of his daughter's murder. Apparently, all their neighbours also agreed that she got what she deserved.

I was amazed that Um Mohammad, obviously traumatized by her loss, was trying to excuse her daughter's murder. 'I am satisfied with her death because it is her fate, but I am worried about my son and the kind of punishment he might get. They say he will get a reduced sentence and will be released soon but I am not so sure. He should return to his wife and children. When his children ask us about his whereabouts, we tell them that he is travelling and should be back soon.'

Sana told me confidently that her sister deserved to die and blamed her for being raped. 'She destroyed our family, our honour and did not think of us or her family's fate when she did it. She was mature and understood what is right and what is wrong. What she did was out of her free will. She deceived us,' said Sana. 'My brother killed her and cleansed our honour. If he did not kill her he would have died of shame and disgrace.' Sana also admitted that she missed Amneh and sometimes felt bad about her death and wished that her family had instead married her off to her rapist.

These surprising attitudes were not uncommon. I had previously interviewed an illiterate sixty-year-old mother of seven for an Arabic article in *Al Hayat* newspaper. She told me: 'Sinning women should be killed and their murder should be announced on the radio. They should also be hung in a public yard so that all the women would see them and be scared so that they would know in their own eyes what would happen to them if they decide to go astray.' She also told me she was prepared to kill her own daughter: 'I would hang her on a tree. It is easier and much better for us and her as well.'

This attitude does not belong solely to the poor and uneducated. Manal, a twenty-five-year-old woman with a Masters degree in Economics, told me she did not consider so-called honour crimes a barbaric act because they help keep the number of 'deviant women' low. 'Women are the source of seduction for men and if all women are chastised then men would become good on their own. We are in a Middle Eastern society and I am for punishing women more than men because men cannot resist the seduction of girls who are dressed improperly ... When women are punished, fear of their families will build up among them and they will think twice before committing any immoral mistake.'

I have been asked many times by people who (understandably) can't fathom how a mother and/or sister is able to assist or justify the butchering of their daughter or sibling. From my experience, it is clear that many immediate female relatives simply go along with the male members of the family out of the fear that the same thing might happen to them. When they speak publicly to a journalist such as myself, then they may also feel compelled to tell me what their male relatives would want to hear them say.

Sometimes, women do carry out honour killings on their own, but I am certain that their motives still stem from the same fear. I reported on one such case for *The Jordan Times* in July 2006. A sixty-nine-year-old mother waited until her twenty-six-year-old daughter, exhausted from giving birth to her illegitimate baby boy, fell asleep. The mother fetched her other daughter and together they murdered the victim with an axe as she slept, turning themselves in to the police immediately afterwards.

Amneh's fifteen-year-old sister, Salma, was at a wedding when the incident took place. She was more sympathetic. 'I felt sorry for her because she died. I love and miss her. We were good friends and she used to help me with my school studies and we went shopping together. My sister is a good and honest woman but she never told us what happened to her,' Salma said.

She went on to insist, as her sister and mother sat silently, that killing was not the solution. 'There is no justice in this life. The neighbour who caused my sister to become pregnant is relaxed and alive and my sister is dead.' She paused for a moment. 'If I saw him, I would try and hurt him.'

Salma's mother took her out of school after the incident because her family was concerned about her reputation and they wanted her always to be within their sight in case the same thing happened to her. 'I am upset that I am no longer going to school. I had dreams of becoming a doctor when I grew up, but now I do not know what my future is.'

As for the man who caused the pregnancy, Um Mohammad told me her son was planning to kill him. However, the authorities had taken him into custody shortly after Amneh's murder on adultery charges. Um Mohammad bowed her head. 'May God forgive him for what he did. He ruined our life and caused the imprisonment of my son.'

The court certainly seemed to forgive Mohammad, thanks to Article 98. The judge agreed that he committed his crime in a moment of rage and was sentenced to one year's imprisonment. Of course, his mother dropped the charges, so he was a free man six months later.

Um Mohammad later told me that her son had been suffering

from depression since he had been released. 'He refuses to talk to anyone. He told me he acted hastily after becoming enraged and that it solved nothing.'

Her son visits Amneh's grave every now and then and prays for his sister's soul, Um Mohammad added. Since the killing, his uncles and neighbours, who had said he had done the right thing, had turned their backs on him.

I was unable to speak to Mohammad myself; his mother told me that he'd sworn never to talk to anyone except his immediate family. 'The killing did not solve anything,' she told me tearfully. 'On the contrary, it has destroyed our family. If I went back in time, I would defend my daughter. She was a good girl. What happened to her was not her fault. It is not fair that she died.'

The confused and miserable outpourings from this poor girl's mother only galvanized me further into action. If I ever needed encouragement to continue our battle, then this experience provided it. I hoped that after hearing Amneh's story many others would join us. And they did …

CHAPTER 6

We Fought the Law …

During the first four non-stop weeks of our campaign, we managed to collect eight thousand signatures. Then in September, the Jordanian Women's Union (JWU) organized a seminar entitled 'Honour Crimes … Any Improvements?' Abdul Hadi Majali, the Speaker of the Lower House of Parliament, attended the seminar and warned us that, as we expected, any attempt to amend Article 340 would face strong opposition. The JWU's vice president Nadia Shamroukh announced that she had received anonymous pamphlets that accused the JWU of encouraging adultery.

At the end of the conference the JWU issued a statement calling on Parliament to cancel Article 340 and to place restrictions on the application of Article 98. They also called for punishment for people who incited false rumours about women, and for an increase in the severity of the punishment for adultery (believing this would add some balance to their call for reforms of Article 340).

Many moderate religious scholars, mostly Muslim leaders, such as King Abdullah's former adviser on Islamic affairs and Chief Islamic Justice, the late Sheikh Izzedin Al-Khatib Al-Tamimi, backed the statement and spoke openly about honour killings for the first time.

Al-Tamimi said, 'If the punishment for crimes of honour is detainment in a five-star prison, I believe we cannot stop these crimes or this bloodshed. A tough punishment must be implemented. Many men and women have been killed because of their relatives' ignorance ... Killers think their victims' blood is a medal representing their act of heroism of honour. They do not know that God's anger and curse will remain with them.'[3]

But despite our regal and rapidly increasing public support, we faced real opposition from the Islamic Action Front (IAF), the political arm of the Muslim Brotherhood in Jordan, along with conservative deputies, who strongly denounced our activism. As was to be expected, they accused us of corrupting public morals and imposing western values in order to appease international human rights organizations. The solution, they argued, was to end this problem by calling for the full application of Islamic law in Jordan.

The then IAF Secretary General, Abdul Latif Arabiat, said, 'This is a western plot to destroy and corrupt our society ... [The west] has occupied us militarily and politically, and now they want to destroy society, our last remaining fortress.'

Lower House MP Mahmoud Kharabsheh told me in an interview for *The Jordan Times*: 'Women adulterers cause a great threat to our society, because they are the main reason that such acts [of adultery] happen. If men do not find women with whom to commit adultery, then they will become good on their own.'[4]

Of course, apart from outright opposition, we also faced a great deal of apathy and *laissez-faire* from various parliamentarians. One deputy who previously occupied an important and influential government position said that he was in favour of cancelling Article 340, but added, 'I am not willing to say it in public in front of my colleagues or to defend it ... There are more important things to discuss in Parliament and surely I will not stand up and defend this article in front of 79 deputies.' (The Lower House was then made up of eighty male deputies. The number has since increased to 110 seats, including six seats that are allocated to women, through a new quota system.) Another deputy said he enjoyed a good position in the party and so he was not 'willing to risk his position to defend such an issue in Parliament'.

Meanwhile, the Al-Tahrir Party (the Liberation Party, which is technically illegal because it has never been granted a licence by the government) issued a statement addressed to the Jordanian Parliament, which openly accused the USA of backing a global campaign to spread fornication in Jordan via our activism.

The statement said: 'Do not be fooled by the few thousands of signatures that were collected by the committee. If you really want to know what Jordanians' opinion is, just organize an opposing campaign and you will collect thousands of signatures in a few days ... People in Jordan do not waste or sell their honour for the sake of a misleading campaign that is run by a few people who are fascinated by western civilization and values.'[5]

On 16 November, less than a week before Parliament was to vote on Article 340, the Al-Afaf Islamic Society organized a one-day lecture entitled 'Preserving honour between Sharia and Law' to express its opposition. The atmosphere was heated and the opposition to our work was strongly hostile. However, popular support turned the lecture into a public rally for our campaign.

On 18 November, a survey we had conducted of twenty-two thousand people was published on a full page in the *Arab Al-Yawm* newspaper. We had by then collected fifteen thousand signatures (fifty-five per cent male and forty-five per cent female).

Around seventy per cent of the people we approached had agreed to sign the petition. Of these, thirty per cent supported changing Article 340 enthusiastically and without discussion. Around fifteen per cent signed for the novelty of the experience and twenty-five per cent agreed to sign after researching the issue. Around eighty per cent of the people we met either did not know about the subject or did not have a clear picture of the size of the problem. Ten per cent of the remaining thirty per cent who refused to sign were afraid (unsurprisingly these were nearly all women), while fifteen per cent simply rejected the idea of cancelling the article. Some were apathetic about the whole issue and simply believed that nothing ever changes in Jordan.

And then, having done everything we thought possible, 21 November 1999, the day Article 340 was to be debated, finally came. There were sixty-three MPs present when the session began. The chamber crackled with tension as many MPs leapt up to oppose virulently any change, describing the cancellation of Article 340 as 'legislating obscenity'. Deputy Mahmoud Kharabsheh (Balqa), who was the *rapporteur* of the House Legal Affairs Committee, was the first deputy to speak. He told the assembly he had the support of twenty-seven of Jordan's most senior MPs who were against cancelling Article 340. 'This draft is one of the most dangerous legislations being reviewed by the House,' he said, 'because it is related to our women and society, especially in light of the threat of globalization.'

Kharabsheh said that activists should focus instead on changing other articles in the law that have granted women lenient punishments, such as Article 341, which reduces the punishment for a woman who kills her child born out of wedlock to avoid being disgraced.

Over a dozen deputies of the Parliament spoke, as well as key figures, including the Prime Minister, Abdur-Ra'uf S. Rawabdeh. The overwhelming message was that this was a western-driven campaign of misinformation aimed at destroying the morals of our society.

One deputy described the draft bill as a document to legalize adultery and destroy Islamic ethics and lashed out at us, saying we didn't represent Jordanian society or its Islamic values.

This was the most heated session ever seen in our parliament. Despite some moderate voices, only one deputy, Nash'at Hamarneh, a leftist from Madaba, was courageous enough to speak directly in favour of the draft, and kept speaking even as opposing members tried to shout him down.

'This article has become a sword over the necks of our women ... we have never once heard of a man being killed in the name of honour,' he said, struggling to be heard. 'We must cancel any legislation that stands in the way of liberating our women.'

By the end of the session, when it was time to vote, I peeked over the balcony to watch the voting. I thought they would count hands and cite names of deputies. I hoped I'd at least be able to question the deputies who claimed during their campaigns that they were in favour of women's rights as to why they were voting against this change.

But then one deputy shouted, 'Why are we wasting more time? Seems to me the majority of the Lower House is against it. Let us vote.'

The voting was carried out as quick as a flash, so fast that I almost missed it. The Speaker of the Lower House asked who was against the amendment. The majority of the deputies waved their hands. That was it. The bill was rejected without even the dignity of a count of hands.

I returned to the newspaper to write the story; the news was already out because the voting session was aired live on TV. I watched my in-box swell as people supporting the cause wrote to express their anger over the deputies' vote.

I opened an email. 'Please don't give up,' a woman had written, 'you highlighted an issue that we really didn't see. The number of killings is obviously going to increase, but you gave it a try, and we'll still support you and fight to banish the murder of the innocent souls.'

The following day, the JWU's vice president Nadia Shamroukh expressed her disappointment to the press and said that she had not expected such an impassioned reaction to an amendment.

Our committee sent an open letter to the Jordanian Parliament voicing our own disappointment and refusal to accept the Lower House's decision.

Notorious columnist and former minister of health Zeid Hamzeh agreed. He wrote in *Al Rai* newspaper in December 1999: 'Instead of standing all together against Article 340, why didn't they find another legal way to prevent the killing of tens of women in cold blood?'

The public indulged in fierce debates following the Lower House decision to sustain Article 340 and one of the most interesting of these was on a website hosted by a local internet company called Baladna. No longer in service, Baladna encouraged public debates and started several chat rooms or forums for people to voice their opinions on various topics. They had started a Women's Forum, which I moderated.

Identities of the participants in this forum could be withheld and so many ordinary people felt they were able to speak freely and in safety. A man named Michael Ibrahim wrote, 'May the blood of every dishonourably murdered girl haunt those of our deputies who voted down the abolishment.'

Sultan Abu Mariam spoke for many people when he wrote, 'Let's move and do something for our country and our children's future … Jordan is our beloved country and deserves the best out of us so let's fight for a better life, so we know that we earned it.' Batir Wardam, a Jordanian columnist, agreed, calling the deputies 'a disgrace to our intelligence'.

In December of that year, we met with the Speaker of the Lower House, Abdul Hadi Majali, to hand him the 15,300 signatures we'd collected in less than six months. Majali criticized the government, saying it had acted hastily and had 'caused the intent of the draft to be misunderstood by the MPs', a statement that I published in an article for *The Jordan Times* on 19 December 1999.

Majali happened to be out of the country when the law was debated in the Lower House. He told us he had since discussed the issue with many MPs and they thought that if a man killed his wife after surprising her in the act of adultery, then the law stated that he would be sentenced to fifteen years. 'That was the main reason they rejected the draft,' he told me, in exasperation.

Almost a month later, the legal committee at the Upper House upheld the Lower House's decision. They debated the idea of giving women the same leniency as men were receiving in Article 340, but decided to do nothing in the end.

But there was one final ace up our sleeve. The Senate, our Supreme Court, is appointed by the King and, thanks in part to royal influence, they upheld the draft bill to amend Article 340 and returned it to the Lower House for a second debate. Senator Leila Sharaf, a much-respected female politician and activist in Jordan, said that keeping Article 340 in the Penal Code was an insult to society. 'Do you think that women refrain from adultery merely to avoid punishment? Why is it always that a woman is the only one blamed for adultery? Doesn't she have a partner who should be punished?'

On the other side, Deputy Mohammad Rafat from the Balqa Governorate criticized the senators' decision: 'The Lower House has already taken its decision, and there is nothing to add. The senators have only worsened the situation.'

Around this time I spoke with the experienced political analyst and adviser to the late King Hussein, Adnan Abu Odeh, who described the Lower House MPs as traditionalists who came from a pastoral culture. He told me during the interview that they would never amend Article 340 because they wanted to keep the status quo. If they failed to keep the status quo, then they would be replaced by people who could.

'They would be afraid of people saying this deputy voted against the law. "Let's see," they would say. "What he would do if his daughter did something wrong? What would he do?" This means someone else would substitute him in his own constituency,' Abu Odeh said.

Former Jordanian Prime Minister Dr Fayez Tarawneh also told me in an interview that the MPs 'did not do a good job on this issue and were immature because ... people were holding a peaceful demonstration to present them with signatures.'

Dr Tarawneh said the problem was that many deputies did not understand the issue and did not even bother to try and investigate or discuss the issue properly. 'When it comes to issues like this, deputies revert back to being individuals, instead of going back to their constituency to ask people what they think. They only go back to their constituency at election time.'

Both Abu Odeh and Dr Tarawneh agreed that the royal family was sincere in its quest for change on this issue. Abu Odeh told me, 'Although the Jordanian monarchy are not traditionalists personally, they are politically because their powerbase is made up of traditionalists. The problem is their powerbase. It pulls them back and they don't want to provoke it,' Abu Odeh said.

At the second hearing, held on 26 January 2000, the debate was over all too quickly. The only deputy who spoke out in favour of referring the article to the Legal Committee for examination was Zarqa MP Bassam Haddadin.

Several deputies said the entire Lower House had already voted once with a sweeping majority to reject the proposal, and that they were not prepared to discuss it again. Sure enough, they voted against the draft amendment again before sending it to the Upper House. It was clear that nothing was going to change any time soon. We had been defeated. Despite this, I felt that our work had proven to be a major success, thanks to the hard work of our committee and other non-governmental organizations (NGOs). Together, we made the debate on so-called honour crimes public and ongoing in Jordan and the subject still regularly filled newspaper columns – expressing both support and opposition.

Very much on the side opposed to reform was *Arab Al-Yawm* columnist Muwafaq Mahaddin, who wrote twice, in November

2000 and January 2001, criticizing financial support provided by the UK's Foreign Ministry to a local NGO called Sisterhood is Global Institute (SIGI), which was headed at the time by the lawyer Asma Khader.

In the first of these columns, written in November 2000, Mahaddin wrote that his readers 'would be surprised to know that women in Britain are in more need of this financial support than women in Jordan. It would be good if the Jordanian Embassy in London would offer support to women in the UK as well.' Many Jordanian columnists were incensed and wrote several opinion pieces criticizing the UK's interference.

During the first few months of 2000 the debate on Article 340 and so-called honour crimes dominated internet chat rooms. I read the comments criticizing and supporting me without comment until I saw that people were starting to blame me for tarnishing Jordan's image and for 'threatening Jordan's tourist industry'. I couldn't let that one pass and so I wrote:

I think every country in the world has its own problems. For example, the crime rate in the USA is one of the highest in the world. But you still see people exerting the utmost efforts to go and live or invest there and, if I am not mistaken, I think that the USA has one of the highest numbers of tourists visiting each year ... I would like to assure you all that I would never do anything to harm my beloved country ...

My work and the committee's work is not 'self-serving' as some have described it; we are trying to serve and keep women safe.

CHAPTER 7

The Royal March for Justice

Two days after the battle for Article 340 had been 'lost', Prince Ali took the extraordinary step of speaking out against the decision. Using an internet chat room, he made an extraordinary appeal for people to take part in a public march to Parliament in protest at the deputies' decision to vote against the amendments:

> As a Muslim, a Hashemite and a Jordanian citizen, I was dismayed to learn that honour killings are still condoned by some of our countrymen. My father the late King Hussein was resolute in his stance against these crimes and my brother King Abdullah and I remain just as determined to end honour killings in Jordan. We support the struggle to change the law, a struggle that began with Rana Husseini who had the courage to expose the truth …
>
> Therefore, we have decided to march to Parliament to protest against honour killings. Please join us, each and every one of you, so that we may make democracy in our country a reality and voice our opinion towards a better Jordan.[6]

To me, this email was the greatest thing that could have happened. I couldn't believe it – the Prince was going to march with us, in a march he had initiated! Perhaps not surprisingly, we had previously been refused permission to organize any kind of march, and although we hadn't given up, we did wonder if it was ever going to happen. Now, with the support of the Prince, who was able to obtain the necessary official clearance, we knew it was most definitely going to happen. It was just the most incredible feeling.

Many others praised the Prince for his move and pledged to be there with their families and friends. My friend and gender and development expert Randa Naffa, who was one of the first to respond to the Prince, spoke for most of us when she wrote: 'Thank you ... your presence will be a valuable support to all the believers of a better life for women in Jordan ... Any democracy cannot be fully consolidated unless just and fair laws exist for the right of all!'

Our committee members were divided on the issue. Some feared that the Prince's participation might cause a backlash. Others were excited that a public march was finally going to take place – especially as we had already lodged a request in November 1999 to organize a silent 'funeral procession' from the Christian and Muslim cemeteries in East Amman to Parliament.

Many of the victims of so-called honour crimes had been buried in unmarked graves, without normal tradition. We wanted to give them a proper funeral while presenting a painful reminder to the Lower House that their inaction meant these murders would continue.

The committee buzzed like a beehive as we tried to persuade as many people as possible to join us. Our press release said:

We call on each one of you to come and join us to express our voice – to make it clear that all Jordanians are against so-called honour crimes and the cold-blooded murder of women and girls. To insist that each one of us has individual rights and that everyone has the right to a fair trial and is entitled to a legal defence. We are counting on your support to prove to the Lower House that they are turning a blind eye to what Jordanians want.

This time, thanks to our royal backers, we won the support of the Mayor of Amman, who even arranged the printing of banners. However, the government remained resolutely against us and forbade Jordan's local TV from advertising the event.

Prince Ali had chosen 14 February. I remember that damp and cloudy morning very clearly. I walked with my friends to the starting point at Sports City. As we arrived, I gasped in astonishment. Thousands of people had already gathered in the huge courtyard behind the football stadium. Dozens of buses were standing by to transport us to Parliament.

It was a huge crowd, the largest I had ever seen in Jordan. Many people were dressed in their traditional tribal robes. Among them were women's rights activists, high school girls, lawyers and civil servants. My heart sang when I saw cameras and journalists absolutely everywhere, from all over the world, and that they were already busy filming and interviewing.

People were carrying black flags to commemorate the murdered women; there were countless banners which read 'Say No to Honour Crimes' and anti-Article 340 slogans were everywhere. It was an overwhelming sight. We had gone from nothing to this truly extraordinary event in Jordan's capital in just a few months. I really believed then that we would win our battle.

I searched the crowds looking for Prince Ali. I finally found the young prince, dressed in a black leather jacket with a black jumper. He was with Prince Ghazi bin Mohammad, King Abdullah's cousin and his adviser on tribal affairs, who wore a red kufia.

It was a dream come true for me. Here were two princes standing shoulder to shoulder with their subjects, fighting for the same cause. Prince Ali greeted me warmly and said he was delighted with the turnout (there were about four thousand people behind us at this point, with more joining the procession every minute). 'Rana,' he said, 'I would be very grateful if you would escort us to our meetings with the heads of the Upper and Lower House and the

Prime Minister.' I was hardly going to refuse! I checked and rechecked that I had my notebook with me, as I wanted to record every word and make sure a true account of the day's historic events was read by as many people as possible.

The level of support was tremendous. At the rally, MP Noman Ghuweiri, also a tribal leader in Zarqa, condemned so-called honour killings: 'Only the rule of God should apply in such cases. These crimes do not occur within tribes. The Bedouin women are well respected and their rights are preserved and secured.'

Some other tribal leaders spoke negatively about the issue during the march, including tribal leader Trad Fayez, who was quoted by the Associated Press as saying: 'There is no harm in killing whoever is proved to have committed a bad act ... A woman is like an olive tree. When its branch catches woodworm, it has to be chopped off so that the society stays clean and pure. We will not become like Europe and western countries and condone dissipation. We are tribes and devout Muslims. We stick to our customs.'[7]

We reached the Parliament building and crossed through the masses to talk with the Speaker of the Upper House. I was just behind the head of the delegation when we reached the door but as I tried to follow them inside, I found myself caught up in a crush as people tried to squeeze through the doors.

Prince Ghazi, who had already entered the building, also with great difficulty, looked back and saw me losing the battle to get inside. He shouted at the guards to help me in. It didn't help that I was carrying a black flag, but somehow I squeezed myself between various people until I popped through the doors like a champagne cork and flew unceremoniously towards the princes; I was about to fall flat on my face when Prince Ghazi caught me.

The Speaker of the Upper House and former Prime Minster Zeid Rifai welcomed us into his office. Prince Ali told him that we were there to express the will of the Jordanian people to cancel Article 340 because it did not reflect our customs, traditions or

Islamic Sharia. Rifai praised our efforts and described the participation of the two princes as marking a new phase for the human rights movement in Jordan.

We then headed with the two princes to the office of the Speaker of the Lower House Abdul Hadi Majali, where several deputies were waiting for us. Prince Ali greeted them and came straight to the point. 'I feel ashamed when we know that such a law exists,' he told Majali and the other deputies, 'a law that was opposed by King Hussein and King Abdullah.' Prince Ghazi added, 'There is no basis for Article 340 in our religion or culture, and we have great hope that the deputies will reconsider their decision.'

But Majali refused to be cowed, and replied, 'We have our own customs and traditions and we deputies insist that if an individual surprises his female relative and kills her, he should benefit from a reduction [in penalty].' He also blamed the government for acting hastily on this issue without examining it thoroughly. But he added, 'We are against any individual who takes the life of a female relative in cold blood on the basis of rumours, suspicion or other hidden motives.'

'Look outside and you will see the people who oppose this law,' Prince Ali said. 'We urge you to reconsider. We ask you to take responsibility and make the decision that [will] push our country forward.'

But Majali's response was the same. 'This is a controversial issue and we have our own customs and traditions.'

'We are not here to attack anyone,' Prince Ali replied. 'We have democracy in Jordan, and you are the people's representatives, and you are in an official's position and you should bear this responsibility. We have much faith in you.'

With that, we left and, driving in a convoy of around sixty buses, we headed to the Prime Ministry. By the time we arrived, Prime Minister Abdur-Ra'uf S. Rawabdeh had left the building, so it was down to Deputy Prime Minister Marwan Hmoud to greet us instead.

Ignoring this rather obvious snub, Prince Ghazi told Hmoud that we were there to express our dismay at and condemnation of the rejection of the amendments to Article 340. Prince Ali added that hopefully this would be 'the beginning of changes to all legislations which have no Arab or Islamic basis and which are hindering the path of progress. We hope that you will face up to these issues.'

Although his reason seemed clear to me, there was a great deal of speculation about why the Prime Minister fled minutes before we arrived. A politician close to the Prime Minister told me that Rawabdeh was never convinced of our cause. He was pressured to pretend to agree with the amendments but that 'Culturally, he belongs with the MPs.' Others said that he had to be objective about the issue and therefore that was why he refused to meet with us.

The following day, Prince Ali posted a piece in several internet chat rooms to explain what had happened:

Contrary to some opinions, the demonstrations were organized and carried out without governmental or institutional help.

In fact, the prime minister [Abdur-Ra'uf S. Rawabdeh] stood against it. He contacted Jordanian TV and the papers and asked them not to publicize the demonstration. When we moved to the government, the prime minister was supposed to meet us. However, he sneaked out before we arrived.

As for the Muslim Brotherhood, who stood with Article 340, they contacted us and said they wanted to do a counter-demonstration, and we said it was all right for them to come. However, they had no idea of our great number and showed up with only a hundred demonstrators, some of whom filtered into our demonstration and approached the media in order to spread misinformation.

In reality, forces both within the government and Parliament had never intended the bill to pass in the first place ... the reason behind it is not about the article itself but fear that the article will lead to reforms … reforms that would hold them accountable, loosen their grip on power, by allowing people to move creatively and freely to move our country forwards.

It is an old game where Parliament and government oppose each other outwardly to give the image of democracy at the expense of the people and our progress. Meanwhile innocents are murdered and our country remains economically stagnant.

What really irked those forces of negativity is the fact that members of the Hashemite family and the people marched together… since they have been trying to use their institutions to create a barrier between the king and his people, so that they may gain more power, by trying to manipulate the king's decisions the way that suits them.

However, in times past, what kept this kingdom together was the fact that the king and the people rallied together to prevent forces of negativity from taking over the country.[8]

Some time later, Prince Ali assured me when I interviewed him in August 2006 that he had received the full backing and blessing of King Abdullah to organize the march. 'Every single member of our family considers this a very important issue because it is against our traditions and religion and is wrong. We are all emotional about this particular issue. King Abdullah is extremely open minded and I told him: "Look, this is an issue and I know this is your government, but is it OK if we make a stand?" He told me to go ahead.'

I asked him what he thought of the deputies' decision. 'Unfortunately, sometimes people take the easier route. They do not want to step on anyone's toes nor stir things up. This is because they cannot deal with this democracy on the one hand and because of their own fears on the other.'

Prince Ali criticized the government's handling of the matter. 'It was not a priority for the government and it brushed it over. This, to me, was very bad especially that the government represents the King and we know very well that the King and the royal family were completely against it. I really thought we could change things in a day; obviously you cannot. The whole culture needs to be changed.'

Prince Ali said that one reason why Prime Minister Rawabdeh refused to face us was that 'none of the officials actually believed that we would go through with it. When we did, they were surprised and confused. They did not know how to react. I was also surprised that the Prime Minister wasn't there. He was a respected politician.'

One of the main criticisms levelled at us that day had been voiced by Islamist Deputy Abdullah Akayleh, who was quoted in an article written by my colleague Dima Hamdan for *The Jordan Times* in February 2000: 'I find it strange that people should be grouped for such demonstrations. Tribal leaders did not join the march on their own accord, they were driven to it.'

Prince Ali said that he saw many tribal leaders who were fully aware of and fully supported what we were trying to achieve. One of the reasons for holding the march, he said, was 'to show that this custom was not a tribal tradition. This is an excuse that has been used by a lot of people before the demonstrations: that this was Jordanian culture.'

I was still buzzing after the march and was still furious that the MPs had refused to listen to the people, to its voters and to the royal family. Something in my gut told me to head over to the Criminal Court, that something would be happening there that day.

I wasn't wrong.

CHAPTER 8

Opening the Floodgates

The month before our march, on 4 October, thirty-four-year-old Samir Ayed saw his sister Hanan walking in the street in the company of two men at around 8 a.m. in the town of Zarqa. Apparently, he 'became enraged', drew a gun and shot her three times in the head. He then calmly sat and smoked a cigarette, gazing at his sister's body while he waited for the police to come and arrest him.

The defence argued that the thirty-two-year-old victim had been divorced twice for her 'poor conduct' and 'immoral behaviour'. I arrived at the courthouse just in time to catch the verdict. The court decided to amend the premeditated murder charge to that of a misdemeanour because he committed his crime in a fit of fury to cleanse his honour. He was sentenced to six months in prison. The court ruled that he benefited from Article 98, and not Article 340. This verdict, given on the day of our march, was a clear message from the judges of the Criminal Court to campaigners like me.

Also on the same day, the IAF held a press conference at which they claimed the government had banned them from holding a counter-march to voice their objection to our campaign. They announced that their scholars committee had issued a fatwa [religious decree] calling for the maintenance of Article 340 because 'it was the last fortress that would protect the morals of our society, and cancelling it was against the Islamic Sharia.'9

The fatwa said: 'Muslims in this country were surprised by a witty and misleading campaign which was aimed at scrapping Article 340, to destroy our Islamic, social and family values, by stripping men of their humanity when they surprise their wives or female relatives committing adultery, a right that was valued by the Islamic Sharia.'

'This article does not encourage killings as much as it encourages preserving one's virtue and the honour of the family,' it continued, and also called on Muslims to stop the 'suspicious campaign' targeting deputies.

The fatwa also questioned what would happen if Article 340 were scrapped. 'What do they expect from a man who is surprised and saw a man committing adultery with his wife or one of his female relatives? This man should not be angry and instead should control his temper and head to the nearest police station and complain, during which time the crime would have ended and no longer can be proven.'

The fatwa said this was against what God stipulated; that cancelling this article would encourage the spread of fornication and constitute a call to kill religious beliefs and Islamic fervour. 'Since foreign legislators also valued the fit of fury status for men and male relatives and offered them leniency in such crimes, and they are the ones living in a lewd atmosphere that allows relationships between men and women, then why should we not give the same excuse in our Islamic, Arab and Jordanian society?'

The Jordanian Ifta Department at the Ministry of Awqaf and Islamic Affairs, the highest religious authority in the Kingdom – the only body endowed with the authority to issue a fatwa in Jordan – remained silent when the IAF issued its fatwa.

The next day a local newspaper reported on a fatwa issued by the Al-Azhar Ifta Council, which was represented by Sheikh Mohammad Said Tantawi, one of the most respected Ifta institutions in the Sunni Muslim world. They said that no individual has the right to take the life of a female relative caught committing adultery or found in an adulterous situation: 'Instead, applying the punishment should be up to the ruler, because if individuals are allowed to take the law into their own hands, then it will create chaos.' The fatwa also said that if an individual stated the reason for his killing, then he would be slandering his victim and would be in violation of the Islamic Sharia which ordered people to keep these issues hidden in order to protect the dignity and honour of families.[10]

The Jordanian government took three months to respond to the IAF's fatwa. The Legislative Bureau at the Prime Ministry ruled that the issuance of fatwas in Jordan was the sole jurisdiction of the Ifta Council.

During our interview, Prince Ali described the Front as a very well-respected political party with a generally decent agenda in Jordan, but said, 'They are politicians and nobody has a monopoly on religion, especially if they are politicians. You can agree and disagree with them and they can agree and disagree with you but because they put the word "Islam" at the front of their name this does not mean they represent in any way anything more than any other Muslim, Christian or other religious person in this country.'

Jordanian political analyst Adnan Abu Odeh said the IAF believed that opposing change was a sure-fire vote-winning policy, while former Prime Minster Fayez Tarawneh said, 'The IAF use certain holy Quranic verses to scare voters into supporting them … The IAF issued a fatwa. They were not supposed to. Fatwas are for the rulers to issue.'

It was clear by now that those who opposed change were a small but powerful minority. A great many events took place and a great many groups spoke out in the wake of the march, including soldiers, politicians and sportspeople. A war veterans association wrote a public letter to King Abdullah, saying, 'There is no shame in talking about our mistakes and backwardness, but what is a shame is to cover it up as if nothing is happening. Crimes of honour are only inflicted on women, and with our respect to the opposing opinions, we believe it is time to cancel Article 340.' I couldn't have agreed more with their sentiment and it was such a boost to see this coming from a highly respected body of army officers.

Centrist Al-Ajial from the Generations Political Party also issued a statement condemning Article 340, which they said was used as 'a pretext for killers to commit all sorts of crimes against innocent women. Justifying a murder that occurred in a fit of fury could not be tolerated by an Arab and Muslim man who was brought up on virtue and preserving his honour, home and religion.'

In an editorial, *Al Rai* sports editor Samir Janakat called on all sports federations to take a 'positive and active role towards a phenomenon, which, according to statistics, mostly victimizes young females'.

Despite this tide of popular opinion, many deputies remained defiant. The fact that two princes had led the march had irked many of them, and they argued that the royal family should not interfere in Parliament's job. Many MPs cited this as the main reason why they had voted against the bill a second time.

On 23 February 2000, some fifty-five MPs signed a petition calling for Islamic Sharia to govern life in Jordan 'to rid the nation of the burden of a bloated bureaucracy, favouritism and dereliction the country is presently suffering'. They also made it clear that they believed the royal family should not meddle in politics.

There was a huge and unexpected public outcry against this petition, which caused thirty of the fifty-five signatories to withdraw their names. Suddenly they started to argue among themselves over how the petition had been worded. Clearly they had not expected it to cause such controversy.

Some deputies stated they had changed their minds on reflection or because they had not paid sufficient attention to the text of the motion. Others said they decided to retract their statement on the motion because it had been 'misinterpreted' by the media. Still others said they had not read the petition before signing it, and some admitted as Muslims they had been 'embarrassed', and had felt obliged to sign when MP Mohammad Bani Hani asked for their support.[11]

A week after our march, the Senate reviewed the draft for the second time and upheld its previous decision, forcing a joint session of the Upper and Lower Houses to vote on the draft law once and for all. But after various delays, the joint session was never held and Parliament was dissolved for the summer vacation in June 2001. It seemed as though the opposition would, like us, never consider giving up for a moment.

This now meant that a joint session could be held only if the King summoned Parliament for an extraordinary sitting. According to the Constitution, in an extraordinary sitting, lawmakers are limited to the discussion of drafts specified in a Royal Decree.

On 22 February 2000, the Islamist weekly newspaper *Al-Sabeel* announced it was conducting what it claimed was a 'comprehensive' three-day survey aimed at determining the public's attitudes towards the cancellation of Article 340.

The questionnaire asked:

Are you for or against the cancellation of Article 340?
Is honour killing a major problem and does it deserve all the attention it has received from the government?
Had you heard of Article 340 before the recent campaign?
Do you believe that these crimes happen because Sharia laws on adultery are not applied in the Jordanian Penal Code?
Do you believe the movement to cancel Article 340 was based on international pressure or internal political strategies?

The editor-in-chief of the newspaper, Assef Jolani, was very honest about expressing his bias. 'Our position is clear on this issue. We are against all this attention and we felt that this movement was not based on the needs of people,' he wrote in his editorial. He said most Islamists opposed the draft law because it was the result of international pressure.

He emphasized that Muslims are opposed to shedding the blood of innocent women and that the government was at fault because it did not apply the Islamic Sharia. 'That is why some people take the law into their own hands, because they know there is no punishment for adulterers,' he explained.

The survey was conducted randomly in the cities of Amman, Zarqa and Irbid, as well as being available online. Two days later, the newspaper issued the results of the survey on its front page, stating that seventy-six per cent of the 163 respondents were against cancelling the article and nineteen per cent were in favour, while the rest were undecided. The survey found that seventy-eight per cent of the women and seventy-seven per cent of the men surveyed were in favour of keeping the article.

Fifty-eight per cent of those surveyed said the government's campaign was the result of international pressure and eighty-one per cent said so-called honour crimes take place in Jordan because the Islamic Sharia on adultery is not part of the Penal Code.[12]

Other deputies, along with the local press, accused the Netherlands of blackmailing Jordan by threatening to cut aid if Article 340 was not changed. The Dutch ambassador to Jordan, Bernard Tangelder, denied these reports, claiming they were merely rumour based on misquotes. Others accused the government of succumbing to the USA, claiming that the USA was going to block a $25 million donation to Jordan.

Prince Ali brushed these accusations aside. 'We are not a country that gets easily pressured by anybody. This is simply a ridiculous excuse. We are a small country and live in a tough neighbourhood. There are many times in our history when we have been besieged. We have been pressured by big and regional powers. But we are not afraid of taking stands that no other Arab country has ever taken. Be it an Arab or foreign embassy, we are much stronger than that.'

Prince Ali went as far as to criticize some foreign missions for their interference, or at least for their bad timing when I interviewed him. 'The US Embassy said a few days before the voting that the law should be changed. That helped the opposition, who used this as the excuse they needed to say they would not be forced to do something because the west wants them to.'

Many people concluded that we failed in convincing the Lower House to cancel Article 340. That is of course absolutely true, but as far as I was concerned, the battle had just begun and we had already succeeded in improving women's rights in many other ways. It was often brought home to me, however, that the opposition to change ran deep and moved in powerful circles.

The government began to promote the idea of introducing a quota so that women would have a voice in Parliament in the upcoming elections. My colleague Alia Shukri Hamzeh from *The Jordan Times* was the only female reporter who attended a debate with the Parliament Legal Committee to discuss the new draft election law with the heads of other women's organizations.

A deputy from Amman Fourth District strongly opposed the idea. He said that being an MP was a man's job; a woman can jeopardize her honour by going out late at night to take part in related social activities. If his daughter stayed out late at night he would shoot her himself, he added. He told the gathering that a woman's presence in Parliament 'would be damaging, since a woman in the house would distract male deputies and stir trouble when male deputies instinctively look at her breasts.'

At that moment, several of his colleagues pointed out to him that there was a female reporter in the room. He later told Hamzeh that had he known she was in the room he would not have made these remarks, but he did not apologize. He also pleaded with her not to mention his name in the article.[13]

But perhaps the most disturbing statement of all came from former Justice Minister and current Deputy, Abdul Karim Dughmi. He told foreign journalist Eliza Griswold in an interview published in *The Sunday Times* on 7 August 2001, entitled 'Death and dishonour', on the topic of so-called honour crimes in the Kingdom: 'All women killed in cases of honour are prostitutes. I believe prostitutes deserve to die.'

* * *

In June and July of 2000, we went back to the streets of Amman and other cities to collect more signatures and to evaluate the level of awareness among ordinary citizens. We headed to Wihdat neighbourhood and entered shops located on the main road, Madaba Street, asking owners and shoppers to sign our petitions. To our delight the result was very positive; the majority of people we spoke to this time had better knowledge of the issue. Many voiced their objection and immediately signed the petition. This time, we didn't find it as hard to convince anyone to sign, as people had already been informed about the subject.

Committee member Maha Abu Ayyash entered a shop in Wihdat where two men were getting ready for noon prayers. She said she was hesitant at first to enter because they seemed to be in a private conversation. But when she entered, one of the men looked at her and noticed the petitions in her hand. His first reaction was, 'Where have you been? I've been waiting for you!' He explained that he had a business partner who had killed one of his female relatives only to use Article 98 to escape justice.

While many local NGOs, professional associations and political parties organized debates and workshops to discuss the issue and the efforts exerted in Jordan, opposing rallies continued. In a lecture organized by the Culture Committee of the Jordanian

Professional Associations, former female senator and practicing lawyer Na'eyla Rashdan accused us of running a 'misleading campaign'.

'The campaigners were calling for the cancellation of Article 340, claiming it was responsible for the killings of innocent women, when in fact the article addresses a certain condition when women are caught committing adultery,' Rashdan said.

'What do people expect from a man who catches his wife committing adultery with another man? Smile for them and apologize for disturbing them? No one has the right to end the life of an innocent woman, who may be the victim of rumour or suspicion ... But in Article 340, when a woman is caught committing adultery there is no innocence.'[14]

Rashdan instead suggested that women benefit from the same exemption as men.

Our lawyer, Asma Khader, who dedicated her entire career to fighting for women's causes in Jordan, responded to Rashdan's suggestions by stressing that no one should have the right to end someone else's life. 'The article is a dangerous clause imposed on women's lives because in almost all these crimes, women are the sole victims. The male partner, if there was any, is rarely harmed.'

The opposition had nothing new to say and simply repeated their old conspiracy theories – the west trying to destroy the east – and their belief in the need for women to preserve themselves in order to protect society from 'moral deterioration'.

Almost two months later, Khader and Deputy Kharabsheh met face to face again at a lecture on Article 340 hosted by one of the Rotaract clubs in the Kingdom. Kharabsheh again accused the west and Zionists of being behind many campaigns aimed at destroying Jordan and exposing misleading information to the international community. He insisted the article remain because 'the control over women prevents sexual diseases and mixed paternity'. He claimed he wanted women to be protected, respected and afforded dignity, but added, 'Jordan is still a male-dominated society and men are more capable than women are. Women have not developed themselves yet; they are not experienced enough, having not held high positions in authority as men have.'

In her speech, Khader said that the campaigns helped raise awareness. One such example of this was that two families whose daughters were murdered had come to her after hearing about the campaign, and had asked her to take legal action against the killers.

* * *

As a result of the increased campaign activity and pressure from so many groups, the government passed two new temporary laws in the summer of 2001.

First, Article 340 was expanded so that women received the same reduction in penalty as men. Needless to say, offering equal treatment for women in this particular case was not one of our aspirations. We were against the concept of pardoning a person for killing another in general.

The second new law, known as 'Khuloe', granted women the right to file for divorce in return for monetary compensation without having to specify the reasons. Under this law, a woman had to return the dowry given to her by her husband before the wedding and waive all of the financial obligations listed in the marriage contract.

The government ignored Article 98 despite the efforts of the Royal Commission on Human Rights, which in November 2001 presented suggestions to the government to curb these crimes by lengthening the period of imprisonment for murderers. As it stood, a person who burgled a house or stole a car would spend more time in prison than someone who had taken the life of a female relative for reasons of 'honour'.

Nevertheless, both temporary amendments were seen as a victory for the women's movement in Jordan, especially the Khuloe law, which had been in demand for a long time. It normally took several years for a decision to be given to women seeking divorce through the Sharia Courts – and the decision was very often a refusal.

Islamist Ibrahim Zeid Kilani, who was the president of the IFA's Fatwa Committee, did not voice any objection to the Khuloe law when I contacted him for a reaction in December 2001, but he strongly criticized amending Article 340, saying it was 'a step to protect unfaithful women and prostitutes'. Kilani said the amendments did not protect innocent women who were killed because of rumours, suspicion or inheritance reasons, and argued that the government should have amended Article 98 instead. Again, Kilani blamed the USA: 'The government amended Article 340 because this is what Americans want. They want to destroy our families.'

Both temporary laws remained effective until a new Parliament was elected in 2003. In the first session of the Lower House on 3 August, MPs reviewed some sixty temporary laws, including Article 340 and the Khuloe law.

The deputies debated and voted on all these laws before referring them to various committees for consideration. When it came to Article 340, in contrast to the 1999 vote, this time there was a hand count. A total of fifty MPs out of the eighty-nine present at the session raised their hands to reject the new amendment.

Khuloe was also rejected outright in the same session. Their excuse this time was that Khuloe was against the Islamic Sharia and amending Article 340 was 'dangerous and would be bad for society'.

Some one hundred protesters, including myself, demonstrated a week later in front of Parliament. We carried banners and handed out pamphlets and intercepted deputies' cars. Whenever I managed to stop one, I told the MP to remember their female relatives when they voted on both articles in future. Most drove on quickly, leaving their windows firmly rolled up.

MPs Mohammad Abu Fares and Mahmoud Kharabsheh stopped to talk to us. They assured us they would always work to see the Khuloe law rejected because it contradicted the 'Islamic Sharia and women will destroy the family if divorce was in their hands'.

When I told Deputy Abu Fares that Egypt's Grand Mufti from Al-Azhar had approved Khuloe in Egypt as part of Sharia since March 2000, his answer was: 'Al-Azhar's Mufti is an agent for the Egyptian government.'

Other liberal deputies, such as Dr Abdul Rahim Malhas and Ghaleb Zuby, promised that they would work hard to convince the deputies who opposed the law to change their minds.

What was most disappointing of all was that two of the six women who had won parliamentary seats, thanks to the new quota introduced by the government, voted against the law because 'although the legislation had some positive aspects, its implementation only facilitated divorce'. Two of the remaining four did not show up for the session and the remaining two voted in favour of amending the law. None of the female deputies showed up for our protest and they all entered the Parliament building via the back door that day.

Lawyer and human rights activist Reem Abu Hassan, one of the organizers of the protest in which the National Council for Family Affairs was also involved, said that this organization planned to co-ordinate their efforts with other NGOs to debate the issue with the Senate's Legal Committee. The same scenario occurred; the Upper House upheld the decision to introduce Khuloe and change Article 340 twice. The Lower House rejected it both times.

On 6 September, the day the Lower House rejected the draft amendment for the second time, newspapers plastered the story 'Lower House rejects honour crime bill' over their front pages.

I found this headline terribly disturbing. I called some of my reliable sources, asking if any woman had been killed so far in

Jordan after the newspapers had been published. The source told me there were none – so far.

My fears, however, soon proved justified. A source called back in the evening to tell me about a horrific murder that had occurred earlier that day.

CHAPTER 9

Changing Attitudes

Two sisters, aged twenty and twenty-seven, had left their family's home three years ago. The eldest married a native Arab in a civil ceremony without her family's knowledge and her younger sister had fled the family home shortly after to join her.

Then, one of the defendants had spotted the sisters shopping in a local market, followed them to discover where they had been living and informed their brothers. They then paid their siblings a surprise visit. When one of the sisters opened the door, they ran inside and hacked the two women to death with axes.

I was unable to sleep that night. I was so enraged. Imaginary scenes from the murder replayed in my head every time I tried to close my eyes. What were the two sisters' last thoughts on that day of horror? To be killed by their own axe-wielding brothers … it nearly broke me, it was just such a waste of life. I felt tired, lifeless; I couldn't go on.

But it turned out there was one vital difference. At the trial, the judge refused to offer the defendants lenience and he sentenced them to death. This was then immediately commuted to ten years in prison because the parents asked to have the charges against their sons dropped.

This, for me, was a landmark case. It was the first sign that the Criminal Court was beginning to change their attitude to these crimes.

One important activity that I think played a crucial role in changing attitudes in Jordan regarding domestic violence at this time was the Family Protection Project, a UK-funded scheme that was implemented in Jordan for almost six years, starting in 2000.

This project focused on training judges, criminal prosecutors, police officers, physicians, social workers and religious scholars to be more aware of and sensitive to domestic violence. It also encouraged and trained police investigators and criminal prosecutors to take crimes against women in general more seriously.

As a result, doctors at one government hospital started paying more attention to cases of accidental or supposedly natural deaths of women. In one of the first cases of its kind, doctors became suspicious when a family arrived with their dead daughter at a hospital claiming that she had been crushed by a vehicle carrying a water tank. When they examined her body, they noticed multiple wheel marks that led them to deduce that she had been run over several times.

The police launched a criminal investigation. The two brothers confessed to murdering their married sister, a mother of a four-year-old child. They drove over her several times to cleanse their family's honour because the victim 'was divorced twice, was known for her bad behaviour and went out with many men'.

One of the most important establishments in Jordan, the National Institute for Forensic Medicine, played a major role in breaking the social and official silence over these brutal murders. I worked with them often, once we discovered that we shared the same goals. The head of the Institute, Dr Mumen Hadidi, has been instrumental in the fight against so-called crimes of honour.

Dr Hadidi became personally involved after the charred bodies of two sisters were brought to his autopsy table in 1996. He had performed a virginity test on the two women when they were alive a month earlier. 'We had reported deaths of women as far back as the 1980s for reasons of honour. We felt that these families thought they were getting rid of something bad in our society. Personally, I had confused feelings about these crimes at that point.'

But he got his answer when he saw the fear and horror in the eyes of the two young sisters, aged eighteen and nineteen, brought to his clinic one morning, escorted by several policemen, as if they had committed a major crime. They had eloped with their husbands to Egypt and hoped this would force their family to accept their marriages, but they were quickly brought back to Jordan with the help of Interpol.

Dr Hadidi was astonished by the swift police action in the case. He attributed it to the fact that the police officers, as men, felt they needed to bring these two teenagers back because what they had done, eloping to another country, was dangerous.

Although his official government report stated that the two sisters were still virgins, it failed to convince the family to spare their lives. 'After examining them, I bade them farewell. I felt it was the last time I would see these two girls. I felt they were like sheep waiting to be slaughtered. I will never forget them. They are always present in my mind. They wanted my help and I could not give it.'

The family pledged not to harm them and returned home, keeping their wayward daughters in the family home until the day they burned to death in the kitchen in an 'accident' a short time later. No one was ever tried.

So much of the problem of violence against women in general, and specifically in so-called honour crimes, revolves around the hymen – the proof of virginity; a literal seal of virtue. It represents the 'honour' of the girl and, more importantly, of her family. For more than a thousand years, women across the world from Europe to the Middle East have been expected to be virgins on their wedding night – often on pain of death. The seal cannot be broken until then and as a result that first night together bears phenomenal importance for Arab women. Some so-called honour crimes are known to occur precisely when a woman fails to bleed as a result of penetration. The bride is then taken back to her family, who might kill her for having shamed them.[15]

This has its roots in numerous ancient texts, including the Old Testament, specifically in Deuteronomy (22:13–21), where proof of the bride's virginity could be presented to both sets of parents in the form of stains on the bedsheets. If an unwed woman was found not to have been a virgin, then she was to be punished by being stoned to death.

Dr Arwa Amiry, a psychology professor at the University of Jordan, pointed out to me during an interview in September 2006 that Arab societies put all the weight of their honour on women and their virginity. In particular, a man's 'honour' derives from the struggle to retain the chastity of the women in his family. When a man is shamed in this context, through female misbehaviour, his masculinity is damaged; it's as if he has been castrated. Husbands-to-be consider virginity evidence of exclusive possession, proof that the 'merchandise' is brand new and that his wife will not be able to compare his performance unfavourably to that of another man.[16]

Dozens of gynaecologists have reported that they have performed many hymen restoration operations either secretly or with their families' knowledge just before a wedding night. In Jordan in 2002, I attended a rare and daring lecture organized by a medical centre at which psychiatrists and physicians discussed this topic. Pathologist Dr Ahmad Bani Hani of the National Institute of Forensic Medicine said the fear of not seeing blood on the wedding night is a joint factor for both men and women. 'We have had families come to the National Institute first thing in the morning after the wedding night, wanting to examine the woman because she did not bleed.'

Psychiatrist Dr Mohammad Habashneh said, 'Women in this part of the world are haunted by the idea of wanting to prove they are virgins from the time they become aware of this issue until their wedding night ... trust between couples should not be based on drops of blood, but it seems that women in our part of the world are guilty of not being virgins until proven otherwise.'

Dr Mumen Hadidi, who performed virginity tests on hundreds of women throughout his medical career, told me in an interview in August 2006 that it is always a tough moment for him, professionally, when a girl is brought to his centre by police where she is 'pressured to do the test because there was no clear cut consent for the examination'. Dr Hadidi's job is to issue a certificate of 'proof' for the family. 'On many occasions we examine a woman and find her hymen to be intact and we write a report stating just that. Still many families are not convinced by our reports and these women are returned to our morgue tables, murdered a few days later.' It is clear that the results of this examination are often considered to be a license to kill, as in the case of Sarhan, described in chapter 2, who killed his sister and was excused in part by the court judgement which cited the medical report as proof that his sister was no longer a virgin, considering this to be a crime in itself.

Dr Hadidi decided to conduct his own scientific research and review the cases of murdered women. 'I felt that there was a message we, at the Institute, should convey to people. Our role is not only to open and close the body; our role is much greater than that. We can provide evidence that helps solve social ills.'

Dr Hadidi also appointed the first female resident forensic specialist, Dr Israa Tawalbeh, in March 2003. Dr Tawalbeh told me, 'I deplore injustice, especially actions that target women and children. At the same time, I wanted to defend people's rights and I felt by joining the Institute I would be able to do both.' She has proven herself to be a valuable addition to the team, paving the way for the appointment of another female member of staff.

Awareness has increased in Jordan. Judges and criminal prosecutors are keen to call to my attention harsh verdicts they have seen against men who have committed so-called honour crimes. On many instances the judiciary has rejected the fit of fury argument that is raised by the defendants and their lawyers during trial. The attorney general, Judge Yassin Abdullat, has started appealing three- and six-month verdicts passed in such cases, demanding justice for the victims. On many occasions, the Cassation Court (Jordan's Supreme Court) has intervened to overturn six-month prison terms and has returned the case to the Criminal Court, demanding a tougher sentence. Of course the system is still nowhere near perfect, and light verdicts still slip through every now and then.

Many Jordanians wanted the 1999 campaign to continue, believing quite rightly that more should be done to improve women's rights. Once the flame had been ignited, it refused to die – and gradually, thanks to the will of thousands and thousands of determined people, we have started to see its positive effect; things have been changing for the better in Jordan.

Since I became known for my work, many schools and universities have invited me to speak about my experiences. In one school, I watched in amazement as children performed a play about so-called honour crimes at the end of the school year. They told me they wanted to be part of the change that was taking place in our society. The expression of such a desire would have been unheard of just a couple of years earlier. More recently, many theatres have staged plays about so-called honour crimes and violence against women, with many of the voices opposing these crimes coming directly from male actors and performers.

During 2005 and 2006, Jordan took part in the Sixteen-Day Global Campaign Against Gender Violence supported by Freedom House, a US NGO. Activities included plays at universities, lectures, training courses and bicycle rides to Parliament to demand just laws for women. The campaign was widely covered in the press and domestic violence was publicly discussed for a long time afterwards.

Nonetheless, Articles 98 and 340 remain in place, unchanged, and are still relied upon by many of those accused of murder. Senator Leila Sharaf told me, 'Without a constructive plan of action, no one [official] will move. The grassroots movement should work on a plan of action and should continue their efforts by collecting signatures, issuing press releases, meeting and sending telegrams to officials and deputies pressing for positive change.'

I, and others, have taken her advice and will not rest until women are protected in law from these horrendous crimes. The former Prime Minister, Dr Tarawneh, has since told me that the government is determined to change Article 340, but 'We are waiting for the appropriate timing.'

Prince Ali is also certain that the day will come when all the laws that discriminate against women will be abolished:

> It is one of a few important things we need to change in this country. You cannot repress, in any way, fifty per cent of your society. You need them to work and be an active part of the society. I hope it changes but there has to be a whole change in mentality.
>
> We are the ones who talked about the so-called honour crimes, not to expose ourselves, but because this is an issue that needs to be changed. We are mature enough as a country to deal with it and many people are voluntarily getting involved with it. You do not see this anywhere else and this is a great sign and what gives us hope.

Many people tell me that the campaign failed in convincing Parliament to vote for the bill to amend Article 340. But I truly believe that by raising public awareness and debate about the issue, we succeeded in setting a precedent for the younger generation to learn from our experience, and paved the way for people to realize

that they are capable of organizing successful marches and petitions – that in our democracy, people can be agents for change.

One thing is for certain. Even though the campaign has brought
the issue of so-called honour crimes in Jordan permanently to the
surface, women are still not safe and, as we will soon see, murder
committed in the name of honour continues around the world to
this day, and many brave activists risk their own lives to help. First,
though, comes the story of an incredible event that very nearly
ruined our cause.

CHAPTER 10

Two Steps Back

One day early in 2003 I arrived at work and, as usual, checked my in-box. I receive emails from all over the world, but I was interested to note that on this occasion there were some from Australia. The first I read was from a woman called Lauren J:

> I wish to express my disgust and horror at the 'honour crimes' in Jordan ... I am especially outraged that girls and women in Jordan are treated with such disrespect and disregard that it is considered acceptable by society that they are murdered for such innocent behaviour as talking to a man ... If society and the Parliament allow it to continue, Jordan will soon be seen as a merciless, evil killer of its own people.

There was another from a woman called Tanya:

> It is shocking enough to hear all about the Arab culture and how women are treated like prisoners having no freedom at all and are treated like dirt, let alone male family members killing them when they have done nothing wrong!! All the men in this country are chauvinist, sexist, self-centered ANIMALS with no feelings whatsoever ... My heart goes out to all Arab women. I wish something could be done and they could all be rescued and brought here to Australia to live. I can certainly say that I live in the best country in the world. At least women are safe here.

Another wrote: 'The Middle East is somewhere I have not yet been to and Jordan in particular was on my wish list of places to go. However, I refuse for my tourist dollars to be spent in a country where male family members kill their own female relatives for any purpose whatsoever, let alone for falling in love.'

I was worried by these emails, as they were so aggressive and unrepresentative of the reality of Jordanian life. Of course we suffer with so-called honour killings but, thankfully, they remain comparatively rare and Jordan is largely a progressive, modern society in which the majority of women, such as myself, are able to speak out. These people were writing to me about a Jordan that I did not know – a country full of evil men who butchered hundreds of women every year. More and more emails continued to arrive from Australia and New Zealand and I was baffled as to why.

I soon received an explanation. Yasmine Bahrani, an Arab-Iraqi journalist, who was working as a features editor for *USA Today*, told me about a book that had just been published and had hit the bestseller lists in Australia. Called *Forbidden Love* in Australia and later published as *Honor Lost* in the USA, by Norma Khouri, it was about so-called honour crimes in Jordan.

Yasmine shocked me with what she had to say next. 'Rana, you have to read this book and do something about it. It's filled with huge mistakes, false accusations and slander directed at Muslims and Arabs. What is worse,' she added, 'is that the book has been translated into fifteen languages and is selling well all over the world! Khouri says that Jordan is bordered by Kuwait and Lebanon and that Arab women do not have a say in what to study and that they are oppressed in every aspect of life.'

Unable to believe what I was hearing, I got hold of a copy.

Forbidden Love tells the story of Khouri and her childhood Muslim friend named Dalia. Khouri, who describes herself as belonging to a strict Christian family in Jordan, claims she ran a unisex hairdresser's shop with Dalia. According to Khouri, Dalia was killed by her father after he discovered she was in love with a Christian (one of her male customers). Khouri also writes that she had to flee Jordan in 1996 to escape death after speaking out against the murder. She says she ran away to Greece and started writing her book in an internet café.

I visited the street in Jabal Hussein where Khouri claimed to have lived with Dalia, the honour crime victim. No one I spoke to had ever heard of these two women or their hairdresser's shop, nor had there been a murder in the name of family honour in that neighbourhood for over twenty years.

There were also gross historic, geographic and demographic errors. On page two, Khouri states, 'Unlike the Jordan River, no longer strong enough to flow down to Amman ...' The Jordan River never passed through Amman; it has always flowed through the Jordan Valley.

On the same page, it is stated that Jordan is bordered by many countries and mentions Lebanon, Egypt and Kuwait, among others. The countries bordering Jordan are Syria, Iraq, Saudi Arabia, the Occupied Palestinian Territories and Israel.

The description of women's lives in Jordan was the thing that really disturbed me the most. Khouri said that the situation of women in Jordan is 'a stifling prison tense with the risk of death at the hands of loved ones and [they] had no right to argue with men in their families'.

But one of the most disturbing statements was: 'Life in Dalia's home was basically like life in all Muslim homes in Amman, regardless of class, money, or neighbourhood.' To illustrate this statement, Khouri claimed that Dalia was not permitted to eat at the same table with, or at the same time as, the men in her household. Dalia was to cook the meal and quietly serve it to them. Only when they had finished and left the room were she and her mother allowed to eat the leftovers. While this family lifestyle could be the case for a few individuals, this sweeping generalization does not in any way reflect the reality of life in the vast majority of Muslim homes in Jordan.

Khouri also said that Dalia was only one of thousands of women who are victims of honour crimes yearly in Jordan, again a gross exaggeration that left my head spinning. Perhaps her most blatant giveaway was Khouri's claim that she ran a unisex hairdresser's shop in Jordan with her friend Dalia; the whole story revolves around this fact. The Hairdressers' Union in Jordan, in charge of issuing operating licenses, informed us that they had never heard of such a hairdresser's, and that it was against the Union's regulations to issue licenses to unisex hairdressers – so none existed in Jordan. Nor did the Greater Amman Municipality have any record either of this shop or of the owners. In addition, families who had brought up their daughters so strictly would never have allowed them to work in a unisex salon, had it existed, let alone handle men's hair.

Khouri also stated that Christians were oppressed in Jordan and had to live according to Islamic law. In reality, all citizens abide by the civil laws that govern the country. When it comes to religious laws, these mostly govern family issues; Muslims abide by a certain set of laws while Christians abide by laws drafted by their own churches.

Khouri wrote: 'We [Christians] must not build new churches or temples, or sound church bells. We must not build any building taller than one belonging to a Muslim, as this would disgrace our neighbours.' Not only are these false statements, they are ridiculous. The bells of Christian churches ring on every religious occasion in Jordan, such as weddings, holidays and Sunday prayers.

Khouri also claimed that from the moment she defended Dalia publicly she became a legitimate target for an honour killing. I never came across any murder whereby the friend of an honour crime victim has been murdered.

There are dozens of other small details: the mention of a 50JD bill (these were introduced four years after the story took place);

she went to a café that did not exist at the time of the story; a ciga-rette brand was mentioned which was introduced years later; she claimed that *The Jordan Times* is a weekly newspaper when in fact it is a daily. The list is very long and I will spare you the majority of the errors, as I'm sure you will have got the idea by now.

The timing of the book's publication (six years after she started writing it) raised some important questions. It was first published in 2002, not long after the attacks against the USA on 11 September 2001, and during the build-up to the war in Iraq.

Yasmine Bahrani wrote an important article in *USA Today* on 24 February 2003, entitled '*Honor Lost* troubles knowledgeable reader', a month after the book started receiving extensive cover-age in the western media and entered the bestseller lists (it went on to sell several hundred thousand copies).

Bahrani wrote:

> One way to end this despicable practice [so-called honour killings] is to call attention to it, and Khouri's tale has some valuable aspects. As the United States prepares for a possible invasion of Iraq, Khouri focuses on a tragic aspect of that region's culture … Khouri asserts that the kingdom's Christians must pay a special poll tax. Such a tax on Christians and Jews is well known in Islamic history, but it hasn't been imposed in Jordan in decades … Honour killing is a serious and wrenching issue in the Middle East. It is certainly helpful to examine such a tragedy, but the context and details of Khouri's case make it appear atypical, if not unique.

Back in Jordan, people began hearing about the book from friends and relatives living in the countries where it had been published. They told of how the book had had a negative impact on their lives, especially in the case of friends and relatives who lived in the USA and Australia.

It is vital to understand the incredible amount of damage Khouri has done by writing this book. She ruined our cause. Those who opposed change, who suspected that a western agenda lies behind our activism, were suddenly presented with 'evidence' that crimes of honour were a fiction and exaggeration and sought to link our campaign to Khouri's book.

Things had already been hard enough for us without this. And then, incredibly, Khouri had the nerve to put my name and email address in the back of the book – and urged people to send letters of objection to me! She had also included, without permission, the Jordanian National Commission for Women (JNCW) and the Jordanian National Campaign to Eliminate So-Called Honour Crimes. We had been well and truly tarnished by this dreadful account.

I had had it with this book. I could not stand by and watch years of work by journalists, activists and NGOs being sabotaged. I grabbed it, marched down to my favourite café and studied the book for several days, listing every single factual error it contained (I eventually had a list of eighty points).

With the help of my colleague Nisreen Alami, I prepared a letter and sent it to the publishing house along with the list. The publishing house responded by saying that they did not plan to consider the points on our list and that they stood by Khouri's story.

Of course, this just made me all the more determined.

The harsh and angry emails from New Zealand and Australia continued to fill my in-box. One person wrote on 22 July 2003: 'Jordan and the royal family claim to be modern, while these crimes still take place in Jordan.' A woman named Natasha H. wrote: 'Jordan is not a society of democracy but one of brutality and its leaders should be ashamed.'

Another person named Ellie from Australia wrote to me three days later: 'We have just had a case here of a paedophile who has indecently assaulted up to six hundred girls from the age of one to 15. Under Islamic law all six hundred girls would have to be killed, while the real criminal walked free.'

Keristi D. wrote an email during the same period saying she had just finished reading Norma Khouri's book and declared that she was puzzled – she had visited Jordan in 2001 and found it to be a very enjoyable and vibrant place with helpful people – it was nothing like the decription in the book. 'Before reading the book *Forbidden Love* I told many people that if given the chance they should discover the wonderful country of Jordan, but now I would consider not even mentioning I went there due to the disgust I feel at the laws and crimes against the women of the country I so enjoyed.'

She continued: 'If I knew then what I have been aware of now through Norma's book, what went on behind the great façade they have built for tourists, I would not have gone. I plan on advertising Norma's book to as many people as I can to make them also aware of the wrongs that are occurring in a country I thought far superior to its neighbours.'

Another woman from Australia wrote on 8 November 2003: 'I am too angry to express my feelings on this particular book, plus I may get into trouble by expressing what I would like to do to Muslim men (Oh yes, I would love to stoop to their levels and show them what they do to these stifled, prisoned [*sic*] women).'

I received emails from children, which made me sad to think that their first understanding of the Middle East was a book full of fictional daily horrors. Sarah, a nine-year-old girl from New Zealand, wrote me an email on 22 May 2003, thinking I was Norma Khouri. She found the book in her mother's car; the minute she looked at it she knew straight away that it was 'the right book for me … when I found out it was true I was shocked and it must have been scary to you. I do not know your friend. I bet she was wonderful … I think it was good to write about that awful story and now you can tell the world your feelings and different religions and what they believe.'

This book was doing irreparable damage both to our cause and to Jordan as a whole. It also had a major impact on the debate about invading neighbouring Iraq, especially in Australia where the book eventually sold 200,000 copies. Ihab Shalbak was a member of the Palestine Human Rights Campaign and member of the No War in Iraq committee. Shalbak, who lived in Australia, sent me the following email: 'As you are aware the debate about the morality of the war against the Iraqi people is a major issue in Australia and western countries, in Australia even the conservative right wing constituents came out to speak against the war, strangely and suddenly Norma Khouri appeared in these very conservative constituents to speak about the oppression of Jordanian, Arab and Muslim women and the need to liberate them.'

Khouri had indeed held a series of readings in Australia (where she now lived) that had 'moved festival audiences to tears'. It was clear that her book succeeded in further embedding the stereotypical image of 'Arab' men. This book was perpetuating the generalizations and misconceptions that 'all Arab men are chauvinists', 'all Arab men terrorize women', 'all Arab women are oppressed', 'Arab women do not have choices', and so on.

'In such circumstances,' Shalbak continued, 'Norma Khouri is providing what [George] Bush, [Tony] Blair and [John] Howard failed to deliver which is the moral case of the war, for attacking savage Arab men and liberate Arab women and the feminized Arab world.'

Shalbak also contacted Malcolm Knox, the literary editor of the *Sydney Morning Herald*. Knox contacted me in June and confirmed the great extent of the book's influence in Australia, saying it was crucial to know how reliable *Forbidden Love* was.

Knox travelled to Chicago and found Khouri's family. He learned that Khouri was married and had two children; she had moved with her family to the USA when she was three years old. He confronted Khouri but she denied everything and claimed that she had lived in Jordan at the time of Dalia's death. Knox wrote a large feature that appeared on the front page of the *Sydney Morning Herald* on 24 July 2003.

Reporters Tony Koch and Paul Whittaker followed this up with an article in *The Australian* on 10 August 2004, entitled 'Khouri ready to defend her honour', in which they stated that her lawyers had confirmed that Khouri obtained a government permit to enter Australia after US Vice President Dick Cheney's eldest daughter, Elizabeth, had supported her application for Australian residency in 2003.

Based on Knox's findings and the list of errors compiled by Dr Amal Sabbagh (then secretary general of the JNCW) and myself, the publishers finally withdrew the book for good after Khouri failed to provide evidence that she ever lived in Jordan. The publishers also shelved plans to publish a second book by Khouri, *A Matter of Honour*, in November 2004. This was to have been about how she fled from Jordan following Dalia's death and about her new life in Greece, the USA and Australia.

'In the absence of conclusive evidence being provided by Ms Khouri, we have no alternative but to acknowledge the considerable doubts that exist as to the truth of events described by the author in *Forbidden Love*,' said Margaret Seale, managing director of Random House Australia in a statement issued on 13 August 2004. The publishers apologized to their booksellers and readers who purchased the book believing it was a true story and offered refunds on all returned books.

I sent hundreds of emails to all the people who had emailed me, attaching the list of errors, the letter sent to the publishing house and Malcolm Knox's story. Only a few people bothered to respond. None were apologetic. One woman wrote, commending my work, and told me that she now understands what really went on in Jordan and concluded that Norma Khouri was a con artist. But the damage had been done.

A woman named Klea wrote this in August 2004:

> I feel that your so-called 'proof' that *Forbidden Love* is a fake can at the least be called questionable. I'm sure that men in Jordan and other Muslim countries were outraged and embarrassed by Norma's words being published all over the world ... You can defend the puny attempt to veil the truth of what is happening to women in these Middle Eastern Muslim countries, but Khouri has already succeeded at opening the world's eyes. Those defending equality and human rights will continue to fight against you and those you shield.

Many international writers and columnists wrote several articles after the book proved to be a hoax, arguing that the Australian government had used it as a means to convince people that there were strong moral reasons (namely, the supposed severely abusive treatment of all Muslim women in the Middle East) for Australia to take part in the war in Iraq.

Nada Jarrar, a Lebanese novelist, wrote an interesting piece in the *Guardian* on 24 November 2004, saying Khouri's book should never have rung true, even as a work of fiction. She wrote:

> In what fictional world are all the female characters victims, and all the men tyrannical or just plain stupid? How did a work of 'non-fiction' so entirely superficial and written in such a facile manner ever get published – and why did it then get such an enthusiastic response from the public?
>
> The tragedy of the terrorist attacks of September 11, 2001, might have increased western interest in the Middle East and in Islam ... It has also fuelled a desire to have certain preconceived prejudices about the Arab world – and Arab women –

confirmed by publishers and the media. There is a whole new market for books, fiction and non-fiction, that depict Arabs as people with no sense of – or vision for – the world around them, who feel no love for life or each other, who have created monolithic societies where nuance does not exist.

She added: 'Khouri's betrayal of her fellow Arab women is only a microcosm of a much larger deception. Greed and hunger for power – in so far as writers can be powerful – seem to have been her chief motivations. It is sad that she was able to find so willing an audience in the west.'

Joseph Wakim, founder of the Australian Arabic Council and a former Multicultural Affairs Commissioner, wrote an article in the *Canberra Times* on 28 July 2004, entitled 'A sexed-up story of honour killings', saying, 'Whether deliberately or not, the book's release in 2002 in the shadows of the September 11 attacks, has undoubtedly capitalized on the tidal wave of Islamophobia that is sweeping across most of the non-Muslim continents … Given the current Islamophobic climate, Khouri did not even need to claim that hers was a true story. The tide was already on her side … she merely reinforced an image that many western readers already possess.'

Ihab Shalbak wrote a piece for the *Sydney Morning Herald* on 2 August 2004, arguing that the book 'helped provide a moral case for war to the hesitant public in Australia'.

'Curiously,' Shalbak wrote, 'while many Australians welcomed Khouri as a refugee, and bought 200,000 copies of her book, large numbers of Australians [have since] voted in a new government with an extremely tough migration policy. What's more, we know there are hundreds of Arab and Muslim women in detention centres around the country.'

Exposing so-called honour crimes in one's own society is like igniting an uncontrolled fire. Sometimes, it is all too easy to play into the hands of other people who have their own agendas. People like Khouri have taken advantage of the huge publicity generated by our campaign to release false information about the issue, in this case portraying all Arab and Muslim men as evil murderers.

Now that publishers have realized the massive interest in and market potential for books on this subject, many other non-fiction books about honour killings have since appeared. Publishers (and authors) owe the world a duty of care to check non-fiction stories before they are published in future. Stories like Khouri's fictional tale have enormous amounts of influence, and the damage caused by misinformation can be incalculable.

CHAPTER 11

A World of Honour

Honour is concept that has been widely interpreted by different societies, cultures and classes throughout history to promote behaviour that is beneficial to the community. The roots lie with early man, who wanted to ensure his genes were passed on. The simplest way for him to do this was to make sure that 'his' woman did not have sex with other men. Men who controlled 'their' women were seen as strong leaders of high status and therefore were honoured by others in the tribe. As time went on, the honour of a group (or individual man) depended on the behaviour and morality of its female members (or his female relatives).

A sexualized form of honour continued to develop, with women being seen as a form of property, a valued commodity to be traded. So women's bodies and sexuality gained a monetary value, which led their husbands and families to regulate and guard their sexual behaviour. Intact women were prized by the community – who all stood to benefit from the alliances and profits that would arise from her marriage to a member of another tribe. As patriarchal notions of morality and culture became more deeply entrenched, these idealizations of women's sexual behaviour gradually came to be reinforced by dress codes and notions of right and wrong. As men created and dominated the religious, cultural and judicial elements of society, women became subordinate, as they were legally, culturally and religiously bound by their husbands and male relatives to keep the family honour. Maintaining this honour meant that women *had* to be restricted so there would be less chance that this precious commodity would be lost.

The advantages of keeping sexual honour intact are numerous. It provides increased security and large families (in the sense that marriage prospects for a family's children will be good); it is used to keep a family stable, particularly in immigrant communities where honour may also help give a sense of superiority, self-awareness and pride; and a family's high status will lead to good business contacts and opportunities.

As we have already seen, honour may be lost for any number of reasons: women having sex before marriage, committing adultery, being raped, defying parental authority and becoming westernized in immigrant communities. However, most commonly in my experience, honour can simply be lost through gossip and rumour about a woman suspected of immoral behaviour. Generally, an immoral act does not become dishonourable until it becomes public knowledge – hence the reason for gossip being so damaging.

The sheer numbers of so-called honour murders are undeniably shocking. As mentioned in the introduction, in 2000 the UN Population Fund estimated that over five thousand women die in honour killings every year. Some experts insist that the true figure is much higher, simply because of under-reporting and because many so-called honour killings are disguised as suicides, accidents and disappearances. In countries where this form of violence is considered an acceptable check on women's behaviour rather than a serious crime, the perpetrators remain unpunished. A 2005 report from the Geneva Centre for the Democratic Control of Armed Forces, prepared by Swiss UN Ambassador Theodor Winkler, entitled 'Slaughtering Eve. The Hidden Gendercide in Women in an Insecure World: Violence against Women. Facts, Figures and Analysis,' stated that around two hundred million women and girls are 'demographically' missing because of gender-related violence. Winkler listed examples of such violence which included abortion of female foetuses, deprivation of food and medical care and honour-related murders.

Thankfully, over a relatively small number of years, it has become apparent that there is a widespread desire for change. In 2002, the UN General Assembly adopted Resolution 57/179 and committed to 'working towards the elimination of crimes against women and girls committed in the name of honour'. The resolution called upon states to 'investigate thoroughly, prosecute effectively and document cases of crimes against women committed in the name of honour and to punish the perpetrators'.

The resolution also urged states to intensify their efforts to raise awareness of the need to prevent and eliminate crimes against women committed in the name of honour and work to change the attitudes towards these crimes within each country's community.

An updated resolution, co-sponsored by seventy-nine countries, was presented jointly by Turkey and the UK in 2004 to the UN General Assembly. This 'Resolution on Working Towards the Elimination of Crimes against Women and Girls Committed in the Name of Honour' acknowledged in its title that girls could also be victims of these crimes, and called on the international community to introduce measures to prevent so-called honour crimes and introduce effective legislation.

Meanwhile, many people in Jordan and countries such as Pakistan and Turkey have voiced their disapproval of the way foreign and sometimes local media have handled the issue of so-called honour crimes.

In Jordan many feel that we are targeted as if ours is the only country where so-called honour crimes take place; that we've been singled out, attacked and blackmailed by western countries who have threatened to block financial aid if the Kingdom does not change its discriminatory laws against women.

These feelings are mirrored in Pakistan where, in September 2005, I attended a regional conference on violence against women in Islamabad. At this conference, the then President, General Pervez Musharraf, pledged to protect and empower women in his country, but spoke strongly against individuals and foreign organizations that 'singled out' Pakistan for criticism on the issue of so-called honour crimes.

'What hurts me is that Pakistan is singled out when it comes to violence against women. I would not be with people who single us out alone. Let us all raise the issue together. Never single out Pakistan. That I will always oppose with my will and power,' the President told the gathering.

This is perhaps because Jordanian and Pakistani campaigners have led the way in exposing the problem and so international coverage of the issue in these countries has indeed been very intense. The sheer volume of work that has since been conducted by governmental and non-governmental organizations in these countries, and by other activists and journalists, has made Jordan a pioneering country in the region in terms of combating violence against women.

Nevertheless, so-called honour killings and other forms of violence against women continue to occur, and not just in Jordan and Pakistan. Reports submitted to the UN Commission on Human Rights indicate that these crimes occur in countries including Bangladesh, Brazil, Ecuador, Egypt, the UK, Palestine, India, Israel, Pakistan, Morocco, Sweden, Turkey, Yemen, Uganda and the USA.

After our campaign became internationally known, I began to receive correspondence from all over the world about so-called crimes of honour. I was invited to speak at dozens of conferences where I was asked for advice about running campaigns to raise awareness or how to effect a change in the law.

It soon became very clear to me that so-called honour crime is one of the most serious global problems currently faced by women. As I visited dozens of different countries and conducted my own research, I was shocked and appalled to learn that the problem was far greater than anyone seemed to realize – particularly those who were in a position to do something about it. The next section of this book describes my experience of so-called honour crimes around the world, starting with the other country that has received as much, if not more, international attention than Jordan: Pakistan.

Pakistan

In Peshawar, in the North-West Frontier Province, twenty-nine-year-old Samia Sarwar was married off to her first cousin in 1989. During her decade-long marriage Samia was subjected to all forms of abuse by her husband. She left her husband briefly in 1995 after he pushed her down the stairs while she was pregnant with their second son.

During this time she stayed with her family. Her father was a businessman who had headed the Peshawar Chamber of Commerce and Industry, while her mother was a gynaecologist. Samia herself had a law degree and her sister studied medicine.

Although Samia and her husband both wanted a divorce, family pressures meant that the unhappy couple were forced to stay together. When Samia told her family she had fallen in love with an army captain and wanted to leave her husband, they allegedly threatened to kill her.[17]

Her parents sent her back to her husband and eventually, unable to stand a life of abuse any longer, she ran away on 26 March 1999, while her parents were on a trip to Saudi Arabia. She hoped to secure her divorce before they returned.

That's when Samia went to see a pair of remarkable lawyers, Hina Jilani and her sister Asma Jahangir, who were known for helping abused women.[18] They had founded an all-female law firm in the early 1980s, which included a training school for lawyers along with a shelter for abused women. They were also the founders of the Human Rights Commission of Pakistan, which they had established in 1986.

Jahangir, at just over five feet in height, was a tiny woman with an enormous mission. Along with her sister and her colleagues, they defended people sentenced to death by stoning (including a fourteen-year-old boy condemned to die for scribbling blasphemous graffiti on a the wall of a mosque) and sheltered women whose families wanted to murder them because they had deserted cruel husbands. She investigated the fate of prisoners who vanished in police custody and battled for their release through the courts and in the press. Needless to say, they had made plenty of enemies on the way. 'People aren't willing to believe that these injustices happen in our society,' Jahangir told *Time* magazine, 'but it's all going on next door.'

Their work was controversial and they were often threatened. Extremists once smashed Jahangir's car, attacked her driver and took her family hostage (they were released unharmed). As a result, the government assigned the two sisters their own police escorts.

The sisters took Samia in. She lived in their shelter and refused to meet with any of her male relatives. Her family then sent word through a government contact that they were willing to allow the divorce to take place and asked if they could meet her.

They also met with lawyer Aitzaz Ahsan, leader of the Opposition in the Senate (the Upper House of Parliament) and showed him the divorce papers they had brought from Peshawar, and assured him they only wanted their daughter to be happy. Samia agreed to meet her mother in the presence of Hina Jilani, but refused to see her father because she 'hated him'.

Samia arrived at Jilani's office at around 6 p.m., while her mother, walking with a stick, arrived a few minutes afterwards, accompanied by Samia's uncle, Yunus Sarwar, and Habibur Rehman, their driver.

Jilani instantly sensed something was wrong and asked the two men to leave the room but Samia's mother said she depended on the driver to help her walk. At this moment Yunus Sarwar stood up and Rehman drew a gun, marched up to Samia and shot her in the head. He then fired at Jilani and fled down the corridor.

Samia's mother screamed and ran out of the room after the killer, her 'limp' forgotten. Someone rang the alarm for the guards downstairs. Samia's uncle took an employee hostage to use as a shield to hide behind in case the security guards tried to stop him.

As he reached the exit, in a desperate attempt to escape the building, the driver fired at the plainclothes policeman who was supposed to be guarding Jilani. The policeman ducked behind a nearby reception counter and returned fire, fatally wounding Samia's killer.

Meanwhile, Samia's uncle and mother escaped with the abducted employee and drove to a hotel where the father was waiting. When they entered the room his first question was: 'Is the job done?'

Back in her office, Jilani was relieved to find herself unharmed – but Samia lay face down in a pool of blood next to her desk, dead. The following day, demonstrators marched to the Lahore High Court, where several prominent citizens addressed the gathering and promised not to 'let Samia's blood be spilt in vain'. They said that even if her own family had disowned her, she would be 'buried honourably by us'.

Asma Jahangir proposed to erect a monument outside her office honouring the memory of women killed for 'honour'. 'We will cherish and treasure their names,' she vowed.

After the shooting Jilani spoke to reporters, saying:

On the two or three occasions that I met her personally to discuss her case, she repeatedly expressed fear of death at the hands of her family ... She seemed well-educated. However, I had the impression that she lacked confidence. I was surprised that a timid woman like her had resolved to take on the enmity of her family by resorting to legal action for divorce, which, according to her, the family was opposed to even after five years of separation from her husband ... Samia was a frightened, unhappy woman who felt very alone in a predicament that she couldn't deal with confidently.

The fact that the shooting incident occurred in my office during a busy afternoon, it is obvious the perpetrators were convinced they were doing the right thing, were not afraid of publicity as they could count on widespread support and were therefore not inclined to hide their identity. They were possibly convinced the state would not take measures to hold them to account.

Jilani's comments proved accurate. Samia's father, who was the head of the Chamber of Commerce in Peshawar, was released on bail along with her uncle and mother. The investigation into their involvement was achingly slow because, the police said, 'the case was complicated'.

The Minister of Women's Development made a statement in Washington on 10 April, four days after Samia's murder, pledging the government's commitment to women's rights in Pakistan. A representative from the Pakistani government also condemned the killing before the UN Human Rights Commission in Geneva.

It is remarkable just how different this reaction was, performed in front of the eyes of the world, compared with the government's reaction at home. The local government didn't issue a statement for three weeks and then produced only a few noncommittal lines.

Pakistani newspapers reported that local people overwhelmingly sided with Samia's family. Many Pashtun said the murder should not be considered a crime since it was committed in accordance with tradition.

Both Jilani and Jahangir demanded proper legal investigations, a fair trial and a judicial inquiry headed by a Supreme Court judge to investigate almost three hundred cases of honour killings reported in 1998 in Pakistan. Instead, the Senate of Pakistan heavily criticized them for interfering. Pakistan People's Party Senator Iqbal Haider tried to present a resolution condemning the killing of Samia but Senator Ilyas Bilour's reaction was typical: 'We have fought for human rights and civil liberties all our lives but wonder what sort of human rights are being claimed by these girls in jeans.'

Israrullah Zehri of the BNP, a secular, nationalist party, and Ajmal Khattak, the supposedly progressive leader of the ANP, shouted Haider down. Zehri held the view that Samia Sarwar had disgraced her family who had acted according to tradition. Some senators physically attacked Haider. Only four senators stood in support of the resolution: the PPP's Iqbal Haider, Aitzaz Ahsan, then leader of the Opposition in the Senate, the late Hussain Shah Rashdi, and the MQM's Jamiluddin Aali. Twenty-four senators, including recent presidential candidate Mushahid Hussain Syed and luminaries like Javed Iqbal and Akram Zaki, stood to oppose it. Perhaps unsurprisingly, the Senate rejected an amended resolution on so-called honour crimes in August of the same year.

The Sarhad Chamber of Commerce, of which Samia's father was the president, and other religious groups demanded in April that Jilani and Jahangir be arrested in accordance with 'tribal and Islamic laws' for 'misleading women in Pakistan and contributing to the country's bad image abroad'. Other religious organizations issued fatwas against the two lawyers, promising financial rewards for anyone who killed them. Even the then President, Pervez Musharraf, railed against Jilani and Jahangir, calling them unpatriotic.

Not long after this, five gunmen burst into Jilani's house, searching for her and her young son; luckily, neither were home. On another occasion, according to a report in *Time* magazine, a policeman was caught creeping up to her house with a dagger in his hand.

Then – incredibly, unbelievably – on 11 May 1999, Samia's father filed a case at the police station accusing Hina Jilani and Asma Jahangir of abducting and murdering his daughter.

But despite this seemingly insurmountable opposition, Jahangir said that all the publicity was helping them to reach women across the country, to let them know that someone was fighting for them. The publicity also led to several television documentaries being aired about so-called honour crimes and violence against women, which have also helped to publicize the case.

Today, in addition to her work for the Human Rights Commission, Jahangir works as a UN Special Rapporteur on extrajudicial killings, a job that has taken her to Afghanistan, Central America and Colombia.

In an interview for *Time* magazine in 2003, Jahangir said, with more than a little optimism, 'Eventually things will have to get better. However, the way they will improve is not going to be because of the government or the political leadership, or the institutions of our country, most of which have actually crumbled. It will be the people of the country themselves who will bring about the change in society because they have had to struggle to fend for themselves at every level.'[19]

Jilani often tells the press that she will never forget Samia's murder. 'I will probably never get over Samia's death. I have never witnessed that kind of violence first hand,' she said. 'But as activists we have to fight back.'

As I wrote this section of the book in August 2008, I read a report about a dreadful killing. This atrocity took place in a remote region of the vast Pakistani province of Baluchistan. Initially, reports said three teenage girls, named Hameeda, Raheema and Fauzia, attempted to marry men of their own choosing, and were then reportedly kidnapped by armed local tribesmen, as were two older women who were with them.

The five women were driven away to a desert area by men belonging to the Umrani tribe. The three teenagers were hauled out, beaten and shot. According to Human Rights Watch, they were thrown into a ditch, injured, but still alive. When the two older women, aged forty-five and thirty-eight, protested at what was happening, they too were forced into the ditch where they were buried with the teenagers.

Unbelievably, these killings were defended by senior politicians. Reacting to a female colleague's attempt to raise the issue in Parliament, Senator Israrullah Zehri said such acts were part of a 'centuries-old tradition' and that he would 'continue to defend them', adding, 'only those who indulge in immoral acts should be afraid.'[20]

Iqbal Haider of the Pakistan Human Rights Commission said the two senators should be removed from Parliament. 'They are as obscurantist as the Taliban ... these men have violated the constitution,' he said. Details of the incident only emerged after the local media began to draw international attention to the crime.

As I wrote this section, women's rights protesters gathered outside Parliament and government buildings in the major cities of Lahore and Karachi. I believe this is the most effective way to make their voices heard and to provoke a response from the government. Three suspects were finally arrested six weeks after the murder, as condemnation and protests against the outrage spread steadily across the country.

Pakistan has one of the worst records when it comes to so-called crimes of honour. As in Jordan, campaigners have fought a long and difficult battle to change the law – specifically to amend the heavily criticized Hudood Ordinance Laws, which governed the punishment for rape and adultery in Pakistan. These laws, enacted by military ruler Zia ul-Haq in 1979, criminalize adultery and non-marital consensual sex. The most appalling aspect of these laws is that a rape victim can be prosecuted for adultery if she cannot produce four male witnesses to the assault.

The new Women's Protection Bill brought rape under the Pakistan Penal Code, which is based on civil law, not Sharia law. The Bill removed the right of police to detain people suspected of having sex outside of marriage, instead requiring a formal accusation in court. Under the changes, adultery and non-marital consensual sex are still offences but judges are allowed to try rape cases in criminal rather than Islamic courts, eliminating the need for the four witnesses and allowing convictions to be made on the basis of forensic and circumstantial evidence.

The amendments change the punishment for someone convicted of having consensual sex outside marriage to imprisonment of up to five years and a fine of ten thousand rupees. Rape is punishable with ten to twenty-five years' imprisonment, but with death or life imprisonment if committed by two or more persons together, while adultery remains under the Hudood Ordinance and is punishable with stoning to death.

Research by the Asian Human Rights Commission makes it clear that there has been almost no change in the number of incidents of violence against women since the Bill came into force in 2006. The Human Rights Commission of Pakistan recorded over six hundred cases of 'honour' killings in 2007, compiled from media reports. The actual number may be higher (various human rights organizations quote a figure of one thousand) as not all cases are reported. Figures presented to the Senate by the Federal Minister of the Interior provide evidence in favour of this. Between 1998 and 2003, the government states that 4,101 people were killed in so-called crimes of honour.

A UN committee noted that so-called honour crimes are on the increase in Pakistan even though the country passed a law banning these crimes in 2004. The committee questioned the sincerity of the Pakistani government in ending these crimes and prosecuting people who are guilty of these murders, and charged the Pakistani government of being 'lenient and tolerant' towards such crimes.[21]

It is impossible to know, but is the level of violence actually rising or is it just that the media are reporting such cases with greater frequency? The media boom is certainly instrumental in bringing more of these stories to light. There is little doubt that the vast majority of perpetrators go unpunished.

Recent cases include a woman who was axed to death by her cousin because he was suspicious of her relations with other people. Just before this murder, two bullet-riddled bodies of women were discovered in Gulli Garhi village with a note, which stated they were of 'loose character'. Hundreds, if not thousands, of jirgas (village courts) have yet to be replaced by courts of law. The 'edicts' ordained by jirgas and militants are in open violation of the laws of the land.

Mukhtar Mai, a thirty-year-old woman who lived in the remote hamlet of Meerwala, knows better than most the terrifying power that the jirga is able to wield. In June 2002, Mai's then twelve-year-old brother Abdul Shakoor had been seen strolling with a girl from the more influential Mastoi tribe; Mastoi villagers demanded Mai's rape to avenge their 'honour'.

The village court sentenced her to be publicly gang-raped by four volunteers. Mai's family sat helplessly while she was dragged into a room. To further humiliate her, and make an example of those who would defy the power of local leaders, she was paraded naked before hundreds of onlookers. Afterwards, her father covered her with a shawl and walked her home.

Incredibly, Mai refused to leave it there and fought a public battle to bring her attackers to trial. She told reporters she would rather 'die at the hands of such animals' than 'give up her right to justice'. Incredibly, despite several threats, she not only brought them to trial, she won the case. Half-a-dozen of the men involved in her rape have been jailed and two of them have been sentenced to death. Mai has used the money awarded to her by the court as compensation to open a school in her village where, according to Mai, 'children will be taught the real meaning of honour'.[22]

In February 2008 an Islamic fundamentalist shot and killed a government minister because of her refusal to wear a Muslim veil.[23] Zilla Huma Usman, the Punjab Provincial Minister for Social Welfare, was shot as she prepared to address a public gathering in the town of Gujranwala. The attacker, Malulvi Ghulam Sarwar, said that he was opposed to the participation of women in politics and the refusal of many professional women in Pakistan to wear the veil.

Speaking to a local TV channel, he said, 'I have no regrets. I just obeyed Allah's commandment. Islam did not allow women to hold positions of leadership. I will kill all those women who do not follow the right path, if I am freed again.'

It is clear to me that as long as the government of Pakistan refuses to challenge fully the brutality of tribal law, along with outdated traditions and values, then all women will continue to suffer. People must be given a voice; it is only by hearing their stories and by public outcry that the legislators themselves will be shamed into doing something about it.

Afghanistan

Things are even worse for women in neighbouring Afghanistan. One of the most famous murders in recent times took place in the middle of the night of 6 June 2007, as Afghan journalist Zakia Zaki lay sleeping next to her twenty-month-old son.

Three attackers sneaked into her house and shot her seven times, sparing her young son and five other children.[24]

One of the few female reporters to criticize the Taliban, thirty-five-year-old Zaki ran the US-funded Radio Peace, launched in

2001. Her colleague and head of the Afghan Independent Journalists' Association, Rahimullah Samander, said 'She believed in freedom of expression, that's why she was killed.' Zaki's killers struck just days after a female newsreader at a TV station was shot and killed for reasons that remain unclear.[25]

On the day she was shot, the US Congress earmarked $45 million – twice the 2002 amount – for Afghan government groups and NGOs dedicated to empowering women. The country needs it. A weak judiciary, a lack of law enforcement and widespread discriminatory practices against women are fuelling a rise in so-called honour killings in Afghanistan, according to a 2006 report from the Afghan Independent Human Rights Commission (AIHRC).

Asma Jahangir, UN Special Rapporteur on religious freedom, said during an international conference in Sweden in December 2004 that approximately four hundred so-called honour killings had been documented in 2004, but only twenty men were arrested and were given mild sentences. Jahangir described so-called honour killings as the most hidden of all crimes: 'The "deadly silence" among people at large is a major cause of the deaths of women, not only the open violence of the perpetrators.'[26]

But things are changing. Afghanistan's government, which says it is committed to human rights and ending discrimination against women, hopes to end the practice but admits there are challenges ahead. Dad Mohammad Rasa, an interior ministry spokesman, said honour crimes were prosecuted, but that the practice was so entrenched that stamping it out would take a long time: 'We have created a commission in the interior ministry to try and eradicate such cases but it will take a long time to overcome such crimes as it has become a part of many people's culture.'

Women can participate in every walk of life, including politics. Of the 361 members of Parliament today, ninety-one are women. Women have also begun talking about forced marriages, honour killings, abortions and rape in this traditionally male-dominated society. Local human rights groups are also now leading the way to change by documenting and exposing such atrocities.

Despite these advances, violence against women, such as immolation, forced marriages and rape, remains widespread in Afghanistan. The AIHRC documented over 1,500 cases of atrocities against women in 2006.

A third of these women were victims of domestic violence, simply called 'beating' in the rights group report. Two hundred of them were married off forcibly, ninety-eight of them set themselves on fire, and over a hundred of them tried to end their lives by taking poison.

Iraq

In Iraq, another war-torn region of the world, women's rights have deteriorated dramatically since the start of the US-led coalition's occupation of the country. Despite the horrific number of honour killings, the status of women may have a chance of improving in Kurdistan (the semi-autonomous region in northern Iraq) where the government is secular, in contrast to Baghdad where the religious parties hold power. The Kurdish police and courts are also more sympathetic than those elsewhere in Iraq to women whose lives have been threatened. There are currently no shelters for women in Baghdad or Basra.

Reliable statistics on honour killings are nonexistent; as in other countries in the Middle East where the tradition is tolerated, such as Egypt and Morocco, honour killings are largely treated as private family matters. Iraq is a tribal society where honour killings are an accepted practice and cases have been increasing because conservative attitudes have spread since the fall of Saddam Hussein.

Under Saddam's laws, which are still in place, men convicted of so-called honour killings can receive up to three years in jail. But because the crime is rarely reported, few are actually prosecuted. And since there is widespread sympathy for the killers among police and judges, those who are convicted rarely serve more than a few months.

When US forces overthrew Saddam Hussein, the Bush administration proclaimed that women's rights would be at the centre of its project to make Iraq a democratic model for the rest of the Arab world. But violence against women is rampant, rising every day with the power of the militias. Beheadings, rapes, beatings, suicide, genital mutilation, trafficking and child abuse (masquerading as marriage) of girls as young as nine are all on the increase – any woman who dares to protest will immediately find her life in great peril. Iraq is without question one of the most dangerous places on earth to be a woman.

Duaa Khalil Aswad, a seventeen-year-old student at the Fine Arts Institute in Bashiqa in Iraq, fell in love with her neighbour, Muhannad, who owned a local cosmetics shop. Like many young lovers they met whenever they could. On most days Muhannad picked Duaa up after her college classes.

In 2007, as their relationship intensified, Duaa tried to convince her boyfriend to elope with her so they could get married after she had converted to Islam but he refused, telling her that her family needed to approve their marriage as well.

Duaa's family were Yazidis, belonging to the smallest of the three branches of Yazdanism, a Middle Eastern religion with ancient Indo-European roots. Yazidis are primarily Kurdish-speaking and most of the religion's 350,000 to 500,000 members live in the Mosul region of northern Iraq. They have been persecuted by a succession of rulers, from the Ottomans to Saddam Hussein. Neither Christian nor Muslim, they worship a blue peacock known as Malak Taus. They are fiercely insular, opposing marriage to non-Yazidis, and it is virtually impossible for non-Yazidis to convert.

When Duaa decided to inform her parents of her decision, they weren't pleased but at the same time they didn't try to stop her. Her uncles and cousins felt differently, and when they heard that she had converted to Islam so she could marry the man she loved, they decided to take matters into their own hands.

Her father, worried for her safety, took Duaa to a cleric. She should have been safe under his guardianship; a tradition supposedly respected by all tribal members. On 7 April, Duaa's uncles arrived at the cleric's home and told him that the family had forgiven the girl and wanted her to return. Duaa, who was dressed in a black skirt with a red jacket, really thought they had forgiven her and got ready to go. As the cleric became suspicious the men stormed the house and dragged Duaa outside by her ponytails to meet her fate.

After just a few yards, Duaa was surrounded by thirteen cousins who started kicking her, punching her and pulling her hair before pushing her to the ground. As she shouted for help her father heard and raced to the scene but was forcibly and violently held back by some of the large crowd that had gathered. Some filmed what followed on their mobile phones.

Duaa's attackers tore her skirt, exposing her legs – an act intended to shame the girl who had damaged her family's honour. One man kicked her between her legs, another painful, degrading symbol. The brutal execution continued for almost thirty minutes. The cheering crowd threw larger and larger stones. Duaa gave up trying to cover her legs with her arms, using them instead to cover her head to try to deflect the dozens of rocks that flew at her.

When a large brick struck the back of her head, she stopped moving for a few moments. She then tried to sit up while screaming for help but her murderers chanted 'Kill her, kill her.'

Finally, one of her cousins picked up a huge rock, struggling under its weight, and dropped it on her forehead. The mob continued kicking her to make sure she was dead. Finally, Duaa's killers took her body to the outskirts of Bashiqa where they burned and buried her remains with those of a dog, to show how worthless she was.

According to the police chief in Mosul, most of the killers were members of Duaa's extended family – mainly cousins and their friends. A post mortem showed that Duaa died of a fractured skull and spine.

As the footage circled the globe, journalists started to arrive in Bashiqa and they interviewed several local people, most of whom expressed support for the stoning. Eyewitness Samir Juma, a teacher, said policemen as well as some Peshmerga soldiers belonging to the Kurdistan Democratic Party stood and watched the killing without attempting to intervene. News reporters also spoke of a small boy who was dragged to the front of the crowd and was made to watch Duaa being stoned to death.[27]

It was not the first love story of its kind, nor was it the first so-called honour killing in a region where women are subject to strong social restrictions and face severe punishment for disregarding family, tribal or religious traditions.

Such cases can no longer be covered up as easily these days, because of pressure from very brave local women's activists – but they rarely cause a stir. Duaa's case was different. This killing has had a much wider impact, thanks to the film footage from a mobile phone being broadcast around the world on the internet, providing horrific proof, finally, of the brutality of these murders committed in the name of honour.

The killing also unleashed new horror and conflict in what had been until then one of the only peaceful areas left in Iraq. On 21 April 2007, a group of gunmen dragged more than twenty Yazidi men off a bus in the northern city of Mosul, about twenty miles south of Bashiqa, lined them up against a wall and gunned them down. The next day, a Sunni insurgent group linked to al-Qaeda claimed responsibility for a car bombing that targeted the offices of a Kurdish political party in northern Iraq, saying it was to avenge the death of Duaa.[28]

Journalists were told that the reason police did not intervene during Duaa's killing, or take action immediately afterwards, was that they believed Duaa was guilty of 'immoral behaviour ... breaking a taboo prescribed by social tradition, rather than changing faith.'

It was only when the police heard that Duaa might have been killed for abandoning Yazidism that they decided to issue arrest warrants. One of the results of the international outrage about her death was the reaction by the supreme religious leader of the Yazidis, Tahsin Saeed Ali, who publicly condemned Duaa's murder as 'a heinous crime'. He sought to minimize the interfaith connection to her murder, saying that Duaa was killed because of 'old traditions', implying that the motivation was social rather than religious.

Eventually, four of Duaa's relations were arrested. Four others, including the cousin thought to have instigated the killing, were still at large. Provincial officials claimed that not much could have been done to stop the killing of Duaa, but confirmed that three officers were being investigated.

Duaa's murder has given a voice to the women's movement in Iraq. Houzan Mahmoud, the spokeswoman for the Organization of Women's Freedom in Iraq, said, 'The religious and social climate is such that people can murder in daylight and that the authorities will stand by and watch.'

'There is a new Taliban controlling the lives of women in Iraq,' said Hana Edwar, leader of the Amal Organization for Women, a non-governmental group in Baghdad. 'I think this story will be absolutely repeated again ... and will become common.'[29]

One contentious issue, which may at first sight seem of little relevance, but which may determine the dynamics of Yazidi–Muslim conflict, is the argument over whether Duaa was stoned to death for converting to Islam or for losing her virginity before marriage.

Sources close to the girl's family claim that she did not convert to Islam, but wanted to run away with Muhannad, and it was this that provoked her cousins to punish her. A hospital autopsy, apart from confirming that she died from a broken skull and spine, also confirmed she was a virgin.

Duaa's case was by no means the first; it was simply the first to be noticed by the international community and the first to inspire public outrage in Iraq. A few months earlier, a family executed their daughter by shooting her in the head because she had converted to Islam. Her case received little attention.

Two months before Duaa's murder, a Yazidi man from Shekan, a village near Bashiqa, eloped with a Muslim girl. She was later found beheaded, allegedly by Muslims from her own village, and several Yazidi houses and religious sites were set alight.

Almost a month after Duaa and the twenty Yazidi workers were killed, the Kurdistan Regional Government (KRG) condemned the murders. A statement released on 2 May 2007 said, 'The murder of Duaa in a so-called honour killing is a tragedy for her family and the entire community in Kurdistan. There is no justification whatsoever for this crime. Duaa's death and the subsequent retaliation against the Yazidi community is a reminder to all of us, as individuals and as a society, that we have to continue to fight against the violent and archaic mindset that sadly persists today.'

The KRG remains extremely concerned that Duaa's killing might still be used as a pretext for the persecution of the Yazidi community: 'We must all work together so that the ongoing violence and images of violence in parts of Iraq do not brutalize our society to the point where killing is seen as the easiest solution to disputes.'[30]

As far as I am concerned, Duaa Aswad is a name that will never be forgotten. Several women's groups have devoted themselves to revive her memory every year on 7 April. A group of activists also opened a forum for Duaa on Facebook to commemorate her tragic death.

Roaa Basil, a human rights activist and programme manager at Al-Yaqeen Centre for Training, Development and Studies, has investigated the murder of Duaa. She told me that her family were now considered 'outcasts' in their own community and that they were forced to move after someone placed a bomb on their doorstep.

One of her brothers has since sought political asylum in a European country while Muhannad is still in hiding. Duaa's mother tries to visit her grave whenever she can; sometimes she is stopped and shooed away by people who still think Duaa has brought shame on the family. She told a reporter that all she wanted to do was water her daughter's grave – the last thing Duaa had said to her was that she was thirsty – and people were even preventing her from doing that.

*   *   *

The Independent Women Organization in central Kurdistan conducted an analysis of 118 honour killings that mostly took place in the Souran Province from 1992 to 1998. They found that around sixty-six per cent of so-called honour crimes were motivated by anger over women's desire for more freedom. For example, a woman named Begard in Malayan, Erbil, was burned to death by her husband. He had done so because she had gone to his brother's wedding party without his permission. A thirty-five-year-old woman named Sakina Haji was shot to death by her brother on 20 August 1993 in Sheikh Wasan village because she had chosen her own husband.

More recently, citing official KRG statistics, the UN Assistance Mission for Iraq (UNAMI) recorded fifteen honour killings carried out with blunt objects, eighty-seven by burning and sixteen by shooting in the first quarter of 2007. In the second quarter, there were eight killings carried out with blunt objects, 108 by burning and twenty-one by shooting.

A new addition to the list of murder weapons is the mobile phone. In Kurdistan, where there has been a sudden influx of cheap mobile phones, men are using them to take photos and record audio and video clips of women and girls who are breaking social codes. These are then widely distributed, damaging women's reputations and putting their lives at risk. The first case is believed to have been in 2004, when footage of a seventeen-year-old girl having sex with a boy circulated in Erbil. Two days after the video was made public, the girl's family killed her. A week after the incident, the boy was also killed by his family. In 2006, 170 cases of mobile phone-related violence were recorded. By 2007, this figure had more than doubled to 350, according to statistics compiled by women's organizations and the Sulaimaniyah police directorate.

For example, Salma, who asked that her real name be concealed, and who was hiding in a women's shelter, said that her boyfriend passed on their intimate conversations on his phone to her family when she refused to marry him. The twenty-eight-year-old's hand was broken during one of the beatings from her brothers, father and uncles.

MPs have ordered legislation that they hope will protect women from mobile phone abuse that includes fines of between seventy-five thousand and one million Iraqi dinars (between sixty and 850 US dollars) or between six months and fifteen years in prison. Victims would also be able to sue for financial compensation.

Banaz Hussein, deputy director of Asuda, a women's rights NGO, said that she does not think that a law will stop the trend. Speaking to the Institute for War and Peace Reporting (IWPR), she said, 'Kurdistan is developing, but people still adhere to the old customs and traditions. And women are still the primary victims.'[31]

Youssif Mohamed Aziz, the Regional Minister of Human Rights, said, 'The regional government of Kurdistan has formed a committee … to address all forms of violence against women and especially the "honour killings".' Since 2007, he said, awareness-raising campaigns have been conducted and human rights education has been introduced in schools.

The KRG Prime Minister Nechirvan Barzani said in July 2007, 'Killing under the pretext of protecting honour is murder', and called on religious leaders to use their influential positions to 'spread a message of peace and tolerance in mosques and society'. Muslim leaders have indeed been denouncing the phenomenon as being against Islam, but there is still clearly a long way to go.

*   *   *

In Iraq, as in Jordan, the law is on the side of those who kill in the name of so-called honour. This was thanks to the late Iraqi President Saddam Hussein, who introduced Article 128 of Law 111 of the Iraqi Penal Code in 1990 in an attempt to win tribal support. It read: 'An appeal for murder is considered commutative if it is cited as a pretext for clearing the family name or as a response to serious and unjustifiable provocation by the victim.' In January 2002, the UN Special Report on Violence against Women stated that more than four thousand Iraqi women have been victims of so-called honour killings since Article 128 came into effect.[32]

Human rights activist Roaa Basil told me in a recent phone interview that there were many more so-called honour murders during Saddam's regime – they were simply never made public. 'The regime then suppressed the issue of violence against women, but women were being killed and subjected to all forms of violence by their families and no one could speak about this issue.'

But judging by the sheer number of reports since the fall of the Hussein regime, violence against women has increased at an astronomical rate, with some professional women being deliberately targeted. The breakdown in law and order has contributed to this increase, because there are fewer restraints on violent young men determined to take the law into their own hands.

In March 2004, US President George W. Bush said that 'the advance of freedom in the Middle East has given new rights and new hopes to women ... the systematic use of rape by Saddam's former regime to dishonour families has ended.' This may have given some people the impression that the US and British invasion of Iraq had helped to improve the lives of its women. But this is far from the case.

In September 2007, Ali Jasib Mushiji, aged seventeen, shot his mother and half-brother because he suspected them of having an affair. He also murdered his four-year-old sister, thinking that she was their child. From a cell in the Baghdad slum of Sadr City, he told a reporter that he wiped out his family in order to cleanse it of shame. He had thought about killing his mother for some time, but stated that it was only when the Hussein regime fell that he was able to get hold of a Kalashnikov and carry out his plan.[33]

Ziyad Khalaf al-Ajely, a journalist writing for the IWPR, interviewed Faeq Ameen Bakr, Director General of Baghdad's Institute of Forensic Medicine, in 2005. Bakr said that all too often he wrote the words 'killed to wash away her disgrace' in the many autopsy reports and investigations that landed on his desk.

Bakr said it is difficult to track the number of such killings because they often go unreported. Sometimes women will try to take their own lives rather than face the wrath of their families, an example of which was demonstrated when the reporter returned to see Bakr at a later date. He noticed a crowd on the Bab al-Muadham bridge in Baghdad. A young girl had jumped from it. When a rescuer brought her out of the water – still alive – she told onlookers, 'I am pregnant. They will kill me.' She was taken to the capital's Medical City hospital, where she had an abortion and was discharged.[34]

According to a study conducted by the Ministry of Women's Affairs that examined four hundred rape cases since the fall of

Saddam's regime, more than half of these victims were later murdered in honour killings. The authorities say they treat honour killings seriously, but punishments, when they are given, are hardly ever severe.

In one case, a police captain was imprisoned for one month and docked a month's pay for lending a gun to a friend who used it to murder his unmarried pregnant sister. The murderer received a six-month prison sentence.

Possibly the most frightening place for any young woman to be taken to is the virginity-testing room in Baghdad's forensics institute. Here, young women lie face up with their feet in stirrups and are examined by three male doctors. The findings are then written down and presented to suspicious family members. Girls often arrive in terror, knowing that the results of the test could result in their death.

Women's rights activist Amaal al-Mualimchi says women are so fearful of falling victim to so-called honour killings that they have become virtual prisoners in their own homes. 'So women have two choices – exposing themselves to the threat of rape, after which they will be killed by their families, or house imprisonment,' she said.

Jwan Ameen of the Women's Affairs Ministry is now trying to help women who face honour killings by establishing safe houses for them. Women's groups are also calling for the protection of women to be included in the new constitution, which will soon be drafted by the National Assembly. 'But we are still facing difficulties in implementing all of this because we don't have a budget for it,' said Ameen.

Iraqi women activists say they themselves now live in fear of violence and can no longer walk in the street without covering their heads. Some female journalists have said they do not take any form of identification with them when they go out, in case they are stopped by extremists who might kill them.

An activist recently told me that usually, when a family decides to kill one of their female relatives, they fill the bath with kerosene and wait for the woman to enter the room. The minute she steps inside, the elected killer immediately locks the door, pours kerosene under and on it and sets it ablaze. The family then claims that their female relative was killed accidentally. Because the current situation is still unstable, it is rare for the authorities to open an investigation into the matter. According to a December 2006 report by the UN Assistance Mission for Iraq in the Kurdish-governed north, 239 women were reportedly burned in the first eight months of 2006. Most of these cases have been investigated as accidents or suicide attempts.[35] In Basra alone, police acknowledge that fifteen women a month are murdered for breaching Islamic dress codes.

Mobile phones, too, can result in violence: a casual glance at the photo suggests that Shawbo Ali Rauf was sleeping peacefully on the grass – if it were not for the blood. The nineteen-year-old Iraqi was, according to her father, murdered by her own in-laws, who took her to a picnic area and shot her seven times. Her crime: having an unknown number on her mobile phone.

In 2007, at least 350 women (double the figure for the previous year) suffered violence as a result of mobile phone 'evidence' in Sulaymaniyah, a city with one million inhabitants, according to Amanj Khalil of the IWPR, citing figures compiled by women's organizations and the local police directorate. In the same city in the previous year, there were 407 reported offences against women, beheadings, beatings, deaths as a result of 'family problems' and threats of honour killings.

Despite these outrages, recent calls to outlaw honour killings have been blocked by fundamentalists and the new Iraqi constitution remains a mass of confusing contradictions. While it states that men and women are equal under law it also decrees that Sharia law – which considers one male witness worth two females – must be observed. The days when women could hold down key jobs or enjoy any freedom of movement are long gone. The fundamentalists have sent out too many chilling messages. In Mosul two years ago, eight women were beheaded in a terror campaign. These crimes are all backed by laws, tribal customs and religious rules. Activists have urged the international community to condemn this barbaric practice and to help the women of Iraq.

Rand Abdel-Qader, a nineteen-year-old English student at Basra University, was working as a volunteer helping displaced families when she met an English soldier, Paul. He was distributing water. Although their friendship involved just brief, snatched conversations over four months, Rand had confided her romantic feelings for Paul to her best friend, Zeinab.

On 16 March 2008, Rand was stamped on, suffocated and stabbed by her father, as her two older brothers, Hassan (aged twenty-three) and Haydar (aged twenty-one), held her down while their mother begged them to stop. Her father, Abdel-Qader Ali, claimed the 'honour killing' was supported by local police, and said his only regret was that he had not killed his daughter at birth.

Abdel-Qader, a forty-six-year-old government employee, was released from police custody after just two hours, and claims officers congratulated him on what he had done. 'They are men and know what honour is,' he said. Speaking at his home in Basra's Al-Fursi district, he told the *Observer*:

Death was the least she deserved, I don't regret it. I had the support of all my friends who are fathers, like me, and know what she did was unacceptable to any Muslim that honours his religion.

I don't have a daughter now, and I prefer to say that I never had one. That girl humiliated me in front of my family and friends. Speaking with a foreign soldier, she lost what is the most precious thing for any woman.

People from western countries might be shocked, but our girls are not like their daughters that can sleep with any man they want and sometimes even get pregnant without marrying. Our girls should respect their religion, their family and their bodies. I have only two boys now. That girl was a mistake in my life. I know God is blessing me for what I did.[36]

Rand's mother Leila divorced her husband after the killing and was forced into hiding for fear of retribution. He had beaten her badly before she escaped, breaking her arm. Leaving him was a courageous move. Few women in Iraq would contemplate such a step. She explained, 'They cannot accept me leaving him. When I first left I went to a cousin's home, but every day they were delivering notes to my door saying I was a prostitute and deserved the same death as Rand. She was killed by animals. Every night when I go to bed I remember the face of Rand calling for help while her father and brothers ended her life.'

The forty-one-year-old, who nicknamed her daughter Rose because of her beauty as a baby, said, 'Now, my lovely Rose is in her grave. But God will make her father pay, either in this world ... or in the world after.'

Leila planned to escape to Amman in Jordan where she would carry on the fight alongside other activists like myself. On the morning of 17 May 2008, two months after her daughter's death, Leila set off to meet 'a contact' who was to help her travel to Amman, where she would be taken in by an Iraqi family. She was anxious but happy to leave Iraq. She was also desperately tired; since her daughter's death she hadn't been sleeping well and told one of the women who gave her shelter that she had terrible nightmares. She had a recurring dream where she was being strangled and suffocated – like her daughter. That morning, because she couldn't sleep, she had risen early and prepared breakfast for her helper, cleaned her house and even baked a cake.

Leila had her entire worldly possessions with her in one small bag as she walked fifty metres up the street to get a taxi. Suddenly, a car skidded to a halt beside her and a series of gunshots rang out. The attack, said by witnesses to have been carried out by three men, was over in moments. Leila was hit by three bullets. She died later in hospital.

Police said the incident was a sectarian attack and that there was nothing to link Leila's death to her family. 'Her ex-husband was not in Basra when it happened. We found out he was visiting relatives in Nassiriya with his two sons,' said Hassan Alaa, a senior officer at the local police station in Basra. 'We believe the target was the women activists, rather than Mrs Hussein, and that she was unlucky to be in that place at that time.'

Since February 2006, two other activists from the same women's organization have been killed in the city. One of them was reportedly raped before being shot. The other, the only man working for this NGO and a father of five who was responsible for the organization's finances, was shot in January 2008. Despite this it seems as though Leila was deliberately targeted; the killers chose her over any activist. Since the attack, the NGO that helped Leila has stopped its work in Basra.

Leila was an orphan, raised by an uncle who died in the Shia uprising against Saddam Hussein in the early 1990s. Sixty-eight-year-old Hamida Alaa, a friend of the uncle, said, 'The poor woman was killed and now her name and history is buried with her. No one wants to speak about it. She is just one more woman killed in our country who has already been forgotten by the local society.'

To me, Leila is a hero, a strong woman who should have survived. The best we can do for her is honour her courage and tell her story and work towards change and fight for a better life for Iraqi women – no matter how hard it might be.

Iran

Iran, one of the more populous countries in which honour killings are thought to be frequent, does not report on incidents. There is a clear legal precedent for the phenomenon. Article 220 of the Iranian Criminal Code states: 'If a father – or his male ancestors – kill their children, they will not be prosecuted for murder.' Likewise, Article 1179 of the Civil Code states: 'Parents have the right to punish their children within the limits prescribed by law.'

Incidents are generally concealed from the independent press. For example, in 2003 a truck driver split his niece's head open with a butcher's knife in broad daylight after seeing her walking with a man he did not know, according to an Agence France Press report. He was immediately arrested. No other details were available. The government has the co-operation of the state-owned Iranian News Agency (IRNA) and controls the information that the police provide.

Stoning for adultery remains a common practice in Iran. In December 2002 Ayatollah Shahroudi, Head of the Iranian Judiciary, declared a suspension of stoning in Iran. Nevertheless, stoning sentences continue to be handed down as no change has been made to the Iranian Penal Code to prohibit them as of 2007, according to the US organization Equality Now.

One recent case reported by CNN on 13 January 2009 involved two men who were reportedly stoned to death for adultery and murder in the north-eastern city of Mashhad in December.

'The majority of those sentenced to death by stoning are women. Women are not treated equally with men under the law and by courts, and they are also particularly vulnerable to unfair trials because their higher illiteracy rate makes them more likely to sign confessions to crimes they did not commit,' CNN quoted Amnesty in its report.

You can find out more about the practice of stoning in Iran on the CNN website.

Another case, reported by *The Nation* in February 2006, involved a man and a woman who were stoned in Mashhad. The government eventually confirmed the horrific event the following year, which took place in the village of Aghche-kand.

A fourteen-year-old girl was stoned to death by her father in Zahedan on 14 February 2008 for having a relationship with a boy. The father said he and his friend took his daughter to a mountain, stoned her to death and fired four bullets at her. Both men were arrested, according to the Iran Human Rights website.

A newspaper report quoted the father as saying, 'When we were taking Somayeh to the mountains, she was scared but still didn't know what she was expecting. Upon arrival at the scheduled place, I threw Somayeh on the ground and started the stoning. She was screaming and begging for her life, but I had to save my honour and didn't have any other choice than killing her,'

In 2004, sixteen-year-old Atefeh Sahaaleh Rajabi was hanged in public in the town of Neka, after being convicted of 'immoral' acts.

The UN Special Rapporteur on violence against women reported after a visit to Iran in 2005 that two hundred of the 397 women then detained in Evin prison had received a death sentence for moral or sexual offences such as adultery, which she attributed to 'the gender biases in the attitudinal and institutional structure of the country'.

There is little reason to expect change any time soon. In September 2008, four women in Iran were sentenced to six months behind bars for campaigning for women's rights. They were accused of 'spreading propaganda', specifically for taking part in the Million Signatures Campaign for equal rights for women. An estimated fifty women have been detained since the petition began. One of those sentenced, Parvin Ardalan, a human rights activist and journalist, had been awarded the Olof Palme Prize this year, but her passport was seized at the airport and she was unable to travel to collect the award.[37]

In July 2008, the National Iranian American Council (NIAC) forced significant alterations to be made to a forthcoming Hollywood film, *Crossing Over*, which stars Sean Penn and Harrison Ford. The plot featured an honour killing in an Iranian family living in the USA. The NIAC wrote to the film's producers stating that if 'significant changes' were not made, then the film would 'generate serious backlash against the Iranian American community'.

The NIAC later submitted its analysis and suggestions to the production team, who changed elements of the script and even re-shot certain scenes. The final product, the film's director says, does not include any reference to 'family honour' and does not depict an honour killing. 'Honour killings are accepted in some Middle Eastern cultures but not accepted in Iranian culture,' NIAC president Trita Parsi said.

On 14 August 2008, in a village called Kani Dinar in the Mariwan region of Iran, a man stabbed his eighteen-year-old daughter, Fereshteh Nejati, and slit her throat, almost severing her head in the street because she wanted to divorce her husband.

Fereshteh had been forced into a marriage when she was fourteen years old.

She fled to her uncle's house to seek refuge after her father threatened to kill her but her father forced her uncle to hand her over and murdered her on the same day.

He was not arrested.

A few days later, more than two thousand people in Mariwan came to the street where she had been murdered and held a demonstration against so-called honour killings. This was one of the first such demonstrations held in Iran. The angry crowd demanded that her father be arrested and face trial. They also asked for a change in the legislation of Iran to protect women like Fereshteh from crimes of honour. They went to the hospital and collected Fereshteh's body and buried her in an emotional ceremony in her home town.[38]

Syria

It is estimated that between two and three hundred honour killings take place in Syria each year. Syrian law is lenient towards a man who kills or injures his female relative if he catches her in 'illegitimate sexual acts with another' or in a 'suspicious state with another'. Most receive little or no attention, but one murder that has sparked an outcry for change in Syria is that of sixteen-year-old Zahra Ezzo in 2007.

Zahra's father was having an extramarital affair. If the clan had discovered this, there was a good chance her father and his mistress would have been killed. A young man, supposedly a 'friend' of Zahra's father, took a liking to the then fifteen-year-old, and threatened to tell the clan unless she ran away with him.

Feeling she had no choice in the matter, Zahra agreed, but her family pursued them when they found out. Luckily, the police captured them first, and put the man in jail, where he faced a possible fifteen-year prison sentence for the kidnap and rape of a minor.

Zahra was sent to a shelter where she stayed for nine months. During that time, Zahra's family tried three times to regain custody of her, but the shelter refused, saying the family could not guarantee Zahra's safety.

The family then asked Zahra's cousin Fawaz to marry her, which, according to tradition, would restore the family's honour. Fawaz agreed to marry her first out of chivalry, then because he fell in love with her. He had no idea what her family were planning.

Once her marriage was formalized, her father signed a sworn statement guaranteeing that neither he nor anyone in the family

would harm his daughter. The newlyweds moved into an apartment one floor below Fawaz's new in-laws in Damascus. A month
later, her brother came to visit. On the morning of his third day
with them, after Zahra's husband had gone to work, Fayez stabbed
his sister to death. The murder created a rare burst of very open
outrage among ordinary people, prompting Syria's Grand Mufti,
Ahmad Hassoun, to condemn her murder and to call for better
protection of girls at risk and for legal reforms. President Bashar
al-Assad promised to find a solution.[39]

One of the key questions in this case has been whether the
brother should go on trial for premeditated murder – as the family
had clearly planned it for months – or as someone who had no
choice because the clan's honour was at stake.

In another case that was reported in *Al Hayat* newspaper in
2003, a twenty-eight-year-old woman was stabbed to death by her
brothers after she started listening to Um Kalthoum (a famous
Arab singer known for her love songs). The brothers believed that
her musical taste was evidence of an illicit affair, and, acting on
their suspicion, killed her and then turned themselves in to the
police. Investigations later proved that the victim's husband had
brought the tapes for his wife to listen to while he was away.

In Syria, Article 548 of the Penal Code states that if a man
witnesses a female relative committing an immoral act and then
kills her, he should not be prosecuted. Work by Syrian activists to
combat these crimes and change attitudes has recently become
more visible. A local organization named Syrian Women
Observatory launched a nationwide campaign entitled 'Stop
killing women ... Stop honour crimes' in 2006, demanding the
abolition of laws that offer leniency to killers. The campaign called
on religious leaders and decision-makers to take a stand against
these crimes.

In 2006 the Syrian General Union of Women released the results
of a field study on domestic violence in Syria. This comprehensive

report indicated that nearly one in every four married Syrian women were beaten by their husbands. More than seventy per cent of women's abusers were fathers, husbands and brothers, according to the report, published by *Ms* magazine in 2006.

Yumun Abu al-Hosn is a founding member of the Association for Women's Role Development, one of the few NGOs in Syria. The association runs the girls' shelter where Zahra took refuge in her final months. 'We may not be able to stop honour killings overnight,' she told the *Christian Science Monitor*, 'but at least if the crime is tried as premeditated murder, then Zahra and others like her will have some dignity in death.'

Yemen

Amran, a bustling governorate of Yemen, seventy miles north of the capital, is home to almost 900,000 people. On 30 May 2008, a local resident, twenty-six-year-old Abdullah Saleh al-Kohali, carried his machine gun to the mosque where he hoped to find Belal Qassim al-Kohali, the man who had made his sister pregnant out of wedlock. He later said he planned to avenge the family honour by killing her lover. When Abdullah spotted his target, he opened fire, killing him – but he fired so wildly that he managed to shoot dead ten other worshippers and wounded fifteen more. In June he was sentenced to death by firing squad.[40]

It is rare that anyone is tried in Yemen for an honour-related crime. Abdullah's sentence was so harsh because he shot so many other people in his appalling attempt at revenge. Article 40 of the Personal Status Act No. 20 (1992) mandates a wife's obedience to her husband, including by restricting her movements outside the marital home, and by requiring her to have sexual intercourse with him. Article 242 of Law No. 12 (1994) says that a man who finds his wife in the act of committing adultery and kills her should receive a maximum of a year in prison or a fine.

In the rural, tribal areas, there is a definite absence of a functioning legal system, and so murderers go unpunished in all but the most extreme cases. There are very few villages where the judiciary is represented by a court and a prosecutor.

Around four hundred women are reported to be victims of so-called honour killings each year in Yemen, said Dr Sherifa Zuhur, Professor of Islamic and Regional Studies, during a conference in 2005. It is thought that many of the 1,211 cases of sudden female deaths presented as suicides between 1995 and 2001 are in fact related to honour.

A Yemeni women's rights organization conducted a study in the capital, Sanaa, in 2005. They quoted a police officer as saying that the number of honour killings has increased in recent years but the majority of cases are hidden and never even reach police stations.

Those cases that do come to the attention of the police are usually withdrawn and are rarely registered officially. In one instance, a woman was referred to the police; she'd been suffering from severe abuse and had escaped her family home, telling the officers that she had been imprisoned because she was in love. An officer was quoted as saying he received orders not to register the case. The woman's family had collected her from the police station and no one knew what had happened to her.

According to a report that was prepared by Sisters Arab Forum for Human Rights in 2005, most women in Yemen are killed only on the basis of suspicion or for marrying a man against their family's wishes. Doctors also said that many families hide the real reasons behind their female relatives' death.

Lebanon

Activists report that almost a dozen women die each year in Lebanon as a result of so-called honour crimes. In 2000, *Al Raida* magazine reported on several incidents, including the case of a nineteen-year-old girl from the Bekaa Valley who was shot by her brother in front of twenty-five men from her clan in 1990.

Her crime was being 'raped' by her first cousin on her father's side. The cousin was twenty-nine years old and married, with three children. The girl's uncle told the *Al Raida* reporter that when the teenage girl told her story at a family meeting and said she was pregnant, 'blood rose in the male member's eyes, and no one can utter a word when there is blood in men's eyes.'

The uncle said everyone present decided that the 'rapist' should marry the teenage girl, since 'her cousin was supposed to save the family honour'. The cousin's father asked one of his sons to slaughter a lamb for the occasion and invited everyone to lunch to celebrate the peace that had been reached. But the teenager's eldest brother grabbed a gun that had been concealed in his pocket and emptied the bullets into his sister, declaring, 'You do not have to slaughter a lamb. Have this one for lunch.'

Three Lebanese women activists and scholars conducted a study of many of the so-called honour crimes that were handled by the courts. They listed quotations from some of the killers and their motives behind the murder.

In one instance they quoted a man who had killed his divorced sister as saying, 'Her repeated absence from home and not obeying me, as well as the fact that the neighbours would tease me about her bad conduct ... All that made me kill her out of honour, especially as she was pregnant by someone other than the man who divorced her.'[41]

They also quoted a mother who said, 'I confirm that it was I who slit my daughter's throat without anybody else's help, to wash away the shame her illegitimate pregnancy had brought on us.'[42]

These murderers relied on Article 562 of the Lebanese Penal Code:

Whoever surprises his spouse or one of his ascendants or descendants or his sister in a witnessed crime of adultery (*flagrante delicto*) or in a situation of unlawful intercourse and proceeds to kill or injure one of them, without deliberation, shall benefit from the excuse of exemption. The person who kills or injures on surprising his spouse or one of his ascendants or descendants or his sister in a suspicious situation with another person shall benefit from the excuse of mitigation.

As is no doubt clear from the cases just described, Article 562 was widely abused – it depended on the element of surprise, catching the offenders in the act and the immediate carrying out of the crime, without thought or reflection.

In 1998, under pressure from women's groups, in particular the Lebanese Women's Council, the then Justice Minister announced that he had referred a draft law to Parliament to amend Article 562 to repeal the 'excuse of exemption' because it encouraged 'private justice' or revenge crimes.

The amended Article 562 read: 'Whomsoever surprises his spouse or one of his ascendants or descendants or his sister in a crime of observed adultery or in a situation of unlawful intercourse and kills or injures one of them without deliberation shall benefit from the excuse of mitigation.'

Of course, this amendment did not relieve women from the burden of being the sole carriers of honour. It is a 'blind acceptance of the assumptions that any sexual relationship outside marriage is a shame and sullies the woman's honour, that her honour is the property of her husband or male relative only, that the woman bears immediate and full responsibility for sullying her honour, whether it happened in her positive or negative will and subsequently deserves the maximum physical penalty.'[43]

The amendment was passed in February 1999. Oddly, it is superseded by Article 7 which states that 'All Lebanese are equal before the law' (men and women alike), and Lebanon has also agreed to be bound by the Universal Declaration of Human Rights, which rejects all discrimination on grounds of sex. Meanwhile, Article 522, which pardons any rapist who marries his victim, remains firmly in place.

The Lebanese Council to Resist Violence against Women (LCRVW) worked on a study of twenty-five so-called honour crime court cases in Lebanon between 1998 and 2003. There were many hundreds of honour killings during this time. However, few made it to court and, of those that did, these were the only cases for which the trial record was complete.

Most of the cases were clearly premeditated – including that of a man who, having divorced his first wife and taken on a second, was unable to support two households, so killed his first wife. Another case concerned a husband who beat his wife for years before killing both her and her sister when she complained to her family. A father killed a daughter when she refused to have an abortion. Another killed his daughter-in-law because his son refused to grant her a divorce. A brother killed his sister because he did not approve of her marriage.

Incredibly, Article 562 was not used in any of these cases. Instead, the defence relied on Article 253, which allows the judge to pass a mild sentence if convinced that the accused had mitigating reasons (as opposed to the 'excuse of mitigation').

Article 562 seems to be redundant, so why such a discriminatory piece of the Penal Code is still allowed to exist is a mystery. All it does is encourage the murder of women, as the perpetrators know that they can rely on this get-out clause if necessary. Even though the courts generally give the perpetrators lengthy sentences, this is doing nothing to stem the tide of killings – so, while the repeal of Article 562 remains essential, it is extremely important to work towards changing the mindset of society as a whole. A promising step forward came in August 2007 when the Associated Press reported that a top Shiite cleric tackled the issue of so-called honour murders in Lebanon by issuing a fatwa banning the practice, describing it as 'a repulsive act'.

Saudi Arabia

In the majority of the Gulf countries, there are no accurate statistics on so-called honour crimes, but cases are starting to be reported regularly in the news media. For example, in August 2007, the *Daily Telegraph* reported a story about a young Saudi girl in Riyadh who was killed by her father after he walked into her room and found her chatting to a man on Facebook. The father reportedly beat up his daughter and then shot her to death.

The case remained unreported in Saudi Arabia until April 2008 when Saudi preacher Ali al-Maliki strongly criticized Facebook and called on the Saudi government to ban the internet site because it was corrupting Saudi youth.

'Facebook is a door to lust and young women and men are spending more on their mobile phones and the internet than they are spending on food,' he said. The story was written up in the local press as an example of the 'strife' that Facebook was causing in Saudi Arabia. Ali al-Maliki said women were posting 'revealing pictures' and 'behaving badly' on the site, which has become very popular with young Saudis.

Saudi Arabia imposes a strict form of Sunni Islam which prevents unrelated men and women from mixing, bans women from driving and demands that women wear a headscarf and cloak in public. Facebook is used by many Saudi women as a vital outlet which allows them to discuss women's rights and to share their thoughts and experiences with people across the world. One suspects that it is this sudden freedom of expression that worries the senior patriarchy. The Saudi authorities block access to websites they deem sexual, pornographic, politically offensive, 'un-Islamic' or disruptive because of controversial religious and political content. At the time of writing, Facebook is still online in Saudi Arabia – for now.

In an echo of the Facebook murder, in August 2008, the father of a young Saudi woman cut out her tongue before setting her alight. The crime? Converting to Christianity and writing about it on a blog. The woman wrote on the 'Al Ukdoud' website, a few days before her death, that the discovery made her family life unbearable, according to a *Gulf News* report.

The father was arrested and an investigation has been launched as to whether this was considered to be an honour crime, which would make it very likely that the man, if found guilty, would be sentenced to between six months and three years in jail. What makes this case all the more remarkable is that the accused is a member of the Commission for the Promotion of Virtue and against Vice, which is responsible for the monitoring of moral behaviour and for the full compliance with the law of the rigid Wahabi doctrine.

Just a month before the Facebook murder, a meeting of experts at a seminar entitled 'Therapy of Abuse Cases and Social Adjustment' in Jeddah revealed that a woman had been taken from a shelter and murdered. This happened because she had been seen on her own with a man who was not her husband or a relative, which is a crime under Saudi law.

Dr Ali Al-Hanaki, Director of the Social Affairs Ministry in the Western Region, said the woman's relatives had not been charged, adding, 'We received news about her death off the record. Such "honour killing" crimes happen secretly and the bodies are buried in the desert. The families usually say that the women in question are travelling or have run away.'

In February 2008, the *Independent* reported a new and disturbing development – forced divorce. They described the case of Fatima al-Timani, sentenced to six months in prison for refusing to be separated from the man to whom she had been happily married for the past four years and with whom she has two children. Fatima was the latest victim of this growing practice, when disgruntled relatives have used hard-line Islamic courts to dissolve matches against the will of the married couple.

Fatima was pregnant when court proceedings began in 2005 and was jailed with her newborn baby. Fatima is now forbidden from seeing her husband, Mansour al-Timani, who now looks after their two-year-old-son, Noha. Noha has only been allowed occasional visits to see his mother. Fatima's relatives have accused Mansour of lying about his tribal background to win their father's approval for the marriage and want it annulled so she can have an arranged marriage to a man of their choosing.

Dr Irfan Al Alawi, a British Muslim and Director of the Centre for Islamic Pluralism based in London, said that the case was not an isolated incident and that as many as nineteen forced divorces were working their way through the courts. Meanwhile, Dr Al-Hanaki was at least optimistic that the situation would change one day: 'even if it takes us ten to fifteen years, we need to change their tribal attitudes toward women.'

Kuwait

Several honour-related murders have recently been reported in Kuwait, a country where women were granted the right to vote in 2005 but where Article 153 of the Penal Code reduces sentences in cases of honour killings. However, as yet, NGOs there have rarely talked about these crimes.

On 11 April 2007, the *Middle East Times* reported that a father slit his thirteen-year-old daughter's throat in front of her three siblings in 2005 because he thought she was no longer a virgin. Adnan Al Enezi, a forty-year-old government employee, blindfolded and handcuffed his daughter Asma and stabbed her repeatedly as she begged for her life. Forensic tests revealed that his daughter was a virgin. Two years later, a court ruled that Al Enezi was not responsible for his actions and he was ordered to undergo psychiatric treatment.

In a second case in 2002, three brothers tortured their sister for ten days, tied her hands behind her back and took her to the desert where they shot and then buried her. The girl had run away from home with a friend and was caught by the police, who turned her over to her family on the condition that they would not harm her. This was after the girl had attempted to commit suicide in police custody, telling a police officer that she feared a much harsher punishment from her family.

The *Arab Times* reported on 10 August 1994 that a young man had killed his sister because she had left the house to look for a job in a commercial area. A man who suspected that the girl had run away from home informed the authorities of her whereabouts. When she was brought home, her brother handcuffed her, drove to the desert, slit her throat and buried her there. He then turned himself in to the police.

Almost a year later, Reuters reported a story of a twenty-one-year-old Kuwaiti man who stabbed his sixteen-year-old sister to death after she told him that three men had raped her in the Kuwaiti desert. The suspect told interrogators that he persuaded his sister to come along with him to the desert by telling her he was taking her to the police station to report the incident. He stabbed his sister thirty-five kilometres north-east of Kuwait City while she was telling him the names of the rapists.

Turkey

According to a report from the Centre for Social Cohesion (a London-based think tank), the Kurdish regions of Turkey have some of the highest rates of honour killings in the world. 'In

Turkey Kurds make up more than a quarter of the population [and] carry out a disproportionate number of honour killings.' Researchers and activists estimate the reported number of women and girls murdered annually at about two hundred. A 1999 survey found that seventy-four per cent of rural women in the south-east of the country believed their husbands would kill them if they had an affair.

As we shall see, when Kurds move to European countries such as Germany and the UK they bring their traditional codes of behaviour with them and exact a terrible punishment if the women of the family do not provide total obedience.

In Turkey the decision to kill the woman is taken at a family meeting, at which a young man within the family, a brother or cousin, is designated to carry out the crime. These crimes arise out of collective and deliberate decision and are carried out in public, reinforcing the fear in other women that they would face the same treatment from their own family members.

One such incident that gave momentum to the powerful lobbying against so-called honour crimes in Turkey was the stoning of Şemse Allak in the town of Mardin in November 2002, according to feminist and human rights activist Leylâ Pervizat.[44] Allak was stoned with her husband, whom she had been forced to marry after he raped her and she became pregnant, according to a Reuters report. The stoning of the couple was ordered by a tribal council which ruled that 'her shame was too much to bear'.

Recently, thanks in part to its efforts to become more European with a view to joining the EU, the Turkish government has placed so-called honour crimes on its agenda. NGOs and Turkish women's groups have been working hard to eradicate some of the laws that offered leniency to killers in such murders. Their efforts paid off. Certain articles in the Turkish Penal Code that used to grant sentence reductions to perpetrators of so-called honour crimes were removed.[45]

Women activists in Turkey have had some success. They targeted the custom whereby men pick a male minor to commit the murder, in the belief that the minor will receive a light sentence. By lobbying Parliament, activists brought about an amendment to Article 38 of the Turkish Penal Code, with the result that any person forcing another to commit a crime will receive the same sentence as the perpetrator. If the person incited is a minor, then the sentence is increased.[46]

Women's movements also reported a positive change in attitudes towards these crimes among the public. They said the year 2004 witnessed a change in both public attitudes and judicial decision-making. Perpetrators of two so-called honour killings were given the maximum penalty of life imprisonment.[47]

Unfortunately, there has since been an increase in so-called honour suicide. Yakin Erturk, a special envoy for the UN, was sent to Turkey to investigate suspicious suicides among Kurdish girls and was quoted by the *New York Times* as saying that some suicides in Kurdish-inhabited regions of Turkey appeared to be 'honour killings disguised as a suicide or an accident' in an effort to evade arrest.

Even today, honour killing remains relatively common in Turkey. A June 2008 report by the Prime Ministry's Human Rights Directorate says that in Istanbul alone there is one honour killing every week, and states that there have been over a thousand cases during the last five years.

Most recently and infamously, Turkey has prompted international newspaper headlines as a result of its first reported gay honour killing. Speaking to PinkNews.co.uk, the victim's partner (who did not wish to be named as he was in fear of his own life) said, 'Ahmet had been receiving threats for as long as I knew him. He told me this has been going on since his coming out a year ago. When he came out to his parents, who had always suspected, they made him feel guilty about it.'

Had Ahmet Yildiz's partner joined him for an ice cream, he is certain he would have been killed too. But it was late and he decided to go to bed. A few minutes later he heard shooting outside his flat and, rushing downstairs, saw Ahmet trying to escape his attackers by reversing down the street.

'I fought through some onlookers just in time to see him with his eyes open,' he said, 'and begged him, "Please don't die"; then he shut his eyes.'

Many of Ahmet's friends, including his partner, believe his family murdered him because he was openly gay. According to Ahmet's partner, homophobia in Turkey is 'unbelievably bad', and he believes it has worsened over the last four years. He's not optimistic about his chances of bringing Ahmet's murderers to justice.

'I know the Turkish system. I know I haven't got a leg to stand on. Human rights are known and accepted in the west but are not freely available in Turkey. I have no claim to his estate and body and cannot even collect my personal belongings from his flat. I cannot even bury my loved one.'

Egypt

One of the most horrific cases of so-called honour killing to be widely reported in the local news media occurred in Cairo in August 1987, when a father decided to kill his daughter for eloping. Marzouk Ahmed Abdel-Rahim chopped off his twenty-five-year-old daughter's head and carried it down the street saying, 'Now, the family has regained its honour.' He then surrendered to police.

Studies of so-called crimes of honour are few and far between. One of the small number of fairly recent reports, published in 1996, came from Egypt's National Centre for Social and Criminal Research. The study found that out of 843 murders committed in 1995, fifty-two were so-called honour killings. Activists have stated on several occasions since that the numbers are very likely to be much higher and in 1999 it was reported that ten per cent of all murders in Egypt were honour killings.[48]

The Centre for Egyptian Women's Legal Assistance (CEWLA), formed in 1995, was created to assist women whose human rights have been violated, as defined by the UN. CEWLA published a study in February 2002, which said *suspicion* of indecent behaviour was the reason for seventy-nine per cent of all crimes of honour. Cases included girls with blocked hymens whose bellies swelled with menstrual blood, killed by their families who thought they'd fallen pregnant, and girls whose periods had been interrupted by illness and whose virginity was only discovered at autopsy.

Only nine per cent of honour crimes followed an actual discovery of betrayal, according to CEWLA, which documented all cases reported in the press from 1998 to 2001. These included Fathiyah, who was burned to death in front of her four children by her brother because she refused to abort her illegitimate child to avoid 'scandalizing her family and husband who worked outside the country'. Khayri locked his sister in the bathroom and poured kerosene under the door before setting it on fire.[49]

Another case involved a thirty-seven-year-old married woman whose brother stabbed her 160 times and slashed her neck because it had been suggested she was dating her brother-in-law while her husband was out of the country.[50]

Meanwhile, according to a study conducted by researcher Mohamed Awad and published in *Al Ahram Weekly* in February 2002, 99.2 per cent of women interviewed in Egypt believed that a woman's honour lies in her virginity, while only 0.8 per cent said that it was based on her principles and values. This concept of honour continues to be reinforced in schools, according to a feature on so-called honour crimes that was published in the *New York Times* in June 1999. Abeer Allam, a young Egyptian journalist, recalled how his high school biology teacher sketched the female reproductive system. After he finished drawing he pointed to the entrance to the vagina. 'This is where the family honour lies!' the teacher declared.

The law in Egypt does not deal specifically with honour killings, but Article 237 of the Penal Code states: 'Whosoever surprises his wife in the act of committing adultery and immediately kills her and the person committing adultery with her shall be punished with a prison sentence instead of the penalties set out in Articles 234 and 236.' This means a sentence of three to seven years for manslaughter and heavier penalties for premeditation (Article 237 allows the judge to provide a sentence of less than three years), but only for a man. If a woman catches her husband in the act of adultery and kills him, she would be sentenced to life with hard labour; mitigating circumstances would not apply. Khayri was only sentenced to three years for murdering his sister Fathiyah because she was allegedly pregnant with an illegitimate child at the time of her death – so her infidelity was proven.

Another two articles, 274 and 277, show the clear judicial difference in the treatment of men and women. Women can be sentenced for up to two years for adultery while the maximum penalty for men is just six months.

Despite being the first Arab state to ratify the Convention on the Elimination of All Forms of Discrimination Against Women (CEDAW), Egypt has yet to deal with inequalities in law between the sexes as well as to encourage the courts to hand out stiffer sentences to discourage so-called honour killings.

For example, in 2000, a man decided to kill a local woman who had fallen pregnant as the result of an adulterous relationship. Once he had found a group of men to help him, they decided to kill the woman's mother too as she had tried to hide her daughter's adultery from the village. They kidnapped the daughter and killed her with a meat cleaver. Then they killed the mother, cut up the bodies and disposed of them in a canal. Only one of the killers, a relative of the victims, was sentenced. He was given three years. In another case, a man who tied up his pregnant daughter in a cattle pen and murdered her by setting her on fire was sentenced to one year – a sentence which was suspended for three years.

As yet, although some honour killings and ensuing trials are occasionally reported in the state-controlled press, there has been no real activity in the media to try and end honour crime, nor to point out how discrepancies in the law mean that men can get away with murder. Article 17 of the Egyptian Penal Code gives judges the authority to reduce sentences if they find that the condition of the accused requires it, without needing to provide any justifications. The article is often used to reduce punishments against perpetrators in cases of rape and so-called honour crimes. CEWLA has done a great job in identifying problems with the law and attitudes in the judiciary, and has called for the revision of Article 17 and for the government to help end so-called crimes of honour, but as yet the law and situation remain unchanged.

Palestine and Israel

Fifteen-year-old Samera's last mistake was to chat to a young man without a male chaperone. She lived in Salfeet, a small Palestinian town on the West Bank, where this sort of behaviour was deemed to be unacceptable and she was forced to marry the young man. Less than a year later, she gave birth. Five years later, unable to bear her husband's domineering and abusive ways, she left and went into hiding. According to the neighbourhood gossips, she stayed with several different men. Samera's family accepted the word of the gossips without question.

In July 1999 Samera was found at the bottom of a narrow well, her neck broken. Her father, his honour restored, told the court that his daughter had committed suicide. They accepted his explanation without question.

On 16 October 1995, Ibtihaj Hasson got out of a car with her younger brother on a main street in Daliat al Carmel, a small Israeli Druze village. A decade earlier, Ibtihaj had committed the unpardonable sin of marrying a non-Druze man. Now, after luring her back to her home village with promises that all was forgiven and her safety assured, her brother pulled out a knife and began to stab her. A crowd of more than a hundred people quickly gathered, some of whom urged him on. Within minutes, Ibtihaj lay dead on the ground while the crowd cheered her killer: 'Hero, hero! You are a real man!'[51]

Ibrahim had agonized over his decision: 'She is my sister,' he told the journalist Suzanne Zima, 'my flesh and blood – I am a human being. I didn't want to kill her. I didn't want to be in this situation. They [community members] push[ed] me to make this decision. I know what they expect from me. If I do this, they look at me like a hero, a clean guy, a real man. If I don't kill my sister, the people would look at me like I am a small person.'

Researchers who have tried to collect data on honour crimes in Palestine have had to contend with poor record-keeping by the authorities. However, they estimate that up to a hundred women were killed in crimes of honour in 1998, although the Palestinian police contend that there were only eight proven cases.

Official numbers released by the Palestinian Women's Affairs Ministry state that about twenty Palestinian women and girls were killed in 2004, with approximately fifty additional cases of 'forced suicide'. The Palestinian Ministry also confirmed that dozens of other killings are covered up each year, according to a report by the *Guardian Weekly*, published in July 2005.

Palestinian activist Aida Touma-Sliman said in a 2006 essay that the first demonstration against so-called honour crimes within the Palestinian community in Israel was held in 1990 after a young woman was murdered by her father when he discovered she was pregnant out of wedlock.[52] He did this even though he knew his daughter had been raped by another relative.

During the trial, a local mayor, justified her father's action, saying, 'the father had no choice because it was the only way he could continue to live in an honourable manner … these are our traditions, and that is how we act.'

His statements outraged many Palestinian activists and groups. As a result, a petition was started and adverts were placed in local newspapers calling for the resignation of the officials who provided the testimony. The resignation never came, but the protests did raise public awareness.[53]

In 1993, an organization named Al Badeel was set up by ten women and human rights activists to end so-called honour killings in Palestinian society.[54] Al Badeel was inspired by a horrific murder that had shaken Palestinian society in 1991, when a father, together with his son, murdered his daughter who was pregnant out of wedlock. It was later revealed that the father had been raping his daughter; when she became pregnant, he feared that he might be exposed, and conspired with his son to burn her to death.

Al Badeel played a crucial role in raising public awareness about this and other cases. According to Touma-Sliman, since this case was made public, protestors have taken to the streets whenever a so-called honour killing is reported. She said that Al Badeel, along with politicians, police officials and finally the public, 'forced the press to take note of the issue, and criticism developed of how the media dealt with the issue – generally the press buried the stories deep in the newspapers, did not go into detail, did not investigate and did not question trial outcomes.'

A further turning point was the 1995 murder of Ibtihaj Hasson. Touma-Sliman wrote: 'This tragic and ugly scene was the impetus behind a wave of articles by intellectuals and human rights activists condemning both this murder and honour crimes in general.'[55]

In March of that year, Maha Abdo, a social worker in the West Bank, told Mary Curtius from the *Sydney Morning Herald*, 'For years we did not want our dirty laundry hung in public. These issues were not discussed. But it is out now because of the growing awareness amongst Palestinian women.'

The Hebrew press used to shy away from covering these crimes because it regarded such incidents as an internal Palestinian issue. Their attitudes changed thanks to the extensive work by women's groups such as Al Badeel.[56]

As was the case in Jordan, Palestinian women's groups attempted to change the laws that provided leniency to murderers who claimed their crime was a so-called honour killing, but their calls were quashed by MPs who argued that reform would lead to a 'collapse in the moral fabric of society'. Religious leaders condemned the crime but blamed immoral behaviour and women's lack of adherence to dress codes, arguing that if religious codes were followed then honour killings would stop.

Judges, meanwhile, continue to practise discrimination. Courts tend to believe that the victim is not free of guilt. For example, when a brother stabbed his sister to death, because she had been the subject of rumour about her chastity, the court ruled that he deserved leniency because she had 'stabbed him in his manhood'.

The struggle to change the law has subsided somewhat since 2000, partly because of the second Palestinian intifada in September 2000, the re-invasion of Israeli armed forces and the growing humanitarian crisis in these territories, which have caused the national political agenda to take precedence over the women's rights agenda.

So the killings continue in Palestine with no real change in numbers. Recent cases include that of a twenty-two-year-old Christian Palestinian woman, Faten Habash. In July 2005, her father bludgeoned her to death with an iron bar because she wanted to marry a Muslim man. Faten had sought refuge with a tribal leader but was persuaded to return home after her father, with tears in his eyes, promised her that there would be no more beatings and no more threats to her life, and that she was free to marry the man she wanted. After her murder, hundreds of Palestinian women held a vigil in Ramallah, making it abundantly clear that they will never cease their struggle to try and save women like Faten.

Southern and Central America

In Brazil, it is widely believed that a man can legitimately kill his *allegedly* adulterous wife on the grounds of honour and such cases are regularly treated with leniency in the courtroom. Human Rights Watch (HRW) has documented cases of women killed by their husbands from the 1970s to the late 1990s for leaving or divorcing their husbands, returning home late from work, refusing to sleep with their husband, suspicion of adultery or because they had been caught in an adulterous situation.

Article 25 of the Brazilian Penal Code states: 'It is understood that it is a legitimate defence for anyone to use moderate necessary means to repel unjust aggression, present or imminent, to himself or somebody else.' Such a defence may be used only if the response is proportional and immediate in respect of the 'unjust aggression'. According to legal doctrine, any and every legal right can be defended legally, including one's 'honour'.

HRW's report indicated that while the 'legitimate defence' argument was used widely and successfully by men, '[it] is rarely used in cases in which wives kill their husbands'. HRW quoted a Brazilian state prosecutor who said, 'In general, women who kill their husbands are always sentenced to a higher sentence than men who kill their wives ... Most men who are accused of killing their wives get simple homicide ... Many of the women accused of killing their husbands get qualified homicide.'

A Brazilian judge said, 'The difference in sentencing between men and women is related to the fact that men kill their wives in the heat of the moment while women in the great majority plan [the crime]. Men normally act in an impetuous moment, although it is important to stress that they also plan.'

This Penal Code has been in place for more than sixty years and was created by a patriarchal society with outdated male-centred morals. The failure of legislators to repeal or modify these laws has allowed judges to defend this outdated patriarchal state in ways that are incompatible with basic human rights.

Brazilian scholars and activists Dr Sylvia Pimentel, Valéria Pandjiarjian and Juliana Belloque have stated that Brazil's judicial system, more than that of any other South American country, accepts the defence of 'legitimate defence of honour' in murders and assaults committed against women by their male spouses and former spouses.

The women's movement in Brazil organized a huge campaign in the 1980s to eliminate this defence under the slogan 'Who loves does not kill'. This came in the wake of an infamous murder case where a rich businessman shot his wife dead but was acquitted by the judicial court because the murder was considered to be a 'legitimate defence of his honour'. The ensuing outrage meant the man was retried and this time sentenced to fifteen years.[57]

Despite the best efforts of many committed activists, the Brazilian courts still issue judgments today that accept the 'legitimate defence of honour'.[58] While Bolivia, Peru and Argentina have changed their classification of sexual offences from 'offences to customs' to 'offences to sexual liberty', Brazil continues to classify sexual offences as 'offences against custom', while Uruguay maintains its classification of 'offences to customs and family order'. For example, in one verdict given in Brazil in March 2002, the Court of Appeal acquitted a man of attempting to murder the lover of his partner with a knife after finding him in his bed with his wife.

The judges said:

Antonio, who had already been offended in his honour, being the laughing stock of his neighbourhood, and labelled a cuckold ... entered the house and saw his wife with J.J. in deep sleep, half naked, in his own bed and in the presence of his son, whose cradle was in the same bedroom ... If he had left that house without doing what he did, his honour would be ineffaceably offended. It cannot be forgotten that the defendant was raised in a different time, during the twenties and thirties when morals and customs were different and probably more rigid than nowadays, which undoubtedly influenced his character, shaping his personality and actions.[59]

*   *   *

Sadly, so-called crimes of honour really do occur all round the world, in so many countries that there is not sufficient space available to deal with them all in detail here. In India, for example, more than a thousand women are murdered in honour killings each year. Most murders happen after a woman marries a man from a lower caste, which is seen as damaging to the family's standing in society. Oxfam has said that 'every six hours, somewhere in India a young married woman is burned alive, beaten to death or driven to commit suicide.'

Many hundreds of women are thought to have been murdered in Bangladesh. Odhikar, a local human rights organization, reported that out of 639 rapes committed in 2006, 126 of these victims were killed and thirteen committed suicide. In the same year, 243 dowry-related killings were reported to the police.

So-called honour killings also persist in many smaller countries, including Papua New Guinea, the Philippines, Fiji, the Dominican Republic, Rwanda, Sao Tome and Principe, and Senegal. While many may not find this surprising, I think most people will be truly shocked to learn the frequency with which they are now occurring in western countries, including the UK and the USA.

CHAPTER 12

Love, Honour and Obey

The streets of Derby in the UK may be thousands of miles from Pakistan, but walking down some of them, one feels a lot closer to Lahore than London. These form some of the most tightly-knit immigrant communities in Europe, where tradition and honour play a crucial role in everyday life.

In 1995, fifteen-year-old Rukhsana Naz was plucked from these streets and married off to an older man in Pakistan. Together they had two children and planned to set up home in the UK. Rukhsana returned first and, as her husband waited for permission to travel, she became pregnant by her childhood sweetheart. She was by then nineteen.

As the pregnancy became obvious, Rukhsana told her mother, Shakeela, that she wanted to divorce her husband. Her mother beat her, kicking her in the stomach and demanding she have an abortion. A few days later, her twenty-two-year-old brother, Shazad, along with her mother, forced Rukhsana to sign a legal document, naming them as the guardians of her two children.

A few days after that, Rukhsana's other brother, eighteen-year-old Iftikhar, returned home from college and heard a commotion coming from the basement. He ran downstairs and found his mother holding down Rukhsana while Shazad strangled her with plastic flex. 'Be strong, my son,' his mother told him. The family put Rukhsana's body in the car and drove a hundred miles to dump it.

Shazad and Shakeela were jailed for life in 1999.[60]

This was one of the first cases of an honour killing to receive serious attention from the British press. But it is now known that such murders have been committed in the UK at least as far back as the 1970s.

As usual, it took one extraordinary case to really alert the authorities and the media to the problem. It came in 2003 when Abdullah Yones received an anonymous letter at the south London offices of the Kurdish PUK (a political party aiming to achieve self-determination for the Kurdish people in Iraq) where he worked as a volunteer. This letter accused Heshu, his sixteen-year-old daughter, of behaving like a prostitute.

The Yones family had fled Saddam's Iraq in 1991 and soon settled in their west London community where Heshu attended the William Morris Academy. Heshu complained repeatedly to her teachers about the threat of forced marriage, but no one took it seriously, and no one (except for her closest friends, who saw the bruising) knew that by 2002 she was regularly beaten by her father.

Her teachers noticed that Heshu was overly terrified of going home with a bad school report. What they didn't realize was that Heshu was even more frightened that her father or brother would find out about her boyfriend, Nazim. As a result of this worry, her schoolwork started to suffer. The school thought it might be down to the influence of her boyfriend and so thought they were helping when they told her father.

Heshu ran away from home. When her family found her in July 2002, they took her on what they later told police was a 'happy family holiday' to Pakistan. What they didn't know was that Heshu kept a video diary in which she said over and over, 'I hate it here,' and described what really happened. They had taken her to Pakistan to marry her to her cousin, but when she failed a virginity test her father held a gun to her head and said, 'I can't give her away now.' Her mother and brother saved her on that occasion.

Upon her return to the UK, her brother discovered letters she'd written expressing her desire to run away again. On 12 October, her father locked her in her room and her brother and sister left the flat. Fearing for her life, Heshu called a friend on her mobile phone. She was interrupted when her father suddenly burst into the room and started yelling. Heshu hung up; her friend didn't try to call back, not realizing what was about to happen and fearing it would just make her father angrier.

Heshu fought for her life – her body was covered in defence wounds – but her father overpowered her, stabbing her seventeen times in her neck and back. Afterwards, Abdullah Yones cut his own throat and leapt from his balcony.

He survived and when he was fit to be interviewed he denied having anything to do with his daughter's murder, claiming that al-Qaeda agents had tried to murder them both. Then, when the police picked holes in this story, he changed his tune and said that Heshu had committed suicide and he had tried to kill himself out of grief.

In the run-up to the trial, the local Kurdish community helped Abdullah Yones raise £125,000 in bail while threats were made against those who planned to give evidence against him. The police also uncovered a plan to help Abdullah flee the country.[61]

The police also recovered Heshu's video diaries and letters, in which she detailed her plan to run away. One of them, used in evidence at the Old Bailey, read:

Goodbye Mum, I will see you again one day. Thank you a thousand times for trying so hard for me. I'm sorry I was such a bad friend. Some day I will try and make it up to you. Keep letting off that gas in your fat stomach. Enjoy life – now that I'm gone, there's no more trouble. I promise you I will be good.

Bye Dad, sorry I was so much trouble. Me and you will probably never understand each other. I'm sorry I wasn't what you wanted, but there's some things you can't change. Hey, for an older man you have a good strong punch and kick. I hope you enjoyed testing your strength on me; it was fun being on the receiving end. WELL DONE.

The time has come for us to part. I'm sorry that I have caused so much pain, but after sixteen years of living with you it is evident that I shouldn't be a part of you. I take all the blame openly – I'm not the child you wanted or expected me to be. DISAPPOINTMENTS ARE BORN OF EXPECTATIONS. Maybe you expected a different me and I expected a different you.

One day when I have a proper job every penny I owe you will be repaid in full. I will find a way to look after myself. I will go to social security to get myself a flat or hostel. I will be okay. Don't look for me, because I don't know where I'm going yet. I just want to be alone. But I will be safe. So have a nice day, have a nice week, have a nice life, because the biggest problem in this house has now left.

Bro, I'm not leaving you forever, just for a little while. I'm sorry to do this to you. I LOVE YOU MORE THAN I KNOW WHAT THE WORD LOVE MEANS. PLEASE FORGIVE ME!!! My problem has always been too much talk, too little action. So goodbye. One day you will see that I will make something good of myself. This isn't an end, it's just a new beginning, so enjoy. I'll come and visit you at school, as often as I can. So you'll be seeing a lot of me, okay?

LIFE, BEING HOW IT IS, ISN'T NECESSARILY HOW IT IS. IT IS JUST SIMPLY HOW YOU CHOOSE TO SEE IT.

Abdullah was tried in 2003, where he changed his plea to guilty at the last moment. Incredibly, when sentencing him, the judge said he was 'taking into account the cultural considerations in this case'. He sentenced Abdullah to twelve years in prison.

Abdullah Yones had murdered his daughter in his own home

and yet the judge had treated the crime as less serious than if he had murdered a stranger in the street.

Metropolitan Police Commissioner Sir Ian Blair issued a statement that read: 'Multiculturalism does not mean accepting the unacceptable.' Home Office Minister Mike O'Brien agreed, issuing a similar statement, saying, 'Multi-cultural sensitivity is no excuse for moral blindness.'

This was the first case that London's Metropolitan Police labelled as an honour killing. And while the case received widespread media coverage, the government was slow to address the issue, perhaps being overly cautious in the post-9/11 climate. The police, meanwhile, under the supervision of Commander Andy Baker at the Serious Crime Directorate, set up a small unit to deal specifically with the issue and work with women's support groups in the UK.

In June 2004, Commander Baker announced that the unit had decided to review 117 murder cases (fifty-two in London and sixty-five in other parts of England and Wales) over the past decade to establish whether 'honour' had been a contributing factor.[62]

Currently, the UK police estimate that around twelve honour-related murders are committed against women in Muslim, Sikh and Christian families in the UK annually, although this figure is widely believed to be a conservative one. According to official figures released in 2008, seventeen thousand women in Britain are victims of honour-related crimes (including kidnapping, sexual assault and murder) every year. The Metropolitan Police said they believe many of the killings were carried out by contract killers hired by the families. Consequently, these crimes also involved so-called 'bounty hunters' as well as women who make a business out of tracking down victims, BBC News World Edition reported in June 2004.

I met Commander Baker in March 2005 when he invited me to speak at an International Conference on Honour Based Violence held in London to examine the extent of so-called honour crimes and to help understand honour-based violence. The conference, which was attended by over three hundred delegates from the UK and abroad, was also aimed at examining proactive interventions and considering the issue of education in relation to honour-based violence. It was evident that the UK, which is more advanced than most other western countries in terms of identifying a strategy to deal with honour killings, still has a long way to go. This was made painfully apparent the following year.

Twenty-year-old Banaz Mahmood was found by the police running barefoot in the street on 31 December 2005. Covered in blood, she begged the officer to help her. When Banaz explained that her father had forced her to drink brandy and was about to kill her when she smashed a window and escaped, the constable was indifferent, thinking instead that Banaz was being 'calculating and melodramatic' and considered charging her for breaking the window.

Although the police clearly weren't going to help, Banaz's boyfriend, Rahmat Suleimani, knew he should take her very seriously. He knew that their relationship was the reason for Banaz's treatment. While Banaz was in the hospital, Rahmat sat at her bedside and used his mobile phone to record Banaz's cry for help.

There really wasn't much more that Banaz could have done. She had already gone to Mitcham police station in south London on 4 December and told police that her family were planning to kill her. She was sent home and two officers came round to her house the next day. Banaz was too scared to open the door and there was no way she was going to talk to the police with her parents standing behind her. Banaz asked the police for help on a total of six occasions; she even wrote them a letter naming those she thought were plotting against her.

Banaz was twelve years old when her family first arrived in England as asylum seekers, fleeing Saddam Hussein's Iraq. She arrived with her parents Mahmod and Behya, brother Bahman (aged twenty-nine) and sisters Beza (twenty-six), Payman (twenty-one), Giaband (seventeen) and Bekhal (fourteen). Mahmood was a former Iraqi soldier who beat his children for the smallest infraction. For example, Banaz was beaten for wearing hairspray.

Her father had, in his own words, found 'the David Beckham of husbands' for Banaz to marry but after two violent years, Banaz left him and returned to the family home.

She met Rahmat Suleimani, who was thirty-one years old, at a family party in 2005. They fell in love but her father disapproved of their relationship because Rahmat was from a different village and less religious.

When Banaz learned of another plot to kill her, she went to the police again. This time they did listen and tried to persuade her to stay somewhere safe but she refused because she believed her mother would protect her.

That was the last time she was seen alive.

On the following day, communication between Banaz and her boyfriend stopped. When police officers first called at the family home her father said she wasn't there. Two days later, the police launched a full-scale investigation after her father refused to report her missing.

It took three months to find Banaz's body. She was found after police tapped the family's phones. Her body had been stuffed into a suitcase and buried in a garden in Birmingham. A post mortem revealed that Banaz had been strangled with a bootlace.

She had undergone an horrific ordeal. Her father had watched for two hours as Banaz was raped and beaten by a pair of hitmen. This was supposed to be a form of humiliation for the woman who had shamed his family.

Banaz's sister Bekhal risked her life to testify against her sister's killers during the three-month trial of her father and uncle at the

Old Bailey. This was a first – a woman making a public stand against her family and community.

Banaz's boyfriend Rahmat also risked his life to testify. Her mother and three other sisters were too scared to co-operate with the police, fearing reprisals from their own community.

Bekhal told the court that she herself had run away from home twice, once when her father attempted to make her marry her cousin in Iraq. They locked her in her bedroom for one week to force her to accept the marriage, but she escaped, went to the authorities and was eventually put into a foster home. She said:

> My parents again tracked me down and kept sending me audio tapes. At first they would be tearful, with my dad calling me his 'little rose'. Then they became more menacing. My father told me that unless I went home he would kill all my sisters first, then my brother, then my mother, then himself, such was the shame I had brought on them. I believed him, so I went back. Did I think he was capable of doing that? Absolutely.

Her father used exactly the same method to lure Banaz back home.

Bekhal told the court that her father was so aggressive that when he saw her outdoors without a headscarf, he screamed at her that she was acting like a bitch, then took her home, spat on her and beat her with his slipper.[63]

Bekhal's only brother, Bahman, had attempted to kill her under direct orders from his father to cleanse their family's honour. She said he had arranged to meet her in a remote area in South London and the minute she turned her back to him he struck her on her head with a steel bar.

She fell, bleeding heavily; she shouted at her brother: 'What are you doing?' Bekhal said her brother, who obviously was against the plan that he was enacting, started to cry and said, 'I've got to do it; you have brought shame on the family. It is my duty.'

Bekhal convinced her brother to spare her life, called her

boyfriend and went to hospital for treatment. She refused to file charges out of fear of shaming her family. She remained in hiding until a few months later she learned that Banaz had agreed to an arranged marriage set up by her father.

'Why should we have to die for wanting no more than for our voices to be heard, to have a say in our lives?' Bekhal said. 'I will never be able to tell people who my father is – not only because of the risk to my life but because I'm ashamed. He is the one who has brought dishonour to our family … As I am separated from my family I have no one to share my memories of Banaz and no one to share my grief.'

On 11 June 2007, Mahmood was found guilty of ordering the death of his twenty-year-old daughter. He was sentenced to life imprisonment along with his brother and the killer, thirty-year-old Mohamad Hama, who later boasted in prison how after torturing and raping Banaz for two hours he finally stamped on her neck to 'get her soul out'.[64]

In the lead-up to the trial the director and founder of the London-based Iranian and Kurdish Women's Rights Organization (IKWRO), Diana Nammi, launched the 'Justice for Banaz' campaign, which forced the police to investigate their failure to help Banaz, and influenced their decision to review police procedures in dealing with family violence, especially in immigrant communities.

The police issued a statement shortly after the trial, stating that they had failed to help Banaz. The Independent Police Complaints Commission (IPCC) agreed. They said Banaz had been 'let down' by the police and suffered from delays, poor supervision and 'a lack of understanding and insensitivity'. Six detectives from the Met and West Midlands received written warnings, and one Met constable received 'words of advice', according to a BBC report on 2 April 2008.

Bekhal and Rahmat now face a future of secret addresses and

identities. Afterwards, Rahmat said, 'My life went away when Banaz died. The only thing keeping me going was to see justice being done for Banaz.' She was 'my present, my future, my hope'.

Bekhal described her murdered sibling as 'one of the most beautiful, loving, caring, easy-going girls you could ever hope to meet. Her only crime was to want to have some say in her life. Where is the shame in that? My life will always be at risk. There are people in my community who want to see me dead, and they will not rest until I am. I will never be safe.'

Bekhal now wears a veil for a different reason: 'so no one can recognize me.'

It is clear that the police in the UK have a mountain to climb in terms of addressing honour killings, and not only because their occurrence in the UK has just recently been recognized. A major problem is that these murders very often have the support of the victim's extended family and community; those of them who are opposed to it are often simply too frightened to speak up.

Nazir Afzal, the lead prosecutor on honour-based violence at the Crown Prosecution Service, said, 'In the case of Banaz ... substantial members of the community actually did not assist and support prosecutors; instead they supported the family members responsible for the killing. They really didn't care and it showed ... The murder of Banaz was so brutal that it was a clear warning to others; it was a way of saying "don't step put of line or this could be you".'

As well as a lack of support for prosecutors, there are also cases where prosecution witnesses were terrorized until they withdrew their testimony. For example, in April 2008, Azeem Mohammad, aged twenty-six, was jailed for twenty-one months after admitting to intimidating witnesses in the case of an Iraqi Kurd beaten to death in an honour killing in Sheffield. Ismail Rashid, aged forty-two, was killed the previous year after having an affair with a married Pakistani woman. Three men were jailed for the killing.[65]

Most so-called honour killings that have taken place in the UK have been carried out by people of Kurdish, Bangladeshi and Pakistani origin. Although many are carried out by first-generation immigrants, it's increasingly becoming the case that the murderers are of the second generation. This suggests that many communities may not be as well integrated into British life as is widely thought. That is where the conflict lies; women are attracted to the liberal western values that promise more independence and equality, while men want to maintain their patriarchal system. This conflict is at the root of many honour killings. Most have been the result of relationships outside the family caste or religion.

It is worth mentioning that there are no known cases in the UK of men being killed by their own families for sexual impropriety – reinforcing the idea that women are responsible for the maintenance of family honour, while men can do as they please. For example, Imran Rehman resisted his parents' efforts to force him into marrying his first cousin when he was sixteen and she was eleven. Instead of telling him he was damaging the family honour, his father said that once Imran was married, the family's honour would be satisfied and he would be free to behave as he wished. Imran is now a support worker at Karma Nirvana, a British charity which helps men and women at risk from honour killing and forced marriage.

As we've just seen, the murders tend to be planned well in advance, with consent being sought from the extended family and volunteers being recruited to do the deed (although hitmen or relatives are sometimes brought in from abroad to carry out the killing). Sometimes the victim is lured or forced to travel abroad where the family feels they have a better chance of getting away with murder.

In May 2007, nineteen-year-old Shawbo Ali Rauf was taken from her home in Birmingham to Iraqi Kurdistan where she was stoned to death. Her crime was having unknown numbers on her mobile telephone – which proved to her family that she was having an affair. The British police refused to prosecute her husband, despite protests carried out by Kurdish women's groups.[66]

There are no figures that state how many of the young women that disappear from the UK are murdered. We don't even know how many British girls are bundled off to Pakistan, India and Bangladesh each year, but according to Jasvinder Sanghera, writing in *The Times*, the figure is in the thousands. 'Some three hundred girls aged thirteen to sixteen have disappeared off the school registers in Bedford alone,' she wrote, 'so many of these girls are intimidated or subjected to actual violence as they try to resist their parents' wishes.'

There may be many other reasons for an honour killing. A twenty-seven-year-old Sikh woman fled her marital home because she feared that her in-laws were planning to kill her for failing to produce a child. She had passed fertility tests but still had fertility treatment forced upon her. She suspected that her husband was infertile and it was this that had sealed her fate.

A more typical British victim was Samaira Nazir, a twenty-five-year-old businesswoman and graduate of Pakistani origin. In April 2005, after refusing to marry a series of potential husbands, and embarking on a relationship with an Afghan asylum seeker, she was summoned to the family home. After an argument, her brother, her father and her seventeen-year-old cousin cut her throat and stabbed her seventeen times.

Nazir's father was bailed and he seized the opportunity to flee to Pakistan. He's still at large and unlikely to face British justice any time soon as there's no extradition treaty between the UK and Pakistan. Thankfully, Samaira's brother and cousin were both convicted of murder.[67]

In 1998, Bachan Athwal, a Sikh grandmother, arranged for her family to murder Surjit Athwal, her twenty-seven-year-old daughter-in-law. Surjit, a mother of two, was a customs officer at

Heathrow airport. She was having an affair and was planning to divorce Bachan's son, to whom she had been married for ten years – the result of a parental arrangement.

Soon after hearing this news, Bachan convinced her son Sukhdave, aged forty-five, that Surjit should die for shaming him – not only for having an affair but because she cut her hair short, smoked and consumed alcohol. Surjit was lured to India under the pretext of a 'family wedding'. Her husband, who remarried after she 'failed' to return from India, took out a £100,000 insurance policy on Surjit the day she left.

After the murder, Bachan boasted to her family that her daughter-in-law's body had been thrown into a river. Bachan and her son sent forged letters in an attempt to fool the police into thinking that Surjit had eloped with another man.

That the case was investigated at all was largely thanks to Surjit's brother, Jagdeesh Singh, who spearheaded a campaign to get his sister the justice she deserved. He learned of his sister's murder from two relatives while on a visit to India. 'She was driven off in a car and taken to the banks of a nearby river,' he said. 'She was pulled out of the car, strangled, suffocated to death and then her body was thrown into the river with a view to it being lost for ever.'

The police travelled to India to investigate but drew a blank; a reward of £10,000 failed to persuade anyone to come forward.

'With the greatest of respect to them,' Jagdeesh said, 'all the leading police investigators at the beginning were white, English officers who did not quite appreciate the subtleties and the unseen aspects of honour violence, the details around honour and family and practices within a Punjabi family culture.'

Singh also criticized the British Foreign Ministry for failing to exert pressure on the Indian government to intensify its investigations. He also made the point that a white British woman who vanished in Japan during the same period received a great deal of attention, not only from the Foreign Secretary Robin Cook (who refused to meet Jagdeesh Singh and his family) but also from Prime Minister Tony Blair. It wasn't until 2003, when Singh finally met the new Foreign Secretary Jack Straw, that the government promised to make a serious effort to catch the murderers and in 2007, nine years after the crime, Bachan and Sukhdave Athwal were tried at the Old Bailey.

Surjit's seventy-year-old mother-in-law claimed she was innocent throughout the trial and wept as she was sentenced to life. Judge Giles Forrester told the pair:

> How you could commit this unspeakable act I do not know. There was no motive worthy of the name. You did it because you perceived she had brought shame on the family name.
>
> In reality you murdered her for no better reason than the existence of matrimonial difficulties and the likely breakdown of the marriage. You decided the so-called honour of your family name was worth more than the life of this young woman.[68]

Surjit's daughter, Pavan, did not learn the truth about what had happened until August 2008, when she turned seventeen. She had accepted that her grandmother and father had been mistakenly convicted and that her mother had simply abandoned her. Her family hid newspaper reports from her and she even visited her father in Belmarsh Prison while trying to keep up with her schoolwork and looking after her younger brother.

In her first interview, reported in the *Independent*, Pavan said:

> For years I was told that my mum didn't love us any more and that we should just forget about her. My brother and I grew up hating her because we thought she'd just left us; why would we doubt our dad?
>
> But after I moved out of my uncle's house in April, they started to threaten me with violence and I began to realize what

they were capable of. My aunt Sarbjit told me everything that had happened but it was when I read my mum's diary that it really hit me. I felt terrible. I was so angry at my dad for telling such terrible lies but I also felt guilty. I wanted to tell my mum that I was sorry for hating her all these years. We used to have so much fun together, even though I know now that she was really unhappy.[69]

Her ten-year-old brother was placed in foster care by the authorities after Pavan found out the truth. 'It's such a relief to know that my brother is safe,' Pavan told the *Independent*. 'It feels like a huge pressure has been lifted from my shoulders. I know telling him the truth is going to be a huge hurdle but I can't wait to see him again and start living our lives without all the lies.'

In December 2008, Pavan organized a memorial service at Heathrow airport (where her mother used to work) to mark the tenth anniversary of her mother's death. She is now waging a campaign to raise £10,000 to bring the Punjab-based killers of her mother to justice.

Sometimes, so-called honour killings can spark violent reprisals – perhaps as the result of the fear that the police are unlikely to bring the perpetrators to justice. In 1999 Haq Nawaz Khan from Walsall shot dead his half-brother 'Big Ali' Nawaz Khan. The two men had been close until Big Ali had shot dead Haq's sister, Shanaz Begum, in Pakistan five months earlier in an honour killing.

On 23 September 2005, Mohammad Shaheen, the co-owner of a taxi firm in Chorlton, Manchester, was shot dead by Khyber Khan, his brother-in-law. Khan, aged twenty-eight, had flown to Manchester from Pakistan to kill Shaheen after his sisters told him that he'd sexually assaulted them. After the killing, Khan's sisters helped him flee the country. He was eventually arrested in Canada and deported to the UK.[70]

Sometimes, children are also murdered, intentionally or unintentionally, as the result of an alleged affront to the family honour. On 2 November 2006, one of the most horrific incidents ever seen in the UK took place in Accrington, Lancashire.

Mohammad Riaz was an immigrant from Pakistan's highly conservative North-West Frontier. He had arrived in the UK at the age of thirty-two after his cousin, Caneze, was sent from the UK to Pakistan to marry him. They had four children together, three girls and a boy.

Thirty-nine-year-old Caneze was confident and successful and was described by her friends as bright and bubbly; she worked as a campaigner for women's rights, helping women who felt suppressed by traditional values, and regarded herself as a role model. Caneze, whose mother was English, was highly sociable; she organized women-only swimming groups and had a wide circle of friends. Mohammad, meanwhile, was illiterate, spoke no English, undertook a wide variety of low-paid jobs and spent most of his spare time in the local mosque.

When Caneze's father died, Mohammad tried to exert his patriarchal authority. He criticized the western dress of his wife and children, and demanded that their daughters finish their schooling as soon as possible so they could be married off in Pakistan. Caneze refused, and also refused to give up work. Mohammad was incensed. Then in 2006 Adam, their seventeen-year-old son, developed leukaemia. This failure of Mohammad to produce a healthy son only added to his rage; the final straw came when his eldest daughter told him she wanted to become a fashion designer.

On 31 October 2006, Mohammad, who had been drinking heavily, locked the doors and windows of the family home, sprayed the rooms with petrol and set it alight. Once the fire had taken hold, he poured petrol on himself and stepped into the flames. Caneze and their four daughters, aged sixteen, fifteen, ten and three, all died. Mohammad was pulled alive from the burning building by firefighters but died two days later. Adam was in hospital at the time, receiving chemotherapy. He died six weeks after being given the news.[71]

Caneze's friend, Shahnaz Hussain, told reporters that the community was frightened that the murders would be labelled an honour killing – there was a fear that if it was labelled as such, then some people would feel that it was in some way justified.

A local police constable and Family Liaison Officer, Steve Cox, who knew Caneze's family said, 'There are men here in East Lancashire who are prepared – and I've seen it first hand – to subject their female children in particular to psychological abuse, physical abuse, forced marriages, and keeping them prisoner in the house.' Barry Khanan, Caneze's brother, said:

> You can't bring the old way of life from Pakistan to England and expect it to work. And I don't think people should give any reason or excuse to this kind of action. It's cold-blooded murder. There was no honour involved ... He was so selfish, and pig ignorant that he couldn't see what he was doing to his family. He was closing himself off from his family. He was isolating himself, all because he wanted things his way. I'm the man; I shall have it my way. And yes it does come from his background, where he's brought up to believe that he is dominant. He's the male, he's the husband, he's the father. That right or wrong, things should be done his way. But where's the honour in murdering five innocent people?[72]

PC Cox agreed:

> Honour is completely the wrong word. It is a control murder. That's what these are. It is not honour crime; it is 'control crime' and fear of losing that control.
>
> It really is beyond belief that he felt this – the five graves – was the answer to losing control of his family. What is honourable

about this? Caneze had done nothing wrong. On the contrary, she was doing so much that was good. Every one of those children there are testament to that, and they have all suffered because of one man and his completely twisted view on life. And I've got to say, that whatever twisted multi-version there was, it is about subjecting your own children to complete and utter brutality, whether it is physical or psychological, just because they've made you feel ashamed. Women are dying and being brutalized in this situation many times throughout Britain at the moment. Cultural sensitivity is absolutely no excuse for moral blindness, and there's too much fannying about going on on both sides, from both communities, and as long as that remains the situation, then young women are going to keep dying. It's as simple as that.

Another of Caneze's friends and a colleague, Mussurut Zia, said:

This had something to do with all of us. It was Caneze who died in the end, but it had something that impacted on all of us. And we all had to rethink our positions within our families and within our homes. The heart of it is that it is a patriarchal society, a male-dominated society, and that dominance is extended to women. Women are chattels to be done with as the owner sees fit, and this type of behaviour that men indulge in is perpetuated from generation through to generation, so that each generation following on is going to think that is the right thing to do, and that is the only way to live.

This wasn't the only case in the UK to involve the murder of innocent children. Thirty-two-year-old Uzma Rahan arrived in Manchester in 1992, thanks to an arranged marriage. She adopted an increasingly western lifestyle, making friends independently and dressing less conservatively. Her husband, Rahan Arshad, who worked as a taxi driver, found her behaviour increasingly frustrating. Uzma told her friends that she was afraid of her husband, that she would be the victim of an 'honour killing', saying, 'Count the days before he kills me.'

Soon afterwards Arshad killed Uzma by hitting her twenty-three times with a baseball bat. He then beat his three children to death. At his trial, Arshad told the court that he had been angered by his wife's decision to wear tight jeans and tops. He said, 'It wasn't right for a mother and someone who came from Pakistan to change the way she dressed all of a sudden. It wasn't right at all.'[73]

On 14 May 2008, IKWRO held a conference in London on honour-based violence and honour killings. Diana Nammi, head of IKWRO, said, 'Our policy is to never turn back any woman. In 2007 we rescued seventy women and two men. There are many more who need our help whom we never get to hear about. There are lots of missing women and many self-harm to try and escape their families.'

According to 1992 figures, South Asian women are three times more likely to commit suicide than white women in the UK. Some of these suicides may be murders disguised as such and in some cases the harassment by relatives/in-laws for alleged failings encouraged victims to commit suicide. Many figures relating to so-called honour crimes in the UK are unreliable as they do not account for cases where women have been taken to Pakistan and elsewhere to be murdered.

Nammi also said:

These women are all victims of family members, fathers, brothers, mothers and sisters. Bounty hunters and contract killers are paid to track them down. Once on they run they are never safe. One cab driver that knew a victim's family took her home instead of to a refuge. There is still a great deal of work to be done. One sixteen-year-old who recently ran away from a forced marriage said: 'If your family doesn't get you then the

British government will.' Her father was arrested and held for two hours before he was released without charge.

Nammi argued that there needs to be better awareness and support from the UK government. Women on the run from their families should not be sent home, as has so often been the case. At the very least, the family should not be told until the woman is safe and her case can be properly investigated. It is hard for many people to understand that these women's worst enemies are those who are closest to them.

A recent case that won a great deal of attention was that of the NHS doctor Humayra Abedin, aged thirty-three, who was held captive by her family in Bangladesh for four months while they plotted a forced marriage to a Muslim man she had never met.

A friend of Dr Abedin, who had lived with her in East London, raised the alarm after receiving a text. 'Please help me. My life is in danger. They have locked me in house. My job is at stake. They are making my life hell,' the message said.

Dr Abedin had a Hindu boyfriend in London, and it was this that had angered her Muslim family.

She was tricked into flying to Bangladesh in August 2008 when her family told her that her mother was seriously ill. Once she arrived she was allegedly beaten, drugged and held against her will. The doctor's boyfriend, a forty-four-year-old Bangladeshi software engineer, said, 'Her family told her they'd prefer her to die than return to London.'[74]

The High Court issued an injunction under the new Forced Marriage Act (2007), demanding that Dr Abedin be allowed to return to Britain. Though the Act is not enforceable in Bangladesh it was hoped that it would place pressure on the Bangladeshi authorities. It worked. In December, Judge Syed Mahmod Hossain ordered Dr Abedin's parents to return her passport, driver's licence and credit card.[75]

In the west, the UK is at the moment leading the way in the fight against so-called crimes of honour and the Forced Marriage Act is a step in the right direction. It is aimed at protecting the victims of forced marriages and preventing these marriages from taking place. Courts will be able to make orders to protect the victim or the potential victim and help remove them from that situation. Anyone breaching the orders can, and most likely will, be arrested.

Bridget Prentice, a minister at the Ministry of Justice said, 'This legislation sends out a clear message that forced marriage, a breach of an individual's basic right to choose who and when they marry, is not acceptable in our society. It will enable us to make better use of civil court remedies to provide protection to those placed in this intolerable position.'

The joint Foreign and Commonwealth and Home Office Forced Marriage Unit (FMU) was launched in January 2005 as the UK's 'one stop shop' for developing government policy on forced marriage, co-ordinating outreach projects and providing support and information to those at risk. The unit handles approximately 250–300 cases per year, fifteen per cent of which involve men. Officers from the unit have travelled abroad on many occasions to try and trace people who they think may have been abducted. In the first nine months of 2008, the FMU was contacted by 1,308 members of the public who alerted them to suspected cases.

Although the FMU sees cases from around the world – including East Asia, Africa, the Middle East and Europe – the majority are from South Asia. Approximately sixty-five per cent of cases involve families of Pakistani origin and twenty-five per cent involve families of Bangladeshi origin. Around a third of cases dealt with by the FMU involve children, some as young as thirteen. The unit also assists reluctant sponsors (those forced into marriage and subsequently forced to sponsor a visa application) and has dealt with over a hundred of these cases since May 2006.

IKWRO was involved in the consultation process in the run-up to the passing of the Forced Marriage Act. Another important aspect of IKWRO's work is raising awareness in the community. Many women are unfamiliar with British law and are unaware that help is available. 'We have got to get the message out. There is help, there are organizations that can offer support as well as long-term counselling, shelter and safety,' Nammi said.

Detective Inspector Brent Hyatt, also speaking at the 2008 IKWRO conference, said, 'Many victims don't realize that the police have different views to those in their own country. Those officers who are fearful of breaking cultural rights need to put these fears to one side.'

The Crown Prosecution Service now has specialist lawyers who deal with honour crimes and have been rolling out training on the issue since the IPCC ruling on police failures in the case of Banaz Mahmood. They are also establishing an inter-agency approach to honour crimes, so the CPS will work with voluntary organizations such as IKWRO.

There is still much to be done. At the time of writing there is no standard police or governmental policy for dealing with so-called honour crimes and this has left many women very vulnerable. Nammi, along with the police and other agencies, believes that one of the best things the government could do would be to scrap or amend the 'no recourse to public funds' rule. This rule ensures that non-EU immigrants cannot claim various benefits for the first two years that they are here. This creates a problem in that a woman who leaves her violent household has no support from the state, and would find it very difficult to get work, especially if her English is poor and she cannot get any references. Nor can she return to her country of origin, as her life may be at risk if she is believed to have brought shame on her family, for example, by divorcing. So women on the run are forced to stay in unsecured guesthouses, are not entitled to council accommodation and have no say in where they live. In one case, a woman was re-housed just two streets away from her family.

Sarah Pepper, a Child Protection Co-ordinator for Islington in North London, said that cases of honour-based violence affecting teenagers were increasing in number. The dangers are sometimes acute. One extreme example of this was an incident in Manchester on 28 June 2001. Faqir Mohammad, a sixty-nine-year-old Pakistani man who had lived in the UK for thirty years, returned from Friday prayers at the local mosque to find his daughter Shahida in her bedroom with her boyfriend. The boyfriend leapt out of the window. Mohammad went and fetched a knife, put his daughter in a headlock and stabbed her nineteen times in the stomach. At his trial he told the court that he was a 'strict Muslim' who wanted all of his daughters to have arranged marriages in Pakistan.

Although Pepper stated that in her experience Bangladeshi and Kurdish teenagers between fifteen and eighteen years of age were at most risk, there is currently no official audit, so the true number of cases is not yet known. 'Often they [women in danger] don't realize that what is normal for them is extraordinary for us. On those occasions where they do come forward, we need to be able to react immediately.' They have dealt with several adult sisters who have run away in order to ask Child Protection Services to try to save their younger sisters whom they've left behind with their abusive parents.

Pepper stated that children must be isolated while their case is investigated. There should be no interviews with the immediate family and community leaders to start with, and local people should not be used as interpreters. Pepper made the point that this is impossible without the invaluable co-operation of voluntary organizations.

Most mistakes are made in the early stages of an investigation. Previously, child protection officers have sometimes argued that it's worse to separate young girls from their family than allow them to be forced into marrying, 'because they can always divorce later'. In one instance where this logic was applied, a sixteen-year-old Pakistani girl returned to the child protection officer after being badly beaten when she was sent home.

In an emotional address, Detective Inspector Hyatt told the 2008 IKWRO conference that 'we need also to look beyond the immediate perpetrators'. He was speaking with particular reference to Banaz Mahmood. Detectives had tried to prosecute two men accused of helping to hide Banaz's body in their back garden. The trial had collapsed because of a lack of evidence. Banaz's cousin Dashti Babaker, aged twenty-one, and his friend Amir Abbas, aged thirty-one, were alleged to have joined the plot to please community elders.

The point is that the wider community must be made aware that if they know about an honour killing and by keeping silent about their knowledge they assist the perpetrators, then the police will come after them too. Two other men involved in Banaz's murder, Mohammad Ali and Omar Hussein, who fled to Iraq, are still wanted. Hyatt remains determined to see them brought to justice.

For far too long the British government has left the burden of dealing with so-called honour crimes to unpaid volunteer organizations. These organizations have been struggling to cope with demand, with the result that many thousands of people have suffered unnecessarily. There are many simple things that the UK government can still do to aid the fight against honour-based violence in the UK.

In terms of foreign policy, extradition treaties with Pakistan and Iraqi Kurdistan need to be put in place; the minimum age for those entering the UK on a marriage visa from abroad should be raised from eighteen to twenty-one; and it should be compulsory for anyone entering the UK to live to achieve a certain degree of fluency in English.

There also needs to be greater support for women's groups; women at risk need to know that help is available; forced marriages should be criminalized; accomplices and advocates of so-called honour killings should be punished; and trusted community leaders should try to educate men on the wrongs of honour-based violence (self-appointed 'community leaders', such as the Muslim Council of Britain, have so far done little or nothing to tackle honour-based violence). Dealing with the root cause of honour-based violence will not only help end human rights abuses but will also have a range of positive consequences for immigrant communities and wider society. Many of these strategies may also help other western countries that are facing the same problem. One can but hope that governments across the world will act soon.

As a footnote to this section on the the UK, I was surprised to discover that there is a discriminatory law in England, similar to the 'fit of fury' Article 98 in Jordan, which allows the reduction of the crime of murder to manslaughter when the case of provocation is successfully argued. Campaign groups have demanded changes to this law but their efforts have been strongly resisted by the most powerful judge in the land.

It has been argued that it is unfair that men can currently rely on a 'fit of fury' as a partial justification for killing their unfaithful wives, while women who have been physically abused by their husbands and who have killed them out of the fear of further abuse have been denied any such defence, and have no choice but to face the straightforward charge of murder.

Calls for a change to the law were made after Sarah Thornton was jailed for life in 1990 for the murder of her husband, who had beaten her repeatedly. She won a retrial in 1996 and was freed after being convicted of manslaughter.[76]

In November 2008, the British government announced plans to change the law so that husbands and boyfriends would no longer be able to use the defence of infidelity to escape conviction.

Introducing the proposed changes (the first to the UK's homicide law since 1957), Harriet Harman, Minister for Women, said that for centuries the law had allowed men to escape a murder charge in domestic homicide cases by blaming the victim.

Under the reforms, men would be tried for murder rather than manslaughter for 'crimes of passion', while women who kill their husbands because of years of abuse would be treated more leniently.

The reforms have been attacked by Lord Phillips, the Lord Chief Justice, who has instead argued in support of the defence of 'sexual infidelity', which he said could help show whether a husband (or wife) had been provoked into killing a spouse.

Lord Phillips was reported in the *Independent* as saying, 'I must confess to being uneasy about a law which so diminishes the significance of sexual infidelity as expressly to exclude it from even the possibility of amounting to provocation. Nor have ministerial statements persuaded me that it is necessary for the law to go that far.'

Under the proposals, men who kill wives or girlfriends will be less likely to escape murder convictions by pleading jealous anger. It is designed to help women like Sarah Thornton, who kill their husbands after a long period of abuse. People will also be able to claim they killed for fear of suffering more violence in the future.

The change would replace the present defence of 'provocation' with a new defence based on 'words or conduct', which made defendants feel 'seriously wronged' or fear violence against them. The new defences will allow killers to be sentenced for manslaughter instead of murder. At the time of writing, the changes are being debated in the British Parliament and, needless to say, I am watching with considerable interest.

CHAPTER 13

Chaos in Europe

European communities have done extensive work and offered professional protection and services for female victims of domestic violence. Unfortunately, they have so far looked the other way when dealing with honour-related violence in immigrant communities. All too often, they see the violence within these communities as culturally based and therefore entirely separate from European laws and value systems.

However, after some brutal incidents, European countries have now started to pay increased attention to so-called honour crimes, forced marriages and other forms of oppression of women within immigrant communities. Murders committed in the name of family honour by immigrant communities had been reported back in the early 1990s, but because it was still a poorly understood phenomenon, it wasn't picked up on by the authorities. Many professional staff who received reports of so-called honour killings and honour-based violence simply regarded it as a 'cultural expression, and nothing to get involved in'.[77]

Asma Jahangir, Special Rapporteur on religious freedom for the UN Commission on Human Rights, told me in a phone interview in November 2006 that activism in the Third World by NGOs and individuals, mainly in Jordan and Pakistan, had contributed to raising the awareness of these abuses within European immigrant communities.

'Western countries did not believe these crimes were happening and thought they were immune and that it only happened in our part of the world until they were confronted with two horrifying so-called honour murders committed by migrants within the migrant communities,' Jahangir said.

Jahangir was referring to Heshu Yones, discussed earlier, and the case of twenty-six-year-old Fadime Sahindal in Sweden, which attracted the attention of European governments, NGOs, the police and activists.

On 20 November 2001, the Violence against Women network arranged a seminar entitled 'Integration on whose terms?' Fadime Sahindal told her story to the Swedish Parliament during that seminar:

> I'm going to talk about how hard it is to be caught between the demands of your family and the demands of society. I want to point out that this is not only about women from the Middle East.
>
> I'm twenty-five years old and come from a small village in the Turkish part of Kurdistan. I come from a happy family with clear role divisions. When I was seven years old, my family came to Sweden. They told me not to play with Swedish children, to come straight home from school every day.
>
> My parents thought that school was a good thing as long as you learned to read and write, but that girls didn't need a higher education. The most important thing was for me to go back to Turkey one day and get married.
>
> But when the time came, I refused because I thought that I was too young. Besides, I wanted to choose my own husband. I told them I wouldn't go back to Turkey. For them, my marriage was for the good of the entire family. Even if I didn't want to get married, it was better for one member of the family to feel disgraced than the whole family. But I considered myself to be a member of Swedish society.

I began to test my limits more and more. I hung out with my Swedish friends and came home later than I was supposed to. It was important for me to stand on my own two feet, to get an education and develop my abilities. My family was against that. They regarded Swedish girls as loose – with no respect for their families. Swedes switch partners without worrying about the honour of their family. My family's opinions were riddled with prejudice. They made me confused and ambivalent. I was forced to lead a double life.

One day I met a Swedish guy named Patrik and we fell in love. But it was important that my family not find out about it. I was afraid of what would happen if my family found out that I had met a Swedish guy.

After being together for a year, we became less and less careful. Then the unthinkable thing happened – my dad caught us. His first reaction was to strike both Patrik and me. According to him, the role of a father is to defend and protect his daughter.

He assumed that Patrik and I had a sexual relationship. It is important to be a virgin – the tradition of showing the spot of blood on the sheet after the wedding night is still alive.

For my family, the purpose of my life was to marry a Kurdish man. All of a sudden, I had been transformed from a nice Kurdish girl into a slut. I decided to break with my family and move to Sundsvall. My brother found me and threatened me. The situation got worse and worse. The reason that my brother came was that he was a minor and wouldn't be punished as severely by the law.

I reported the incident to the police, but they didn't take me seriously. They advised me to talk with my family and ask them not to threaten me any more. So I turned to the media instead. This attracted a great deal of attention. A number of similar cases had arisen around the same time. I gave a voice and a face to the oppression.

When I went to the police a second time, I was received by a policeman who had experience with similar cases. He understood the seriousness of the situation and offered me protection.

My report led to a court case. My father was convicted of making unlawful threats. My mother got the blame for my having left the family. She also blamed herself.

Today I feel strong and stable, but it has been a long process to get this far. I have had to give up my background and create a new identity. I have had to leave my family.

I've paid a high price for that. My friends have become my new family. I don't regret having left, but I'm sad that I was forced to do it. My family lost both their honour and a daughter.

It could have been prevented. If society had assumed its responsibility for integrating my family, it could have been prevented. If the Kurdish Association had helped my family, it could have been prevented.

I don't feel any bitterness, but I think it's important to learn from what has happened to me. I hope that it doesn't happen again. I think it's important not to shut our eyes to the situation of girls from immigrant families.

Her case became known in Sweden in 1998 when Fadime and Patrik filed a lawsuit against her father and brother after they had threatened to kill them. They won the case. But a month later, on 3 June 1998, the day Fadime and Patrik had planned to move in with each other, Patrik died in a car accident.

Bam Bjorling, the President of Kvinnoforum, a Swedish women's organization, met Fadime several times. 'She told me she was leaving Sweden. She was returning to her family's home to say goodbye to one of her sisters with whom she was in direct contact, she also said it was because she loved her mother and wanted to tell her goodbye.'[78]

Fadime left to see her mother and sisters in Uppsala on 21 January 2002. Her father, alerted by Fadime's mother, was waiting for her and shot her in the head in front of her mother and two sisters. He was arrested the following day when he confessed and said he had acted to save his family's honour. He was sentenced to life imprisonment on 3 April 2002.

When Fadime was alive, she provoked sympathy among Swedes but there was little willingness to get involved in what was seen as a family matter. It was only once she was murdered that this young victim of an 'honour killing' drew a lot of attention to the cultural double standards she had battled for so long against.

The Scandinavian newspaper *Aftonbladet* said the immigration and integration debate had previously been dominated by so-called expert opinion-makers – noticeably middle-aged Swedish men – but after Fadime's murder, the floodgates opened. Young immigrant women started relating their experiences in newspapers, while immigrant organizations were suddenly given airtime on TV and radio stations.

Aftonbladet led the way, stating that the debate revealed that the divide in Sweden was not between 'Swedes' and 'immigrants' – 'us' and 'them' – but between those who challenge and those who preserve the patriarchal structures which killed Fadime.

'Many immigration organizations can do a hundred times more to help the women,' said Niklas Keleman from the Red Barnet (Save the Child) Dialog project. This project was started five years ago to prevent violence against women and children in immigrant communities by focusing on changing the attitudes of men. 'Officially almost all [organizations] say "yes, of course we want to do something about this," but they have to address the problems associated with the way women and children are looked upon,' Keleman said.

Parvin Kaboly, the Kurdish spokeswoman of the Committee of Iranian Women's Rights, describes many NGO immigrant organizations as 'patriarchal breeding-grounds'. 'I hope that the government will examine them. The message the organizations are generating to their members must be considered. Of course many of them are doing very good jobs, but many of them do not have the courage to challenge the oppression in the immigration communities.'

On top of this are institutional flaws, such as the two years it takes to reach a decision on asylum requests. This encourages waiting immigrants to band together in bleak housing estates, a self-imposed segregation beyond the control of the police. And there are plenty of them; almost one million of Sweden's nine million residents are non-Nordic. Somalis, Kurds, Bosnians and dozens of other groups live in ghettos about thirty minutes from Stockholm.

Sweden has hosted a number of high-profile conferences on honour-related violence in Europe. I attended one in 2004 that was organized by Kvinnoforum. Its purpose was to learn how Middle Eastern countries such as Jordan have dealt with the phenomenon so far.[79]

These conferences were an important step in recognizing, facing and then dealing with the problem. People listen when someone like Anita Gradin, a member of the Swedish Parliament for twenty-four years and a cabinet minister for nine, refers to incidents of so-called honour killings in Europe as a 'reality for us today' and as a 'concern with deep ramifications for democratic Europe'.

Meanwhile, the County Administration of Sweden presented a study that showed that around 1,500 immigrant girls were exposed to honour-related violence between 2002 and 2004.[80]

In a paper on honour-related violence and cross-cultural encounters and power conflict that was presented to the conference organized by Kvinnoforum, Professor Mehrdad Darvishpour pointed out that there is a generational conflict among immigrant families in Europe. 'Males in immigrant families tend to live in the past, women live in present and their children live in the future,' he said.[81]

Meanwhile, Hilde Bakker from Transact in the Netherlands who examined honour-related violence in Europe concluded that many immigrant communities strongly adhered to their traditions in their new country and sometimes even more fiercely than those back home for fear of losing their dignity. Bakker also pointed out that the second and third generations of immigrant families often do not have good knowledge of the traditional base of honour since most of them have never lived in their country of origin and thus (wrongly) think that certain behaviours are religion-based.[82]

According to interviews in Sweden, immigrant girls and boys expressed concern over a change of attitude in their parents' behaviour after arriving in Sweden, which sociologists attributed to the parents' loss of power over their children, who integrate quickly and become fluent in Swedish much faster than their mothers and fathers.[83]

Researcher and sociologist Muna Dahl, as part of her Master's degree research, interviewed four Muslim immigrant men from 'traditional families' in Sweden in 2003. She asked them about their relations with their children and their view on honour. She concluded that those men who had adapted well to their new lives in Sweden had paid a high price. Some of them had to move away from the Muslim community to save their reputation and to avoid interference and gossip. One man said he chose to live in a Christian community because it would guarantee his daughter's freedom from the obligation of covering her hair and meant that he could live in peace without constant reminders that he was a 'bad Muslim'.[84]

Fear of the new culture and fear of losing their children forced these men to compromise between their Islamic beliefs and Swedish law. Most did not want to break Swedish law by enforcing traditions related to so-called honour, which might mean losing their children if the authorities found out. Breaking the 'Islamic law and their social bonds with their countrymen were sadly necessary and painful sacrificial processes but a necessary step for those fathers to avoid gossip, bad reputation, and above all, to save "their faces", to save "their honour".'

Torn between their traditional community and the new country, many such immigrant families find themselves isolated. As Dahl puts it: 'they are different than the minority and yet stranger than the majority.'[85]

The government of Sweden held a conference in December 2004, which concluded that there were men all over the world who distort the teachings of both Islam and Christianity to justify domestic violence, which results in thousands of 'honour' killings a year internationally. Imam Abdal Haqq of the Swedish Islamic Society said that while traditional Islamic Sharia law does impose stricter dress codes on women and stresses their household duties, 'We must free ourselves from these honour killings and the "Islamophobia" they create.'

In my opinion, one of the most important endeavours that has made a significant impact on the issue of so-called honour crimes is the Swedish project 'Sharaf Heroes' (Heroes of Honour). It aims directly to influence boys and young men who 'control girls, including their sisters and other female relatives' to question the 'honour culture' and actively take a stand against it. They are then trained to talk to their peers. The project started in 2001 and also has a useful website and a telephone hotline, and provides meeting points for girls in need of advice and counselling.[86]

The Sharaf Heroes perform plays in schools where they also lead discussion groups. I saw this at a conference I attended in Sweden. They made the very salient point that young boys are also victims because they are forced to take part in a system that makes them watch over and oppress their sisters and cousins. They illustrated how young men can both be 'beneficiaries' and victims of patriarchal structures; for example, in being able to take advantage of and exploit their perceived 'rights' to oppress their sisters and female cousins, but also being obliged to marry against their will.

Addressing the conference, they said:

> We want you to understand that all the Sharaf Heroes love our culture. It is a wonderful culture. It is a culture unlike any other, but it is marked by a little black stain – the problems associated with the honour culture – and that stain must be washed away with our help – and with yours. Here in front of you are eight Sharaf Heroes who are full of willpower and ambition. But we need support. Support from people who work counts just as much as support from mothers on maternity leave. And support from university students is just as important as support from government ministers. Please give us your support and not just empty applause and false smiles. Open doors for us; do not slam them in our faces. *Nothing* is impossible if we work together.

Following the play, I spoke to the actors and they told me that although they faced strong opposition from other men in immigrant communities, they were able to win people over to their side – mainly men from the younger generation.

Sweden has continued to host numerous conferences on so-called crimes of honour and NGOs have found many ways to alert people to the plight of women in immigrant communities. For example, Kvinnoforum initiated a pilot project, as part of the European project on honour-related violence in 2005, producing a resource book from seven European countries (Sweden, Germany, the UK, Cyprus, Bulgaria, the Netherlands and Finland) aimed at increasing and improving support for people suffering from such violence.

Awareness and activism in Sweden has borne fruit. Courts and the police, for example, have finally started to take these crimes seriously. But there is still a long way to go. Honour-related violence is still rampant across Sweden. A study carried out by *Sveriges Radio* and published in June 2008 revealed that sixty per cent of the country's social services have helped victims of honour-related violence, or those threatened with it, to hide from their families.

And the killings continue. In April 2008, *The Australian* reported on the case of nineteen-year-old Pela Atroshi, a Kurdish Swede, who was executed in front of her sister and mother. The decision to kill her was made by a council of male relatives, led by Pela's grandfather, Abdulmajid Atroshi, a Kurd who lived in Australia, who decided Pela should be killed for moving out of the family home in Sweden. Pela, who had moved to Sweden with her family in 1995, was lured to Kurdistan. One of her uncles, Shivan Atroshi, helped pull the women away from Pela so his younger brother could get a clean shot. Shivan, too, lived in Australia.

This was the first time an honour killing with an Australian connection was officially reported in the media. It is likely that there have been other honour crimes connected to Australia that have been concealed by the tight-lipped Australian Kurdish community.

Pela Atroshi's murder, which took place in Dohuk, in Iraqi Kurdistan, was officially deemed an 'honour killing' by both Iraqi and Swedish authorities. The Swedish detective inspector who investigated the murder, Kickis Aahre Algamo, said she had since heard of another honour crime with a connection to Australia, this time the attempted killing of an Australian Kurd that went awry when the girl escaped.

Two of Pelas's uncles living in Sweden were sentenced to life imprisonment. Her father and another uncle were tried and convicted in Iraq. They were given a one-year suspended sentence. The court referred to a medical report that said 'her hymen was broken' and to the 'defendants' honourable motivation'.

Bam, a Kurdish woman living in an undisclosed country in Europe, is another brave woman who shared her horrific experience, for the first time, at the 2004 Swedish conference. Speaking in Kurdish, Bam was accompanied by a translator.

She began her story by recalling her childhood. Continuously oppressed by her family for as long as she could remember, she was forced to marry her cousin at the age of fifteen. Her cousin turned out to be violent and beat her almost every day after accusing her of infidelity.

'My life was about humiliation, oppression and abuse … on one occasion, he kicked me on my back. The beating was so bad it broke my backbone. I was hospitalized for three months. I went back to my husband. We had three children and I did not want to destroy my children's life, so I continued to accept what was happening to me,' she said.

One day he kicked her out of the house. She went to her family home but received little sympathy from her father and brothers. 'They told me it was my fault, not my husband's,' Bam said. 'I decided to take my husband to court to get my rights but his family threatened to kill me because I would bring shame to the entire tribe.'

Bam had reached the point where she knew it was simply impossible to continue living with her abusive husband. She sought the help of the head of the tribe, who told her she had no honour and that she had behaved in a shameful manner by coming to him. Then, incredibly, he beat her.

'He dragged me by my hair in front of my father and brother and beat me up, banged my head on the floor and kicked me on my back. He did not stop even when I told him I had just had an operation on my back.

'Twenty days later, there was a big gathering at my house. It seemed they were planning my death, when my father suddenly entered my room and asked me to prepare for the evening prayers,' she said. She heard shouting near the house and asked her father what was going on. Her father told her to go out and look for herself.

'I went to the front door and opened it. I saw my seventeen-year-old brother walking towards me; he was pointing a gun at me. I was shocked and could not say anything. He shot at me three times; I ran outside, he followed me and shot me once more.'

One of her sisters tried to stop him. She screamed at her father, asking him why they were doing this. 'My father responded by claiming that my brother wanted to kill me because I had an affair with a man. He said that my husband was at the same moment killing the man I allegedly had an affair with,' Bam said.

As Bam lay injured, her brother was shooting at anyone who attempted to help her. It was only when the gun was empty that her mother was able to get near her. 'I knew I was badly injured from the look on my mother's face. Then I saw blood on her hands … On the way to the hospital I was praying for God to save my life for the sake of my mother,' she recalled.

Bam's chest and stomach were riddled with bullets. Bam was placed under police guard, and with good reason. Some of her family members even attempted to enter the hospital to finish the job.

'I was depressed and desperate and attempted to take my own life but was saved again. I stayed in hospital for seven months. Afterwards, a woman in the centre who had connections with foreign organizations helped me escape and seek asylum with my kids in a European country.'

Bam would not reveal the name of the country of her residence, out of fear that some of her family members would learn of her whereabouts and kill her. 'I was told that my brother-in-law had promised to burn my body after I died. I dream of this every night, and every night I worry that someone will come and kill me.'

'The seventh of December 1998 was the day my family tried to kill me to cleanse their honour. But this day has since become my birthday.

'It is the day I became free.'

Despite there being much still to be done in terms of protecting women in immigrant communities, Sweden is ahead of most other countries on the European continent when it comes to dealing with so-called crimes of honour. Sadly, most of Europe is only just waking up to what is a very serious problem.

Somali-born Dutch MP Ayaan Hirsi Ali was forced into hiding after the Dutch filmmaker Theo van Gogh was murdered in Amsterdam in 2004. Van Gogh was shot eight times as he cycled to work. The attacker then cut his throat and stabbed him twice in the chest before attaching a five-page note to the body. The note threatened western governments, Jews and Ayaan Hirsi Ali, who had scripted the film *Submission*, directed by van Gogh, which was about the abuse of Muslim women.

The Netherlands is known for its tolerance, but Hirsi Ali believes that the price of this may be the murder of fifty women each year – the result of so-called honour killings. Hirsi Ali began speaking out in 2002, after she encountered several abused women while working as a translator at various women's refuges. Muslims only account for about six per cent of the Dutch population but Muslim women make up sixty per cent of those in women's shelters.

Hirsi Ali's claims were confirmed the following year when the media got hold of the story of eighteen-year-old Dutch-Turkish student Zarife, taken out of school and to Ankara 'on holiday'. Her father shot her shortly after she landed. Zarife's crime was hanging out with Dutch girls and going outside without her headscarf.

Then it emerged that three women staying at a Dutch women's shelter were murdered in honour killings within just ten months of each other. Two of them were trying to divorce their violent husbands. Suicide attempts among Dutch Muslim girls is five times that of non-Muslim girls.

Hirsi Ali and psychiatrist Carla Rus blame the Dutch, whose 'misplaced respect' for different cultures has allowed honour-based violence and killings to flourish. When, in 2003, a thirty-six-year-old Afghan woman was murdered by her estranged husband in Maastricht, along with her ten-year-old daughter, law-makers struggled to find an appropriate response. Should the killer be prosecuted according to standards of Dutch law or Islam? As yet, they still haven't made up their minds and the debate is reignited every time a killing takes place.

As a VVD (Libertarian Party) MP, Hirsi Ali has demanded much more thorough investigations of suspected honour killings, including the prosecutions of all of those involved, not just the actual killer. A register has since been introduced whereby honour crimes will be monitored and then investigated by specially trained police.

Thanks to an initiative by the Turkish Islamic Cultural Federation (Turks Islamitische Culturele Federatie, TICF), Turkish imams in Dutch mosques now declare their aversion to honour killings during prayers. Eighty per cent of Dutch mosques belong to the TICF. This sort of support is absolutely crucial to ending so-called honour killings. When people regularly hear their spiritual leaders preaching against these crimes, the message gets through, making it much harder for an individual to kill in the name of honour.

In Paris, thirty thousand sympathizers marched on International Women's Day in 2003 to protest about violence committed against migrant women. Over sixty-five thousand people also signed a national petition. The march came about in the wake of the brutal murder of a nineteen-year-old woman, who was burned alive in her housing estate.[87]

According to Sihem Habchi, vice president of Mouvement Ni

Putes Ni Soumises, most of the violence against women, including rape and murder, occurs among frustrated migrant communities living in the suburban ghettos that surround large cities. Immigrants, mostly Arabs from the Maghreb countries, had been placed in housing projects that segregated them from the rest of the community and created a 'physical separation that resulted in building a wall that is very hard to break'.[88]

In Spain, the government has so far ignored violence in the immigrant community. Women's groups have reported that three hundred women have been murdered in suspected crimes of honour between 2000 and 2004.[89]

Hatin Sürücü was a twenty-three-year-old German-Kurdish woman originally from Erzurum in Turkey. Hatin was forced to marry her cousin when she was sixteen. She gave birth to their son in 1999, and in October of the same year she fled her home, found sanctuary in a women's shelter in Germany and divorced her husband. She rebuilt her life and studied to become an electrician. Hatin was about to graduate in 2005 when she was shot dead as she waited for a bus.

A few days later, at a high school near the scene of the crime, some male students of Kurdish and Turkish origin applauded the crime. During a class discussion on the murder, one allegedly said that she 'only had herself to blame', while another remarked, 'She deserved what she got – the whore lived like a German.' The director of the school, Volker Steffens, sent a strongly worded letter to students of the school and their parents, warning that the school would not tolerate inciting statements.

Ayhan, Hatin's youngest brother, confessed to the murder. 'It was too much for me. I grabbed the pistol and pulled the trigger,' he told the German court. 'I don't even understand what I did any more.' He was sentenced to nine years and three months in prison. Hatin's murder was the sixth honour killing in Germany since October 2004.[90]

Berlin-based Muslim leaders were at pains to stress that there is no basis for honour killings in the Quran. But they've also been criticized for not expressing clear condemnation. 'We've preached twice in the last year on human rights, saying that it is forbidden to kill, and so on,' Huseyin Midik, a representative of Germany's largest association of mosques, told the BBC. 'Our job is to explain Islam. That's what has a permanent effect – clearing up certain false ideas about Islam in people's minds.'

But the killings continue among Germany's Turkish and Arab minorities. The police have pointed out that there have been forty-five cases between 1996 and 2004, including thirteen in Berlin. One woman was drowned in her bath, and another was stabbed to death by her husband in front of their three-year-old daughter.

A social worker, who runs a centre for runaways and who wanted to remain anonymous, said:

Some were raped – by an uncle, by a cousin, even by the father – and when they should get married they are worried that someone will find out they're not a virgin anymore. They are afraid that they will be murdered.

All these girls who come to us are locked up, in the house, by their families. They only go to school because they have to by law – otherwise they wouldn't be allowed. They have to stay at home and cook, and care for the sisters and brothers. The parents don't accept that the girl decides anything by herself.

Berlin's Turkish community numbers 200,000. Despite protests and much debate, the killings continue at the same rate. An Iraqi who repeatedly stabbed his twenty-four-year-old wife dead in a Munich street and then, in front of her five-year-old son, set her body on fire, was given a life sentence in 2007. Hours before the attack, a court had granted the couple a divorce. The killer told the court he had no regrets because he believed his wife had cheated on him. 'I am very happy that I did it. She betrayed me, she deserved it,' he said on the first day of the trial.

The debates started again after the honour killing of a sixteen-year-old Afghan immigrant by her brother in 2008 in Hamburg, which is home to more than twenty thousand Afghan immigrants, more than any other European city. The girl, Morsal Obeidi, was ambushed in the parking lot of a McDonald's restaurant by her twenty-three-year-old brother Ahmad, who stabbed her twenty times.

Morsal Obeidi had long experienced a tug-of-war between her desire to live like her friends in Germany and her family's desire to preserve their Afghan lifestyle. Obeidi's arguments with her brother and father, over things like her appearance, smoking and drinking, often turned physical. She reportedly sought the protection of a child and youth welfare agency to escape the violence on more than one occasion.

Ahmad reportedly told police that he had killed his sister because she had become too comfortable with western life, as shown by her uncovered hair, makeup and short skirts.[91]

While there is excellent (but limited) support from NGOs in Germany (such as Papatya, established in 1986 in Berlin for female immigrants, which offers excellent security and social support), the government still needs to make a massive effort to end so-called crimes of honour.[92]

Today, there is now widespread concern across Europe about how many young immigrant women have disappeared and how many of these women have in fact been murdered, abused or forced into marriage. Perhaps most worryingly, the female suicide rate among immigrant communities in Europe is currently three or four times higher than among the native population. Some of these may have been successful attempts to disguise murders, or forced suicides, or actual suicides where women were so desperate to escape abuse that they took their own lives.

In April 2003, the Parliamentary Assembly of the Council of Europe acted against so-called honour crimes, adopting a report by the Committee on Equal Opportunities for Women and Men, entitled 'So-Called Honour Crimes'. In its resolution, the Parliamentary Assembly expressed its concern regarding the increasing number of crimes committed against women in the name of honour 'which constitutes a flagrant violation of human rights based on archaic, unjust cultures and traditions'. The resolution also stressed that it was important and urgent to 'make a distinction between the need to protect minority cultures and turning a blind eye to unacceptable customs that amount to torture and/or a breach of human rights'.

On the basis of this resolution, recommendations were made for the member states to work actively to end honour-related violence. The Council of Europe called on members to amend national asylum and immigration laws to allow women the right of residency or asylum on the grounds of needing to escape from so-called crimes of honour. It was suggested that all crimes committed in the name of honour should be penalized and that the sentences should reflect the seriousness of the crime.

Most importantly, the Council called on courts to refuse 'honour in mitigation, or as a justifiable motive of the crime'. The Council also recommended preventive measures to be adopted by its members, such as awareness campaigns and the provision of special educational programmes for women and men from communities where such crimes occur.

It also recommended providing support for victims and potential victims who request asylum and personal protection and other services, as well as offering support to NGOs that provide such services. These recommendations remain just that, however, and Europe still has a very long way to go – and action is imperative if we want to save countless young women from a senseless and horrific death in the future.[93]

The Parliamentary Assembly acknowledged that the majority of cases in Europe were reported among Muslim or immigrant Muslim communities, but there are a few exceptions.[94] One such example of non-Islamic honour-based patriarchal society is found in Italy where, until 1981, the 'honour' argument was an admitted legal defence. Men were offered a reduction in penalty from three to seven years if they killed their wives, sisters or daughters to cleanse their or their family's honour. In Sicily there is still a minimum penalty of three years in prison for murders of 'honour'.[95] Giovanni Morabito, a twenty-four-year-old member of the Mafia, turned himself in to police in Reggio, Calabria, after shooting his older sister Bruna four times in the face in March 2006 because she became pregnant out of wedlock. He told police calmly that he wanted to kill her because she had a son two weeks before the murder with a man who was not her husband. 'It is a question of honour. I would have shot her in the back, but she turned round. I am not sorry. On the contrary, I am proud of what I did.' Investigators believe that Morabito had in fact shot Bruna because she tried to distance herself from the Mafia. Morabito insisted that his actions were based on the 'dishonour' his sister brought on his family. Miraculously, she survived.[96]

More recently, in 2006, Italy's highest court ruled that it was a less serious crime to sexually abuse a teenager if she was not a virgin, a sign that chastity is still a serious concern in Italy. The court ruled in favour of a man who appealed his forty-month sentence for forcing his fourteen-year-old stepdaughter to perform a sex act. His mitigating circumstances were that the victim was not a virgin; he ended up receiving a lower sentence, according to a report that appeared in *Ms* magazine in the summer of 2006.

In April 2008, a Sardinian who came to Britain to kill his wife's lover was jailed for life. The killer stabbed RAF Flight Lieutenant Stephen Keen, aged fifty-four, four times in the throat and neck in front of his wife, Susan Matta, aged fifty-three, at the home they had moved into days earlier in Tiverton, Devon. Stephen bled to death within minutes.

Prosecutor Martin Meeke QC said that when police arrived Matta calmly told them, 'I came here to kill the man. I have done what I needed to do. I have done my job. He added that it was an 'honour killing – that is what I am, an executioner'. Matta denied murder, claiming diminished responsibility, but was convicted by the jury and must now serve at least eleven years before being considered for parole.[97]

CHAPTER 14

Honour in the USA

When police arrived at a St Louis family home on the evening of 6 November 1989, they found a mother and father distraught. In the living room, covered in blood, was the body of their sixteen-year-old daughter Palestina, known to all as Tina. A nine-inch knife lay by her side.

Tina was most parents' dream daughter. She was a popular, straight-A student with ambitions to become an airline pilot. Her parents told the police that Tina was working for a fast food restaurant and had arrived home at about midnight. Her father, Zein Isa, said that she had recently become rebellious. That night, he said, Tina had come home late and told her parents that she wanted to move out, demanding that they give her five thousand dollars.[98]

When they refused, Zein said, Tina pulled a knife from her backpack, and threatened and then attacked him. Zein said he turned the knife on his daughter in self-defence, killing her. His wife Maria supported her husband's statement.

News of Tina's death stunned her classmates. They told the police that Tina had often rebelled against her parents and their 'old-world traditions'. They also said Tina's family objected to her choice of boyfriend, a popular honours student – an artist who painted and wrote poems. He was also black, but the trouble arose, her friends said, not so much as a result of his colour but because she had a boyfriend and they felt they could no longer control her. Her friends also said that the daughters of the family were only supposed to work for their parents and they were not supposed to date out-side the Muslim faith, nor leave their home without permission.

Tina was their last daughter who was still living at home and was the most American of the family. She played football at high school, despite her father's objections. She also defied him to go to the junior prom, from which family members later removed her.

When the police pointed out that Zein was covered in blood and had cuts on his hands, he said they were defensive wounds. Although the police clearly suspected Zein of murder, they needed to secure proof if a jury was going to be convinced.

Forensic pathologist Dr Philip Birch performed a wound-pattern analysis on Tina's body. He found six stab wounds in close proximity in her solar plexus. He later told reporters, 'She was supposedly involved in a wild, free-for-all fight with a knife and it seemed very odd that all of the injuries were tightly-clustered in a specific area of the body.'

That's because stabbing victims usually thrash about, moving their arms and legs. It was highly unlikely that Tina had stayed still and also highly unlikely that her father, who was smaller than her, would have been able to hold his daughter still and stab her at the same time.

Investigators interviewed the paramedics who were first to arrive on the scene. They said Tina's arms were stretched out above her head, as if she had been restrained. The only other person in the room who could have held Tina's arms was her mother, Maria. Forensic analysis revealed Tina's blood and hair on the inside of the jumper that Maria was wearing at the time.

The prosecutors were convinced, but had a problem – would a jury believe that a father and mother could kill their own daughter, rather than their own claims that they had acted in self-defence?

Then investigators were hit with a bombshell. The FBI called them to say that US intelligence had photographed Zein Isa attending a meeting in Mexico with individuals who were known to have ties to the Palestinian Liberation Organization. The FBI suspected that Zein was maintaining a safe house for any Middle Eastern 'terrorist' who needed a place to hide.

As part of their surveillance of Zein, the FBI had placed recording devices in the family home. The tapes had run twenty-four hours a day, seven days a week, but because the Bureau did not consider Zein to be a serious player, they hadn't yet listened to the recordings.

The police then had to get the permission of the then Attorney General, Richard Thornberg, to release the recordings, as the publicity surrounding the case would alert others close to Zein and across the USA to the fact that they might be under surveillance.

Thankfully, Thornberg immediately gave them permission. The seven-minute tape provided them with damning evidence. It appalled the jury of seven women and five men and shocked court officials, who thought they had seen and heard everything before.

'It's worse than any movie, any film, anything I thought that I would ever hear in my life,' assistant prosecutor Bob Craddick told the *New York Times*. It was also totally unique. This was the first time that the entirety of an honour killing and its run-up and aftermath had been recorded in full terrible detail.

The crucial part of the transcript started with Tina returning home from work.

Maria: 'Where were you, bitch?'

Tina: 'Working.'

Zein: 'We are telling you that if you want to marry that black guy we won't accept that he marries you. Don't you have a conscience? It's fornication! What about your chastity, isn't it a scandal? ... Here, listen, my dear daughter, do you know that this is the last day? Tonight, you're going to die.'

Tina: 'Huh?'

Zein: 'Do you know that you are going to die tonight?'

[There is a pause, then screaming from Tina.]

Tina: 'Mother, please help me! Mother, can't you make him stop?'

Zein: 'Keep still, Tina!'

Tina: 'Mother, please help me!'

Mother: 'Huh? What do you mean?'

Tina: 'Help! Help!'

Mother: 'What help?'

Maria: 'Are you going to listen? Are you going to listen?'

Tina: 'Yes! Yes! Yes, I am!' [coughs] 'No. Please!'

Maria: 'Shut up!'

[Tina continues to cry and scream, but her voice is unintelligible.]

Zein: 'Die! Die quickly! Die quickly!'

[Tina moans, briefly goes quiet, then screams one last time.]

Zein: 'Quiet, little one! Die, my daughter, die!'

Tina was stabbed six times in the chest with a boning knife, which pierced her heart, a lung and her liver. The timing of the tape revealed that her parents waited for thirty minutes before calling the ambulance.

Zein admitted on the witness stand that he put his foot on his daughter's mouth to keep her quiet. His wife held her daughter's arms so she couldn't escape.

Further analysis of the tapes in the weeks leading up to the murder revealed that Zein was planning the murder of his daughter during this time. 'She threatened me,' he told his wife, 'and I'll put the knife in her hand after she falls. Leave the story to me.'

Soraia Salem, one of Tina's sisters who no longer lived at home, said the system had failed her sister. She said the family sought help from the police in the months before the murder, even asking for Tina to be placed in a foster home. But prosecutors said they found only one police report.

Her parents were both given the death sentence. Zein Isa died of diabetes while on death row on 17 February 1997. Maria's death sentence was later commuted to life imprisonment without parole.

After the verdicts were read, a friend of the family who called herself Mrs Abraham expressed her dismay at the jury's failure to acknowledge the Palestinian culture. 'I feel it's not right. We follow our religion.' She said the Isas had to discipline their daughter or lose respect. 'They'd be embarrassed in front of everybody in the country like somebody when they go without their clothes outside.'

Amazingly, the USA seems to be startlingly unaware of so-called honour killings. The UK's Metropolitan Police and the Foreign and Commonwealth's Forced Marriage Unit regularly receive calls from US law enforcement officers looking for information on these crimes. That officers feel obliged to search abroad for answers highlights just how little honour killings are understood in the USA, a country with more than its fair share of incidents of domestic abuse as well as one of the largest immigrant populations in the world.

A UNIFEM report issued in 2003 stated that the health-related costs of rape, physical assault, stalking and homicide by intimate partners against their spouses in the USA amount to more than $5.8 billion every year. The US Department of Justice has found that women are far more likely to be the victims of violent crimes committed by intimate partners than men, especially when a weapon is involved. Moreover, women are much more likely to be victimized at home than in any other place.[99]

The Violence Policy Centre prepared an annual study detailing the reality of homicides committed against women and entitled *When Men Murder Women*. The latest study by the centre involved an analysis of the most recent Supplementary Homicide Report (SHR) data submitted to the FBI in the ten states with the highest female victim/male offender homicide rates in 2004.[100] According to the centre, there were 1,807 females murdered by males in single victim/single offender incidents. For homicides in which the victim-to-offender relationship could not be identified, ninety-two per cent of female victims (1,547 out of 1,689) were murdered by someone they knew. Of female homicide victims who knew their killers, sixty-two per cent (966) of were wives or intimate acquaintances of their killers.[101] There are no known figures for murders within immigrant communities, or for honour killings. It is interesting to note, however, that there have been cases that seem to demonstrate an inequality in how men and women are sometimes treated by US courts.

For example, Jacqueline Hunt of Equality Now said her organization adopted a case of a woman who was killed by her husband in Maryland on 9 February 1994 several hours after finding her in bed with another man. Kenneth Peacock, a trucker from Maryland, kicked the man out of his home at gunpoint and then shot his wife Sandra in the head with his hunting rifle a few hours later.

Peacock fired once at his wife but missed her and he had to reload his rifle before fatally shooting her. He pleaded guilty to voluntary manslaughter. Judge Robert Cahill made some extraordinarily sympathetic statements when passing judgement: 'I seriously wonder how many married men ... would have the strength to walk away ... without inflicting some corporal punishment, whatever that punishment might be. I shudder to think what I would do ... I am forced to impose a sentence . . . only because I think I must do it to make the system honest.' He sentenced Peacock to eighteen months.

Action Alert criticized Judge Cahill, saying his statements in the Peacock case indicated a disregard for violence against women and a devaluation of the victim's life, as well as perpetuating the notion that married women in particular were the property of their husbands who had the right to inflict violence on them or kill them. 'When such statements are made by a judge acting in an official capacity, they represent state authority and are particularly dangerous to the rule of law and the fundamental right of all women to equality and equal protection of the law.'

Hunt said, 'It is the changing of perception from that of women as property with no rights to that of women as equal partners that is the biggest challenge in our work to stop these crimes.'

The effectiveness of US law enforcement agencies is undeniable. In almost all of the cases reported, the perpetrators are in jail, but nothing has been put in place for the purposes of prevention. Immigrant community groups are seemingly reluctant to draw attention to a phenomenon they feel will further exacerbate the hostility already directed towards them since 9/11 and the onset of the wars in Afghanistan and Iraq.

This is despite the fact that the US media have woken up to the problem and have reported on scores of recent cases. For example, in January 2008 in Chicago, firefighters were called to a blaze at an apartment complex where more than seventy people were inside. Some people raced downstairs while others jumped from balcony windows. Remarkably, most escaped without serious injury.

The culprit was Subhash Chander, who confessed he had started the blaze after his daughter, Monika Rani, and her husband, Rajesh Kumar, married without his consent, which he saw as 'a cultural slight'. Kumar was from a lower caste than Rani.[102]

Monika, aged twenty-two, her husband and their three-year-old son perished in the fire. The autopsy revealed that Monika was five months pregnant with their second child.

Chander, aged fifty-seven, was charged with three counts of first-degree murder, aggravated arson and intentional homicide of an unborn child.[103]

Smita Narula, the faculty director of the Centre for Human Rights and Global Justice at New York University School of Law who has studied the effects of the Indian caste system, said violence over caste differences and inter-caste marriages still occurred in

India, although discrimination against the lowest caste has been outlawed for decades. 'What is surprising,' Ms Narula said, 'is that it might happen here.'

It is happening a lot more often than people realize. Also in January 2008, a double honour killing rocked the small town of Lewisville, Texas.

'Ma'am, what is your address?' the emergency line operator asked. A woman had just called in to report that she and her sister had been shot.

'I'm dying,' she said, crying. Then the line went dead.

The police spent the next hour trying to pinpoint the location of the phone signal when another call came in from a hotel employee to report a taxi in the hotel's cab queue with no driver and a body slumped in the passenger seat and another in the back seat.

At the scene, police found the bodies of seventeen-year-old Sarah Yaser Said and her eighteen-year-old sister, Amina Yaser Said. The car was quickly traced to their father, Yaser Abdel Said, a fifty-year-old Egyptian-born cab driver.

Yaser Abdel Said has been on the run since that night. Police believe that he may have successfully fled the country.[104]

The teenagers were inseparable and popular students. Their mother, Patricia Said, called for her husband to turn himself in to authorities. Their nineteen-year-old brother, Islam Said, simply said his father 'messed everything up'.

There had been conflict between father and daughters over their adaptation to western life, including relationships they may have had with non-Muslim boys. This clashed starkly with the strict Middle Eastern culture in which Yaser Abdel Said grew up. Said immigrated to the USA in 1983 and was granted citizenship in 1997.

In 1998 the girls, still children, accused their father of sexual abuse, according to an investigation carried out by the *Dallas Morning News*. The charges were later dropped after the girls said they had made up the story. Fellow students described their classmates arriving to school with injuries consistent with abuse. One student said Amina told him about her father walking into her bedroom waving a gun.

The month before he killed them, in December 2007, Yaser Abdel Said reported his two daughters and their mother missing to the Lewisville Police Department. According to a police report, the next day Patricia Said called police to say that she and the two teens were safe but that 'she was in great fear for her life' and that concern for their well-being had prompted them to flee.

The missing persons' case was closed. 'We were able to verify that their welfare was no longer in question, so we closed that report,' Captain Keith Deaver, a spokesman for the Lewisville police told ABC News. The three returned to Lewisville on New Year's Eve, the day before the fatal shooting.

Significantly, in October 2008, the FBI used the term 'honour killing' for the first time when it made Yaser Abdel Said the 'featured fugitive' on its website. This is the first official recognition that honour killings take place in the USA and represents a welcome and long overdue change.[105]

Later that same year, on 5 July 2008, in Jonesboro, Georgia, Chaudhry Rashid strangled his twenty-four-year-old daughter Kanwal with a bungee cord. On 1 July she had filed for divorce from the man she had been forced to wed in Pakistan. Police found Rashid sitting behind a vehicle in the driveway. 'My daughter is dead,' he told police. He said he could not accept the 'disgrace' a divorce or affair would bring on his family, according to a police spokesperson. In court, a detective quoted Rashid: 'God will protect me. God is watching me. I strangled my daughter.'[106]

A few weeks earlier in Monroe County, New York, Waheed Allah Mohammad, an immigrant from Afghanistan, was charged with attempted murder after repeatedly stabbing his nineteen-year-old sister, Fauzia. Afterwards, he told Monroe County sheriff's investigators that he attacked his sister because she had disgraced their family and was a 'bad Muslim girl'.

His lawyer said that Mohammad, who emigrated to the USA with his family from war-ravaged Afghanistan, may be suffering from a stress-inflicted mental disorder that could mitigate the attack on his sister. 'It was getting to be quite a heated argument,' he said. 'I suspect that at least some element of this triggered something in him related to his past.'

Mental illness first became a defence in a so-called crime of honour when, on 15 April 2004, Ismail Peltek, an immigrant from Turkey, stabbed and beat his wife to death and wounded two daughters at their home in Scottsville. He told investigators that he was attempting to restore family honour that had been lost when his wife and one daughter were sexually assaulted by a relative and the other daughter was 'sullied' by a medical exam. Peltek was allowed to plead not guilty by reason of mental disease or defect and was transferred to a psychiatric centre.

The defence of temporary insanity, which in some ways parallels Article 98 in Jordan, is starting to be used in this context. Prosecutors need to be aware of the psychology of honour crimes, and in particular that perpetrators may have been plotting them for some time.

Perhaps the most clear-cut case of premeditated honour killing was that committed by Chiman Rai, a sixty-nine-year-old businessman of Indian origin living in the USA. Rai emigrated with his family from India in 1970 and taught mathematics at Alcorn State University in Mississippi for a decade before opening a supermarket and a hotel in Kentucky.

He was sentenced to life in prison without parole for paying two hitmen $10,000 to murder his son's black wife as he felt shamed by their inter-racial marriage. The murder was carried out in April 2000, just weeks after his son Rajeev and Sparkle Michelle Rai had married, and a few months after Sparkle had given birth to their child.[107]

Twenty-two-year-old Sparkle was home alone with their seven-month-old daughter when a hitman used a young girl as a decoy to get her to open the door. He strangled her with electrical cord before fetching a knife from the kitchen and stabbing her thirteen times, while her baby was in the same room. Jurors deliberated for less than two hours before delivering the guilty verdict. Rai was sentenced to life without parole.[108]

It is clear that when US law enforcement officers investigate an honour killing they make every effort to catch the killers. But they have been slow to recognize the problem officially and to take any steps towards prevention. When a woman complains to the police about being in mortal danger from her husband or parents, they need to take it seriously and employ similar tactics to those suggested at the end of chapter 12. Unfortunately, it seems as though we will see many more horrific honour killings in the USA before policy-makers get round to legislating for their prevention.

Honour killings have also taken place in Canada, where again no reliable figures exist. Recent cases include that of a fourteen-year-old girl who was raped and strangled in March 2004 by her father and brother because she had tarnished the family name. The following month, a man brutally murdered his wife and daughter after finding out that his brother had molested them. A teenage girl with a Turkish background had her throat cut by her father after he found out she had a Christian boyfriend.

Dr Amin Muhammad, a professor of psychiatry at the Memorial University of Newfoundland who has studied these killings in Canada, said, 'We discovered through our different discussions with lawyers in Canada that it happens here ... When people come and settle in Canada they can bring their traditions and forcefully follow them.' Presciently, he warns, 'You will see, ten years down the road, this will not be very new even for a society like Canada.'[109]

We need to act now.

CHAPTER 15

The Road to Real Honour

'Violence against women is perhaps the most shameful human rights violation, and it is perhaps the most pervasive. It knows no boundaries of geography, culture or wealth. As long as it continues, we cannot claim to be making real progress towards equality, development, and peace.'

Kofi Annan

Today, many crimes of honour are fed by the clash of old and new. As the old world has migrated to the west, countless conflicts have arisen between adolescent children and their parents. In Middle Eastern countries, where concepts of honour have played a part in traditional life for thousands of years, sudden, headlong and rapid urbanization coupled with speedy population growth has meant that millions of people must adapt to a radically different, ever-evolving lifestyle, dependent on a highly volatile and competitive market economy.

Part of this conflict comes from the ongoing worldwide transition in women's status and roles, with women becoming a vital and fast-growing part of the labour force. This change in the status and role of women has been very rapid and the related empowerment it brings clashes with long-established conservative attitudes.

Victimization of and discrimination against women happens at all levels worldwide, so it is important to understand the links between so-called honour crimes and other forms of discrimination against women. There is much work to be done here.

In western Europe, activists have convinced some legislators and governments to alter laws to provide more protection for immigrant women and children. Amendments have included introducing stiffer punishments for families that force their daughters to undergo female genital mutilation and for perpetrators of so-called honour crimes regardless of the 'cultural and traditional excuses' that killers usually hide behind. Other amendments have been made to raise the legal age of marriage in order to prevent forced early marriages for migrant men and women alike. Changes in the law to remove various clauses that provide leniency, such as Article 98 in Jordan, are an essential part of ending so-called honour killings. Of course, education is another vital tool in ending so-called crimes of honour and I believe the Sharaf Heroes project in Sweden provides an important and successful model to follow. Including men in the drive to change cultural attitudes to and beliefs about these crimes is essential and will help many communities to question their acceptance of these murders. Governments need to follow this example and must work with groups like the Sharaf Heroes to change the attitudes and beliefs of those people who use outdated ideas of honour to stifle and control women. Governments must provide financial support for hotlines and shelters for abused women. Far too much reliance is placed on overstretched and underfunded NGOs and charities, such as IKWRO in the UK, which saves the lives of dozens of men and women each year, but could do so much more with increased funding and support.

The education and emancipation of women is of course also fundamental to change. A huge part of this comes about as women use the chances available in this changing world to fight to improve society – and to educate their sons and daughters. Women are now occupying more powerful positions in the workplace, not because of who they know, but thanks to their own merits. I hope this will help move the focus from women's virginity and chastity to their skills and education.

There also needs to be a focus on raising public awareness and I strongly believe that one of the most effective methods in reducing honour-based murder is to highlight and humanize each killing and crime and make it known to everyone, including legislators, the media, the public and the relevant authorities.

NGOs need to start looking beyond the dismissive statements often fed to them by politicians; that 'there are more important issues to tackle', for example. The protection of every woman's life should be a key issue for the government and community alike. Activists must question and hold officials in decision-making positions publicly accountable for the souls of murdered women and men.

There also needs to be more in-depth research into the root causes of these murders, including the consequences for the entire family, the psychological and economic impact on the killer, close relatives and extended family members. Such knowledge could be used effectively as part of a preventative educational strategy in schools and other institutions. In traditional societies where family unity is strong, respected figures such as mothers, uncles and fathers should be enlisted to speak out publicly against the crime, especially to teenage boys who are all too often called upon to murder their siblings in the name of honour. Families know that their teenage sons will most likely be sentenced to spend a short period of time in a juvenile centre from which they will be released without a criminal record.

It has become obvious to me, from all the cases I've reported on, that no relative, male or female, *wants* to kill or be involved in killing a wife, mother or daughter. It is absolutely against human nature. They do it because of a mis-defined concept of honour that has been nurtured since birth. All too often the psychological consequences of murder leave these young men and women deeply troubled, wracked with guilt and alienated by a community who cannot and will not help them come to terms with what they have done.

A case in point is that of Sarhan, described in chapter 2, who wished the 'solution' to restoring his family's honour were anything but the murder of his own sister. His wish was to be incarcerated for a long time so that other families would think twice before turning one of their family members into a murderer. Governments and NGOs need to utilize murderers like Sarhan who have expressed remorse or regret and encourage them to become advocates for this cause and publicly speak out against these crimes.

Finally, governments and NGOs also need to be aware that what might work in one country might not work in another. On the surface, so-called honour murders in Pakistan may seem similar to those that occur in Turkey, for example, but the social, political and economic aspects of the crime in each country are quite different and require different solutions. Wherever possible, initiatives should be home-grown and supported by national organizations rather than being enforced or imported from other countries, a strategy that can often cause resentment.

So-called honour killings are only just starting to receive the attention they deserve and I think any reader can tell from this book, which only scratches the surface of the situation around the world, that there is still an enormous amount of investigation as well as political and social change needed to end these dreadful crimes.

There are many countries across the world where the prevalence of honour-based violence has yet to be assessed, one prominent example being China. A Chinese billionaire placed an ad in a newspaper in Shanghai in January 2006 seeking a female virgin to marry and received six hundred applications. He interviewed twenty before finally choosing the 'lucky' bride. The *New York Times* noted in a January 2006 report that this kind of ad has been common since 2004, and they are usually placed by rich Chinese men seeking virgin brides. These ads and a report by a Chinese newspaper drew mixed reactions from the Chinese community, ranging from one woman who said the purpose of saving her virginity was to get a good price for it, to others who described the girls as selling themselves like merchandise. The obsession with female virgins in China prompted a forty-three-year-old man to purchase the virginity of seventeen schoolgirls in Nanyang, Henan Province, according to a report in the *Shanghai Daily* in May 2006. In China, suicide has become the main cause of death among people aged between twenty and thirty-five, with twenty-five per cent more women than men taking their lives. It is not currently known whether this has anything to do with honour.

*   *   *

While writing this book, I have often asked myself, 'What is real "honour"? Can "honour" be attributed to a reputation, a social, financial or professional status? Is it the quality of being respectable and deserving of a good name and adhering to moral principles? Or is it exclusively dependent on the behaviour of female relatives?'

It is clear that people across the world have very different definitions of honour. For example, these statements were published in a UN report in November 2005:

> Honour is the reason for our living now. That means we live for the cause of honour now. I don't know, but without honour life has no meaning … it is okay if you don't have money, but you must have dignity.
>
> (Sanliurfa, a participant in a group interview with male university students aged between nineteen and twenty-two)

Honour surpasses everything, especially among us Kurdish people or people from the East, the concept of honour is at the foreground.

> (Adana, female, aged thirty-one, from Siirt)

Why should a person work? Why should he live anyway? This is first for his honour and second for daily bread. If a person has hunger, he can eat something small and feel satisfied. However, if one loses his honour, there is nothing to be done, no return...

> (Istanbul, male, aged twenty-five, police officer)

These statements about honour, taken on their own, sound noble, sound proud – like virtues worth aspiring to – yet they were taken from a report about honour crimes in Turkey. They make a very stark contrast to the following group of statements, from the same report:

As the older people say, 'horse, woman and gun': these three things are sacred. Honour is the betrayal of your wife, she starts to have relations with other men ... in the event, a person lives for his honour and dignity. And your honour is your wife. If she betrays you, your dignity is trampled.

> (Adana, male, aged thirty-nine, police officer)

Honour is everything for me ... if I were married, in that case, the girl whom I married would be my honour. My sister is my honour too, so are my relatives, the daughter of my aunt and the daughter of my uncle are also my honour. That is, all of them are my honour. Everything happening around me and all my family line are my honour.

> ('Batman', male, aged twenty-four, imam)

These statements graphically illustrate people's differing definitions of honour across the world today. Beliefs relating to women as the bearers of family honour are still embedded in many people's minds, making so-called crimes of honour acceptable. But these beliefs are about control, not honour. Women are placed in fear, knowing that one false move or one malicious piece of gossip could end their lives in a moment. A killing made in the name of honour is a murder, plain and simple, and must be punished as such.

As far as I am concerned, real honour is for women and men to get a decent education that is based on equality between the genders. Real honour can only flourish when people stop gossiping and interfering in other people's business. Real honour is when young women decide to break the social norms by fighting for their rights, taking up jobs as teachers, doctors, engineers, journalists, mechanics, plumbers or electricians to earn a decent living for themselves, their families and their children. Real honour is about tolerance, equality and civic responsibility.

Some governments, NGOs, religious groups and so on prefer not to debate such issues because they believe it gives a bad name to their country, religion or ethnic group – no doubt they're frightened of damaging their own honour. But how on earth can the human race hope to move forward, to evolve, with our heads in the sand?

The media has so far played a very important role in raising awareness about so-called honour killings in many countries. The staff and editors at *The Jordan Times* were true pioneers when it came to these crimes and this newspaper continues to lead the way; their support showed how a media organization was able to make a huge difference in their own community and beyond. Journalists across the world need to keep the momentum going: rather than focusing on extreme cases that make for especially tragic stories, every case needs to make headlines. Every honour killing is an outrage. Pictures of the victim need to be shown, and their friends and families should be interviewed in order to humanize the victim, so that these cases will stick in people's minds and so that people will ask questions and demand that their leaders do something to end these crimes.

It is for that reason that I have included as many human examples as possible in this book, to show that this is a very real tragedy, that every day, all across the world, bright young women are being slaughtered for no good reason. Remember seventeen-year-old Heshu Yones from the UK? She hoped that, although running away from her family was breaking her heart, it would lead to a new beginning. Despite everything she had suffered, this courageous, eloquent young woman remained determined to live life to the full. Who knows what she would have gone on to achieve if the support had been in place to help her survive?

And remember Inas from chapter 3, wasting away in the so-called 'correctional institute'? The last time I saw her she had served ten years and was thirty-four years old. Today she remains in prison – still waiting, still hopeful. A group of activists, including myself, have since launched the Jordanian Coalition to Help Women in Protective Custody; the campaign has been fierce but progress is achingly slow. We will not stop, however, until women like Inas receive the help they so desperately need.

After all, we're the only hope they've got. I don't want to let them down.

Notes

1 Although victims of honour killing are predominantly women, men are killed as well; in Pakistan for example, according to official figures, roughly one-third of victims are men, but the proportion varies from region to region. There has been no attempt by the UN to calculate the numbers of men murdered in the name of honour worldwide.

2 It would be a mistake to assume that the murder of women by immediate male relatives is exclusively a Muslim phenomenon. In her book *Dislocating Cultures* (Routledge, 1997), feminist scholar Uma Narayan states that 1,400 American women are known to be murdered as a result of domestic abuse annually, while the deaths of 5,000 Indian women (largely Hindu) are suspected to be the result of dowry murders each year. Similarly, John Bowen, in his book *Why the French Don't Like Headscarves* (Princeton University Press, 2006), explains that in the French legal system when European French men kill women it is listed as a crime of 'love', whereas when Muslim French men kill women it is listed as a crime of Islam or 'culture'. Unfortunately, men in every society across the world murder thousands of women annually for a variety of reasons, irrespective of cultural and religious differences.

3 Rana Husseini, 'Sheikh Tamimi outlines Islam's position on honour crimes', *The Jordan Times*, 19 September 1999.

4 Rana Husseini, 'Government refers amendment to Article 340 to Parliament', *The Jordan Times*, 29 September 1999.

5 'An open letter to Parliament members, Tahrir Party', *Arab Al-Yawm*, 18 November 1999.

6　Internet posting by HRH Prince Ali, 'Taking a stand vs Article 340', 'Ask the Government', *Culture*, 3 February 2000.

7　Alia Shukri Hamzeh, 'Jordanians protest against killing women in the name of honour', Associated Press, 14 February 2000.

8　Internet posting by HRH Prince Ali, 'What really happened?', 'Ask the Government', *Culture*, 16 February 2000.

9　Islamic Action Front Fatwa, 'Cancelling Article 340 is against Islamic Sharia', issued by the IAF's Islamic Sharia Scientific Committee, Amman, Jordan, 13 February 2000.

10　Fathi Khatab, Sheikh Al Azhar: 'Applying punishments is the right of the ruler and not the individual', *Arab Al-Yawm*, 16 February 2000.

11　Dima Hamdan, 'About 30 deputies withdraw signatures from petition calling for applying Sharia', *The Jordan Times*, 25–26 February 2000.

12　Rana Husseini, 'Al-Sabeel survey weighs in against amending Article 340', *The Jordan Times*, 23 February 2000.

13　Alia Shukri Hamzeh, 'Press stays away from House debate on Elections Law, Deputy says women's "honour" could be "jeopardized" if they are elected to Parliament', *The Jordan Times*, 15 November 2000.

14　Rana Husseini, 'Lawyers, judges, intellectuals condemn campaign against Article 340', *The Jordan Times*, 10–11 March 2000.

15　Lama Abu Odeh, 'Crimes of honour and the construction of gender in Arab Societies', *Feminism and Islam: Legal and Literary Perspectives*, edited by Mai Yamani. New York University Press, 1996, p. 149.

16　Evelyne Accad, 'Honour-related violence and patriarchy: honour stronger than life', paper presented during a European Conference on Honour-Related Violence within a Global Perspective, Stockholm, Sweden, organized by Kvinnoforum, October 2004, p. 2.

17　'Pakistan: violence against women in the name of honour', Amnesty International, 22 September 1999.

18　'Pakistan indifference as lawyers defending women's rights are threatened with death', Amnesty International, 15 April 1999.

19　Tim McGurk, 'Asma Jahangir, the pocket protector', *Time*, 28 April 2003.

20 'Five women beaten and buried alive in Pakistan "honour killing"', *Independent*, 2 September 2008.

21 Sarah Di Lorenzo, 'UN women's rights group criticise Pakistan for honor killings, trafficking', Associate Press, 9 June 2007.

22 'Pakistan embassy in US honours Mukhtar Mai', *Hindustan Times*, 26 April 2008.

23 'World Briefing Asia: Pakistan: Gunman kills provincial minister', *New York Times*, 21 February 2007.

24 'Journalist killed as she sleeps with baby', *Daily Mail*, 7 June 2007.

25 'A brutal fight for equality', *Time*, 9 June 2007.

26 'Report from the International Conference on Combating Patriarchal Violence against Women – Focusing on Violence in the Name of Honour', Swedish Ministries of Justice and Foreign Affairs, Stockholm, 7–8 December 2004.

27 'Duaa Khalil Aswad was killed for loving the wrong man', *Daily Mail*, 16 August 2007.

28 Tina Susman, 'Faith-based taboos, ethnic intolerance nag Iraqis: stoning of teen girl in North underscores sectarian discord that stirs nearly every issue', *Los Angeles Times*, 22 May 2007.

29 'Honor thy father (news commentary)', Off our backs, 1 July 2007.

30 Susman, 'Faith-based taboos'.

31 'Kurdish women tortured by "mobile phone abuse"', IWPR [http://www.iwpr.net/?p=icr&s=f&o=344448&apc_state=henh].

32 Dr Sherifa Zuhur, 'Gender, sexuality and the criminal laws in the Middle East and North Africa: a comparative study', Women for Women's Human Rights, 2005, p. 28.

33 'Marked women', *Time*, 26 July 2004.

34 'Killing for honour', IWPR, 17 May 2005.

35 Bay Fang, 'The Talibanization of Iraq: under mounting repression, courageous women fight for their rights and their lives', *Ms* magazine, vol. XVII, no. 2, Spring 2007.

36 'My daughter deserved to die for falling in love', *Observer*, 11 May 2008.

37 '2000 demonstrate against "honour" killings in Iran' [http://www.stop-stoning.org/node/378], 10 January 2008.

38 '"Honor" killing spurs outcry in Syria; a 16-year-old's killing spurred the country's grand mufti to call for legal reform and protections', *Christian Science Monitor*, 14 February 2007.

39 Rasha Elass, 'Honor killing spurs outcry in Syria: a 16-year-old's killing spurred the country's grand mufti to call for legal reform and protections', *Christian Science Monitor*, 14 February 2007 [http://www.csmonitor.com/2007/0214/p07s02-wome.html].

40 'Yemeni claims "honour" motivated mosque slaughter' [http://www.stophonourkillings.com/?name=News&file=article&sid=271 8], 8 June 2008.

41 Lynn Welchman and Sara Hossain, eds., *Honour, Crimes, Paradigms, and Violence against Women*, Zed Books, 2005, p. 131.

42 Ibid.

43 Danielle Hoyek, Rafif Sidawi and Amira Abou Mrad, 'Murders of women in Lebanon, crimes of "honour", between reality and the law', Lebanese Council to Resist Violence against Women, April 2004, p. 18.

44 Maria Corrêa and Érica Renata de Souza, eds., 'Family life: a comparative perspective on "crimes of honour"', Centre for Gender Studies, University of Campinas, 2006.

45 'Turkish Civil and Penal Code Reforms from a Gender Perspective: the Success of two Nationwide Campaigns', Women for Women's Human Rights, 2005.

46 Ibid., p. 63.

47 Ibid., pp. 63–4.

48 Zuhur, 'Gender, sexuality and the criminal laws', p. 23.

49 Carin Benninger-Budel, 'Violence against women, for the protection and promotion of the human rights of women', 10 Reports/Year 2000, World Organization against Torture (OMCT), printed by Abrax, France, p. 250.

50 Ibid.

51 Suzanne Zima, 'When brothers kill sisters,' *The Gazette* [Montreal], 17 April 1999. See also Walter Rodgers, 'Honour killings: a brutal tribal custom', CNN World News, 7 December 1995.

52 'Honour's victims', *Chatelaine*, March 2000.

53 Welchman and Hossain, eds., *Honour*, p. 193.

54 Ibid.

55 Ibid., p. 195.

56 Ibid., p. 196.

57 Corrêa and de Souza, eds., 'Family life', p. 40.

58 Ibid., p. 162.

59 Ibid.

60 'Love, honour and obey – or die', *Guardian*, 8 October 2000.

61 'Life for father who cut girl's throat for "shaming family"', *Evening Standard*, 29 September 2003; 'Boyfriend tells of his pain over girl killed by father', *Evening Standard*, 30 September 2003.

62 'Police probe dozens of murdered brides killed for "honour"', *Evening Standard*, 21 March 2005.

63 James Brandon and Salam Hafez, *Crimes of the Community: Honour-Based Violence in the UK*, Centre for Social Cohesion/ Cromwell Press, 2008, p. 56.

64 Karen McVeigh, '"Honour" killer boasted of stamping on woman's neck, Kurdish victim was raped and tortured for two hours, jokes and laughter heard in description of murder', *Guardian*, 20 July 2007 [http://www.guardian.co.uk/uk/2007/jul/20/ukcrime.uknews4]; 'Police errors led to murder; Body in suitcase: Victim said 4 times that her life was at risk', *Birmingham Mail*, 12 June 2007; 'Victim called police before she was killed; honour killings plight of young women who fear death at the hands of their own family; *Sunday Mercury* investigates', *Sunday Mercury*, 17 June 2007; '"Honour killing" rapists are on the run in Iraq', *Evening Standard*, 12 June 2007.

65 'Man jailed for intimidating witnesses', *Sheffield Star*, 16 April 2008.

66 'On the run in Midlands ... refugee who shot, stoned and battered woman for falling in love', *Sunday Mercury*, 17 June 2007.

67 'Brother found guilty', *Newcastle Journal*, 17 June 2006.

68 'Matriarch guilty of ordering family honour killing', *Birmingham Post*, 27 July 2007; 'Guilty, evil matriarch who lured son's wife to her death', *Daily Mail*, 27 July 2007.

69 'Daughter keeps alive memory of mother murdered for "honour"', *Independent on Sunday*, 14 December 2008.

70 'Gun killer's revenge over sex attack allegations', *Asian News*, 26 January 2007.

71 'Man killed family in house arson', BBC News, 20 February 2007 [http://news.bbc.co.uk/1/hi/england/lancashire/6379833.stm]; 'Murder probe as five die in fire', BBC News, 1 November 2006 [http://news.bbc.co.uk/1/hi/england/lancashire/6106712.stm].

72 *Honour Kills*, BBC3 television documentary.

73 'International hunt for father of dead family', *Birmingham Post*, 23 August 2000.

74 'Freedom for doctor in "forced marriage kidnap" by parents', *Daily Mail*, 15 December 2008.

75 'Parents return passport to Bangladeshi doctor', Associated Press Worldstream, 14 December 2008.

76 'Sara Thornton is cleared of murder', *Independent*, 31 May 1996.

77 'Honour-related violence', *European Resource Book and Good Practice*, based on the European project 'Prevention of Violence against Women and Girls in Patriarchal Families', Kvinnoforum, Stockholm, 2005, p. 37.

78 'Honour-related violence with a global perspective: mitigation and prevention in Europe', organized by Kvinnoforum/Foundation of Women's Forum, Stockholm, Sweden, 7–8 October 2004.

79 Ibid.

80 Ibid., p. 30.

81 Ibid., p. 3.

82 Ibid., p. 83.

83 'Honour-related violence', *European Resource Book*, pp. 45–6.

84 Muna Dahl, 'Muslim men between protection and control: how do four Muslim men experience their fatherhood in Sweden?' Qualitative study, International Master of Social Science Work, University of Göteborg, Spring 2003, p. 44.

85 Ibid., p. 45.

86 'Honour-related violence', *European Resource Book*, p. 64.

87 'Honour-related violence with a global perspective', p. 42.

88 Ibid., p. 89.

89 Ibid., p. 75.

90 'Only one of Hatin Sürücü's brothers jailed', International Campaign Against Honour Killings, 27 January 2009.

91 'Honor killing victim wanted to live like other German girls', *Spiegel Online*, 27 May 2008 [http://www.spiegel.de/international/germany/0,1518,555667,00.html].

92 'Honour-related violence', *European Resource Book*, p. 166.

93 'Parliamentary Assembly of the Council of Europe, Resolution 1327 (2003): So-called "honour crimes"', 4 April 2003.

94 Ibid.

95 Germaine Tillion, *The Republic of Cousins: Women's Oppression in Mediterranean Society*, translated by Quintin Hoare, Al Saqi Books, 1983, p. 34.

96 Richard Owen, 'Mafioso shoots sister over "dishonour": an old Sicilian tradition is revived as a young woman who had a child out of wedlock is shot', *Times Online*, 27 March 2006 [http://www.timesonline.co.uk/tol/news/world/europe/article696820.ece].

97 'Sweethearts' reunion ended in murder', BBC News, 18 April 2008 [http://news.bbc.co.uk/1/hi/england/devon/7352380.stm].

98 *Murder in the Family: Honor Killings in America*, Fox News, 26 July 2008.

99 'When men murder women: an analysis of 2004 homicide data: females murdered by males in single victim/single offender incidents', Violence Policy Center (VPC), September 2006 [http://www.vpc.org/studies/wmmw2006.pdf].

100 Ibid.

101 Ibid.

102 'Father says he set fire that killed three', *New York Times*, 3 January 2008.

103 'Man says he didn't approve of marriage: Subhash Chander is accused of setting fire, killing daughter, her husband, their child', Associated Press, 2 January 2008.

104 'Manhunt continues in Texas; Father sought in girls' deaths', *Washington Times*, 4 January 2008.

105 'For the first time, FBI admits Texas murder was a case of honor killing', *Hindustan Times*, 15 October 2008.

106 '"Honor" killing comes to the US', *Boston Globe*, 10 August 2008.
107 'An American "honor killing"', *New York Post*, 23 July 2008.
108 'Man charged with killing his wife', PR News, 16 April 2004.
109 'Cultural "honour" killing brought to Canada', *Vancouver Post*, 11 June 2007.

Acknowledgements

I first thought of writing a book on so-called honour crimes in Jordan nine years ago. The idea was constantly postponed because of the political turmoil that seems to be a constant backdrop to our lives in this region. There have been many developments across the world in those nine years, and during this period I was able to further my research and include valuable information and consult specialists. I hope it will prove to be an informative documentary reference for those interested in learning more about this issue, as well as a tool to help end so-called honour killings.

This work was made possible thanks to the support and help of my close friends, colleagues, government officials, local organizations and the international community. Thanks first go to Jane Fonda for her generous contribution. For me, it's a real honour that such an outstanding, genuine and truly committed human rights activist such as Jane agreed to write the foreword.

I would like to thank Diala Khasawneh, my editor in Amman, who put her heart, mind and remarkable editorial skills into this book, as well as adding her own rich insights.

I am also indebted to my editor in the UK, Kris Hollington, who helped shape and update the book through his professional work. Special thanks also go to Nina Hollington, who conducted interviews in the UK and maintained and updated a database of the most recent cases of honour killing across the globe. I am especially grateful to Kris and Nina for their belief in this project and their eagerness to take it to another level, so that awareness about this horrific practice will be spread worldwide.

My thanks and appreciation also go to my publisher and editor in the UK, Juliet Mabey at Oneworld, who used her talent and commitment to the cause of worldwide human rights issues to edit my work and produce a true and honest image of so-called honour crimes around the world, and in our part of the world in particular.

I would like to thank my UK agent, Adrian Weston, who believed in me, as well as my cause, and who worked tirelessly to secure the best possible publisher.

I am also thankful to the following people who dedicated much of their time over the past seven years to either helping me to formulate the outline or edit the early drafts of this book, and contributed hours of their time to assist with my pursuit of information, opinions and guidance: Amy Henderson, Dr Manal Hamzeh, Sana Abdullah, Mary-An Denis, Rima Cortbawi, Christine Arab, Jane Taylor, Muna Darwazeh, Maha Abu Ayyash, and Frances Abu Zeid, in particular, who provided me with numerous morale boosts.

Special thanks go to Their Majesties King Abdullah II and Queen Rania for their faith in my work as well as for championing the cause of women in Jordan and speaking out against so-called honour crimes, and for working tirelessly to introduce non-discriminatory laws to improve women's status. My appreciation goes to Her Majesty Queen Noor who was among the first in Jordan to acknowledge my work openly, and did so again in her book, *Leap of Faith.*

My thanks also go to Her Royal Highness Princess Basma bint Talal and her daughter Mrs Farah Daghestani for believing in me and supporting women's causes in Jordan. I would also like to thank His Royal Highness Prince Ali for his personal commitment to the cause in Jordan and for his constant support. My thanks also go to every member of the royal family who has supported this cause, including Prince Hassan, Princess Sarvath, Princess Sumaya, Prince Ghazi Bin Mohammad, Prince Raed, Prince Hamzeh, Prince Mired, Prince Zeid, Prince Firas and Princess Dina Mired.

I would like to thank Jordanian officials, influential persons and activists who have often expressed their support for and belief in what I was doing and had pivotal roles in bringing the issue of so-called honour crimes and domestic violence to the fore. They include Their Excellencies Zeid Rifai, Dr Fayez Tarawneh, Dr Zeid Hamzeh, Dr Bassem Awadallah, Dr Nabil Sharif, Asma Khader, Laurice Hlas, Leila Sharaf, Inam Mufti, Dr Marwan Muasher, Dr Abdul Rahim Malhas, Suhair Al-Ali, Hala Latouf Bseiso, Fadi Ghandour, Naser Judeh, Nader Horani, Samir Hiyari, Dr Adnan Abu Odeh, Dr Reem Badran, Maha Khatib, Dr Sima Bahous, Dr Haifa Abu Ghazaleh, Dr Munib Werr, Judge Subhi Abbadi, Dr Nabil Sharif, Judge Ihsan Barakat, Haifa Bashir, and Muhieddin and Amineh Husseini.

I would also like to thank those whose have provided me with their tireless support: Judge Yassin Abdullat, Karen Asfour, Amneh Zoubi, Nadia Shamroukh, Inam Asha, Dr Arwa Ameri, Dr Sari Nasir, Dr Nawal Faouri, Dr Hamdi Murad, Archimandrite Christoforos Atallah, Rania Atallah, Nadine Shbeilat, Ja'afar Touqan, Patricia Salti, Hala Kheir, Kathy Sullivan, Malak Anabtawi, May Abul Samen, Marwan Jumah, Samer Naber, Nadia Hashem Aloul, Emily Naffa, Laila Hamarneh, Toujan Faisal, Samar Haj Hassan, Salwa Nasser, Ethar Khasawneh, Lina Kutob, Reem Abu Hassan, Afaf Jabiri, Eva Abu Halaweh, Nadia Bushnaq, Basma Abdul Jaber, Shirin Mired, Mahasen Imam, Muna Mufti, Salma and Simon Issa, Rihab Malhas, Susan Phillips, Jeanette Jounblat, Myassar Saadi, Suhaila Khouri, Captain Amin and Nadia Husseini, Captain Nasri and Randa Jumeian, Ghada and Abed Husseini, Dalal Etoum, Najwa and Wael Karadsheh, Rami Oweiss, Farid Share, Suleiman Sweiss, Dr Rula Kawas and Vera Salti.

I would like to take this chance to extend my thanks to my close and dear friends who stood by me and with whom I have shared many highs and lows; they were great believers in this cause, and their support helped me tremendously in the writing of this book. They include Najwa Ghannoum, Sahar Aloul, Widad Adas, Randa Naffa, Dima Darwazeh, Suha Snober, Haya Taher, Mona Abdeen, Razan Khatib, Maya Khalaf, Rania Tamimi, Dima Annab, Ola Khalidi, Lamia Fakhouri, Aline and Sevan Bannayan, Alma Khasawneh, Hania Kayal, Rasha Yaish, Ghassan Ghandour, Rula Saadi, Ghada Ziedan, Kais Asfour, Rana Masri, Mohammad Sabbagh, Dina Saad, Shadi Zaayadin, Rania Ay, Maysa and Reem Abu Lughod, Sed Haddad, Ramez Shatara, Runa Sundaha, Sahel Hiyari, Reem Hammouri, Oreib Toukan, 'Dana Khan' Malhas, Shatha Mahmoud, Nadia Abu Judom, Basma Amawi, Luai Qunash, Maro Calis Sahouri, Nadia Naffa, Tala Abu Taha, Sadouf Faraj, Lana Saman, Rula Abu Taha, Alia Nusseibeh, Rania Abu Hijleh, Fatima Issawi, Hala Khalaf, Dima Fayyad, Sultan Abu Maryam, Yasmin Naber, Sally Shalabi, Jan Sherdan, Alex Naber, Cherien Dabis, Amy Amahl Khouri, Aseel Sawalha, Ani Orfali, Alida Orfali, Maha Ghannoum, Samer Nasser, Aline Orfali, Lara Damarjian, Fairouz Abu Ghazaleh, Hala Ghosheh, Reem Hejjawi, Hala Muhaisen, Tala Al Mauge, Jumana Salti, Hala Ghatas, Taroub Khoury Kalis, Lina Sharaiha, Zahra Taher, Mays Shakhshir, Dana Tarawneh, Lara Dajani, Njoud Haddad, Corky Huffine, Kate Wilson, Heidi Elger, Maryum Saifee, Rama Ishaq, Amani Khatib, Arto Baghdayan, Amber Ridden, Nadia Oweidat and Nisreen Alami.

I am also indebted to my editors and colleagues at *The Jordan Times* for adopting the cause of so-called honour crimes and other human rights issues. Special thanks go to my former editor-in-chief, Jennifer Hamarneh, who was always supportive and made it possible for me to focus on finishing this book, and my former editors-in-chief George Hawatmeh, Rana Sabbagh-Gharghour,

Ayman Safadi, Rami Khouri and the late Abdullah Hassanat, from whom I also learned a great deal.

I would like to thank my current editor-in-chief, Samir Barhoum, who constantly encouraged me to work on this book. I would also like to recognize other colleagues who had a great impact on my career, including Walid Saadi, Ellia Nasrallah, Ica Wahbeh, Lamis Andouni, Ara Voskian, Alia Shukri Hamzeh, Dalia Dajani, Ghalia Aloul, Francesca Ciriaci-Sawalha, Ranjana Usta, Victoria Macchi, Paul Tate, Dina Wakeel, Saeda Kilani, Nermeen Murad, Maryam Shahin, Taylor Luck, Mahmoud Abed, Natasha Twal and Jeff Tynes. To these people and other staff members I owe all the good things that happened in my life while working at *The Jordan Times*. It is due to their constant guidance and support that I have reached the stage where I am today. Other colleagues at local media outlets were also instrumental in supporting me: Randa Habib, Musa Kilani, Tareq Masarweh, Ali Abunimah, Cynthia Atrash, Atef Itmeh, Nabil and Yousef Gheishan, Hala Boncompagni, Linda Maayeh, Suhair Tel, Caroline Faraj, Shafika Mattar, Aroub Soubh, Qais Elias, Eman Abu Qaoud, Khalid Nueimat, Ahmad Kreishan and Reem Zumut, to name only a few.

I also thank the forensic medicine team at the Jordanian National Institute of Forensic Medicine represented by its director Dr Mumen Hadidi, and pathologists Isra Tawalbeh, Ali Shotar, Hani Jahshan, Mahmoud Shreideh, Ahmad Bani Hani, Ahmad Odeh, Muwfaq Muti, Azzam Haddad, Ibrahim Obeidat, Iwad Tarawneh, Hussein Abul Samen, Mahmoud Hirzallah and the rest of the pathologists working there who employed their expertise and scientific knowledge to help end so-called honour killings in Jordan.

Special thanks and appreciation go to members of the Jordanian National Committee to Eliminate So-Called Honour Crimes for being the first collective in Jordan to raise the issue of so-called honour crimes publicly and make a real stand on this issue.

Other Jordanian women's groups which played a vital role in supporting the cause and recognizing my efforts include the Jordanian Women's Union, the Jordanian National Commission for Women, Sisterhood Is Global Institute, Mizan Law Group, Princess Basma's Women Resource Centre, Zarqa Family Guidance Centre, Arab Women Organization of Jordan, *JO* magazine, Ammannet and the Arab Women Media Center. Much appreciation should be expressed to the Rotary Clubs, UN agencies, the diplomatic missions and embassies in Jordan for their support for and appreciation of my work and the cause in general.

I am indebted to Equality Now in the US and the UK, its director Jessica Neuwirth and its staff Jackie Hunt, Amanda Sullivan and Taina Bien-Aime, for offering all kinds of support to me throughout my career and for making a strong and positive impact on the lives of women worldwide.

Other international bodies, media outlets and individuals include Amnesty International, Freedom House, the Nobel Women's Initiative, the United Nations Development Fund for Women (UNIFEM), the Carter Centre, *Marie Claire* magazine, Spanish city of l'Hospitalet, *Ms* magazine, Women's News, RAND Corporation, Feminist Majority Foundation, Terre de Femmes, Kvinnoforum, Iranian and Kurdish Women's Rights Organization, Gloria Steinem, Diana Nammi, Asma Jahangir, Mahnaz Afkhami, Rita Henley Jensen, Commanders Andy Baker and Brent Hyatt of Scotland Yard, Gudrun Sidrassi-Harth, Nanci Rafai, Paul Peters, Lesley Carson, Brigitte Schmid, Nicole Choueiry, Isis Nuseir, LaShawn Jefferson, Mariana Vos and Alasdair Soussi.

Special thanks go to Kerry Kennedy for including me in her important project on human rights activists in the world, 'Speak Truth To Power', and the Robert F. Kennedy Foundation. My gratitude also goes to the following people who are associated with the project: Nan Richardson, Ariel Dorfman and Dr Ghada Karam.

I would also like to thank the former Secretary General of the Jordanian National Commission for Women, Dr Amal Sabbagh, for her tireless efforts; we went through a lot together for over a year to expose the false story of Norma Khouri in her hoax novel *Forbidden Love* [*Honor Lost*]. I would also like to thank the former literary editor of the *Sydney Morning Herald*, Malcolm Knox, who worked professionally and objectively in exposing Khouri's story as fake in Australia. I also thank Mustafa Khreishan, Dr Ihab Shalbak and Yasmine Bahrani for their help with this story. Special thanks go to the Australian film producer and director, Anna Broinowski, who travelled the globe, including a trip to Jordan, for her documentary *Forbidden Lie$* and conveyed an objective message to western viewers by portraying the real lives of Muslims and Arabs.

I also need to acknowledge one of the first organizations that recognized, supported and awarded me for my work: the Reebok Human Rights Foundation. The prestigious Reebok Human Rights Award, given to me in 1998, enabled me to achieve so much. It was the turning point of my career and helped me investigate, learn and understand the so-called honour crime issue from a human rights perspective. It was also the starting point for this book.

My deepest appreciation also goes to the Embassy of the Netherlands in Jordan and Second Secretary Bianca Zylfiu-Niccolson for providing me with financial support in 2006 that enabled me to finish my book.

My love goes out to my late grandmother, Wajiha Saifi, whose warmth and kindness engulfed me endlessly, and to my uncles Yacoub Husseini, the late Sameh Saifi and his wife Mukaram Malas, my late aunt May Midani and my aunts Lamis Adem, Umayya Sigilmassi and Ikram Husseini. My thanks go to my cousins who constantly expressed pride in their cousin and her accomplishments, including Reem Saifi, her husband Khalid

Murad and their children Lara, Aya and Sameh, Samar Saifi, her husband Jamal Budeiri and their children Sameh and Abdul Karim, Widad 'Dolly' and Muhanad Midani, Rasha, Samar, Louie and Udai Husseini and Ahmad Budeiri.

Last but not least, my gratitude goes to my dearest lovely mother, Randa Saifi-Husseini, who always wanted what is best for me and gave me the strength to remain a positive person throughout my career. I thank my brother, Moutaz Husseini, for being one of my greatest advocates, along with his wife, Sura Madani.

Index

Note: Names appearing in italics denote victims and their killers. The prefix
'Al-' is ignored in the alphabetical ordering of names.

Aali, Jamiluddin 109
Abbas, Amir 180
Abdel-Qader, Ali (killer) 128–9
Abdel-Qader, Hassan (killer) 128
Abdel-Qader, Haydar (killer) 128
Abdel-Qader, Rand (victim) 128–9
Abdel-Rahim, Marzouk Ahmed
    (killer) 147
Abdo, Maha 152–3
Abdul Aziz, Samir 32
Abdullah II of Jordan 35, 38–9, 51,
    60, 64, 66, 70
Abdullat, Yassin 86
Abedin, Humayra (victim) 176
Abu Ayyash, Maha 32, 75
Abu Fares, Mohammad 79
Abu Hassan, Reem 79
Abu al-Hosn, Yumun 136
Abu Mariam, Sultan 32, 43, 56
Abu Odeh, Adnan 57–8, 70
Abu Rayyan, Muna 32
Abu Risheh, Zuleikha 42
accidents, killings disguised as
    82–3, 102, 127, 146
Action Alert 208–9
Adas, Widad 20

adultery:
    blamed on women 41, 51, 52
    penalty for 33, 37, 51, 57–8, 76,
        136, 139, 149, 154
    rape seen as 112
    and Sharia law 69–70, 72–3
    and stoning 131–2
Al-Afaf Islamic Society 53
Afgani, Hana 27
Afghan Independent Human Rights
    Commission (AIHRC) 115–16
Afghanistan, honour crimes in
    114–16
Aftonbladet (newspaper) 187
Afzal, Nazir 166
Al Ahram Weekly 148–9
Ahsan, Aitzaz 106, 109
Al-Ajely, Ziyad Khalaf 125
Al-Ajial 71
Akayleh, Abdullah 67
Alaa, Hamida 130
Alaa, Hassan 130
Alami, Nisreen 94
Al Alawi, Irfan 142
Algamo, Kickis Aahre 192
Ali, Mohammad 180

Ali, Prince 60–7, 70, 71, 73–4, 87
Ali Rauf, Shawbo (victim) 129,
    167–8
Allak, Semse (victim) 145
Allam, Abeer 148–9
Amal Organization for Women 120
Ameen, Jwan 126
Amiry, Arwa 84
Amman, and honour killings 1–7
Amneh (victim) 45–7, 49–50
Amnesty International 131
Annan, Kofi 214
Arab Al-Yawm (newspaper) 41, 53,
    58–9
Arab Times 144
Arabiat, Abdul Latif 52
Ardalan, Parvin 132–3
Arshad, Rahan (killer) 174–5
Article 98 (Jordan) 33–4, 49, 51, 68,
    75, 77–8, 87, 181, 212, 215
Article 340 (Jordan) 33–8, 41, 51–9,
    62–6, 68–9, 71–6
    amendment 77–9, 87
Article 341 (Jordan) 54
Asha, Inam 14
Asian Human Rights Commission
    112
Al-Assad, Bashar 135
Association for Women's Role
    Development (Syria) 136
Asuda (women's rights NGO) 123
Aswad, Duaa Khalil (victim)
    117–22
Athwal, Bachan 168–70
Athwal, Pavan 170–1
Athwal, Sukhdave 169–70
Athwal, Surjit (victim) 168–70
Atroshi, Abdulmajid (killer) 192
Atroshi, Pela (victim) 192
Atroshi, Shivan (killer) 192

Australia:
    and honour crimes 192
    impact of Khouri's book 89–90,
        93, 94–9
The Australian 192
Awad, Mohamed 148–9
Ayed, Samir (killer) 68
Al-Azhar Ifta Council 69–70
Aziz, Youssif Mohamed 123–4

Babker, Dashti 80
Al Badeel 152–3
Bahrani, Yasmine 90, 93
Baker, Andy 161–2
Bakker, Hilde 189
Bakr, Faeq Ameen 125
Baladna internet company 56
Bam (victim) 193–5
Bangladesh:
    and forced marriages 176
    honour crimes in 104, 156
Bani Hani, Ahmad 84
Bani Hani, Mohammad 72
Barzani, Nechirvan 124
Basil, Roaa 122, 124
Basma bint Talal, Princess 40
Begard (victim) 122
Begum, Shanaz (victim) 171
beheading of women, in Iraq 117,
    121, 127–8
Belloque, Juliana 155
Bilbeisi, Bashir 42
Bilour, Ilyas 109
Birch, Philip 204
Bjorling, Bam 186–7
Blair, Sir Ian 161
Blair, Tony 170
bounty hunters 161, 175
Brazil:
    honour crimes in 104, 154–6

Penal Code 154–5
Burgan, Basil 31–2, 38
burning *see* immolation
Bush, George W. 117, 125

Cahill, Robert 208
campaign against honour crimes
    (Jordan) xii, 29–30, 31–44,
    68–77
  opposition to 51–4, 63, 68–9
  and Parliament 31–2, 37–8, 40,
    52–3, 69–71, 74–6, 87
  petition 32–8, 41–4, 51, 53–4,
    56–8, 76
  royal support for 35, 38–40, 51,
    58, 60–7, 71, 73–4
  setbacks 89–100
  support for 52, 54–5, 69–71, 86
  and western pressure 37–8, 52–3,
    72–4, 76, 94
Canada, honour killings in 213
Canberra Times 99
Centre for Egyptian Women's Legal
    Assistance (CEWLA) 148,
    150
Chander, Subhash (killer) 209
Child Protection Services (UK)
    179–80
children:
  and forced marriage 117,
    210–11, 215
  involved in honour crimes 26,
    146, 185
  as victims of honour killings
    172–5, 209
China, honour crimes in 217–18
contract killings 161, 175, 212–13
Convention on the Elimination of
    Discrimination Against
    Women (CEDAW) 35, 149

Cook, Robin 169–70
Council of Europe 200–1
Cox, Steve 173–4
Craddick, Bob 205
Criminal Court (Jordan) 68, 81,
    86
Crossing Over (film) 133
Curtius, Mary 152–3

Dabis, Ruba 32
Dahl, Muna 189–90
Daily Telegraph 141
Darvishpour, Mehrdad 188
Darwazeh, Muna 32
Deaver, Keith 211
discrimination, gender 214–15
  in Afghanistan 115
  in Brazil 154–5
  in Egypt 149–50
  in Jordan x, xiv, 32, 34–7, 87,
    103
  in Lebanon 140
  in Palestine 153
divorce 82
  forced 142–3
  and Khuloe law 77–8
Dughmi, Abdul Karim 75

Ecuador, honour crimes in 104
education:
  role 162, 200, 215
  of women 215–16
Edwar, Hana 120
Egypt:
  honour crimes in 104, 116,
    147–50
  Penal Code 149–50
Al Enezi, Adnan (killer) 143–4
Al Enezi, Asma (victim) 143–4
Equality Now ix, 131, 208

Erturk, Yakin 146
Europe:
    honour killings in xii, xiii–xiv,
        183–202
    and legal protection 215
Ezzo, Fayez (killer) 135
Ezzo, Zahra (victim) 134–5, 136

Facebook 141–2
Family Protection Project 82
Fathiyah (victim) 148, 149
fatwas 68–70, 78, 109, 141
Fauzia (victim) 110–11
Fayez, Trad 63
Forced Marriage Act (UK; 2007)
        176–8
Forced Marriage Unit (FMU; UK)
        177, 207
Forrester, Giles 170
France, honour crimes in 196–7

Generations Political Party (Jordan)
        71
genital mutilation 117, 215
Germany:
    honour crimes in 197–9
    Kurdish immigrants 145
Ghannoum, Najwa 32, 43
Ghazi bin Mohammad, Prince 62,
        63–5, 72
Ghuweiri, Noman 63
Global Campaign Against Gender
        Violence 86
Gradin, Anita 188
Griswold, Eliza 75
The Guardian 98–9
Guardian Weekly 151

Habash, Faten (victim) 153–4
Habashneh, Mohammad 84–5

Habchi, Sihem 196–7
Haddad, Hamzeh 35
Haddadin, Bassam 58
Hadidi, Mumen 82–3, 85
Haider, Iqbal 109, 111
Haji, Sakina (victim) 122
Hama, Mohamad (killer) 165
Hamarneh, Jennifer 6
Hamarneh, Nash'at 54–5
Hamdan, Dima 31, 67
Hameeda (victim) 110–11
Hamzeh, Alia Shukri 74–5
Al-Hanaki, Ali 142–3
Hanan (victim) 68
Hannoun, Nisreen 32
Haqq, Imam Abdal 190
Harman, Harriet 182
Hassan, Prince 39–40
Hasson, Ibtihaj (victim) 150–1, 152
Hassoun, Ahmad, Grand Mufti of
        Syria 135
Hawatmeh, George 6–7
Al Hayat (newspaper) 135
Henderson, Amy 42
Hirsi Ali, Ayaan 195–6
Hmoud, Marwan 64–5
homophobia, and honour crime
        146–7
honour:
    definitions 218–20
    as excuse xiii, 19–30, 71
    and rumour xiii, 51, 64, 76, 78,
        102
    sexual 101–2
    and virginity 83–5, 143–4, 148–9,
        185
honour crimes:
    acceptance of 46–8
    in Afghanistan 114–16
    in Bangladesh 104, 156

in Brazil 104, 154
in Canada 213
children as victims 172–5, 209
in China 217–18
committed by minors 26, 146, 185
committed by women 48–9
demonstrations against 151–2
in Egypt 147–50
in France 196–7
gay 146–7
in Germany 197–9
in India 104, 156
investigation xii, 2–3
in Iran 131–4
in Iraq 116–30
in Israel 104, 150–1
in Italy 201–2
in Kuwait 143–4
in Lebanon 137–41
and mental illness 212
in Morocco 104, 116
in Netherlands 195–6
numbers xi, xii, xiv, 41–2, 92, 102–3, 112, 115
opposition to 6–7
in Pakistan 103–4, 105–14, 217
in Palestine and Israel 104, 150–4
psychological impact on killers 217–18
and reprisals 171
and role of education 162, 200, 215
in Saudi Arabia 141–3
and Sharia 16, 35, 52, 64, 68–70
in Spain 197
in Sweden 104, 184–7
in Syria 134–6
in Turkey 144–7, 217, 219
used as justification for war in

Iraq 93, 96, 98–9
in Yemen 104, 136–7
see also punishment
Hossain, Syed Mahmod 176
Hudood Ordinance Laws (Pakistan) 111–12
Huffin, Corky 2
human rights:
in Afghanistan 117
in Egypt 147–8
in Iraq 116–17
in Pakistan 108
and western values 37–8, 52–4, 76
Human Rights Watch 27, 29–30, 111, 154
Hunt, Jacqueline 208–9
Hussain, Shahnaz 173
Hussain, Banaz 123
Hussein II of Jordan 39, 40, 60, 64
Hussein, Leila (victim) 129–30
Hussein, Omar 180
Husseini, Rana:
accusations against xii–xiii
awards 31
criticism of 59
education 2–3
as journalist ix–x, xi, 1–7, 8–18, 20–4, 26–30, 89–100
royal support for 60, 62–7
threats against xii, 8
see also campaign against honour crimes
Hyatt, Brent 178, 180
hymen, importance x, 83–5, 148, 192

Ibrahim (killer) 151
Ibrahim, Michael 56
IKWRO *see* Iranian and Kurdish Women's Rights Organization

immolation 116, 122–3, 127, 142,
    148, 150, 152, 172–3, 196
imprisonment of women, protective
    custody 27–30, 221
Inas (victim) 26–30, 221
The Independent 142–3, 170–1, 182
Independent Women Organization
    (Kurdistan) 122
India, honour crimes in 104, 156
inheritance, and murder xiii, 21–3
insanity, temporary 212
Institute for War and Peace
    Reporting (IWPR) 123, 125,
    127
internet:
    accused of corrupting youth
        141–2
    and campaign against honour
        killings 43, 56, 59, 60, 65–6
Iqbal, Javed 109
Iran:
    Criminal Code 131
    honour crimes in 131–4
    Million Signatures Campaign
        132–3
Iran Human Rights 132
Iranian and Kurdish Women's
    Rights Organization (IKWRO)
    165, 175–6, 178, 180, 215
Iraq:
    and honour crimes 116–30
    Penal Code 124
    war in 93, 96, 98–9, 125
Isa, Maria 203–7
Isa, Palestina (victim) 203–6
Isa, Zein (killer) 203–7
Islam:
    and honour crimes 10, 36–7,
        39–40, 43, 65–6, 69, 124, 190,
        198

law *see* Sharia
    and role of women 114
Islamic Action Front (IAF) 52
    fatwa 68–70, 77
Israel, honour crimes in 104, 150–1
Italy, honour crimes in 201–2
IWPR *see* Institute for War and
    Peace Reporting

Jahangir, Asma 105–7, 109–10, 115,
    183–4
Janakat, Samir 71
Jarrar, Nada 98
Jilani, Hina 105–10
jirga (village court), in Pakistan 113
Jolani, Assef 72–3
Jordan:
    discrimination against women x,
        xiv, 32, 34–7, 87, 103
    harm done by Khouri's book 90–8
    honour killings ix–x, xi–xiii, 1–7,
        8–18, 19–30, 31–44, 103–4
    inaccurate depictions of 90–3
    Penal Code *see* Article 98
        (Jordan); Article 340 (Jordan)
    tourist industry 59, 90, 95
    see also campaign against honour
        crimes
The Jordan Times xi, 2–7, 8, 48–9,
    67, 93, 220
    and campaign against honour
        crimes 31, 39, 41–2, 52, 56–7
    and women in Parliament 74
Jordanian Coalition to Help
    Women in Protective Custody
    221
Jordanian National Commission for
    Women (JNCW) 94, 97
Jordanian National Committee to
    Eliminate So-Called Honour

Crimes 32–44, 51–3, 55–6, 59,
94
petition 32–8, 41–4, 51, 53–4,
56–8
and royal march for justice 61
Jordanian Professional Associations,
Culture Committee 75–6
Jordanian Women's Union (JWU)
51, 55
Juma, Samir 119
Jweideh Correctional and
Rehabilitation Centre (Jordan)
9–11
Jweideh Correctional and
Rehabilitation Centre for
Women (Jordan) 27–9

Kaboly, Parvin 187–8
Kasih, Khalid 32
Keen, Stephen (victim) 201–2
Keleman, Niklas 187
Khader, Asma 32–3, 59, 76–7
Khalid (killer) 1, 6, 15–16
Khalil, Amanj 127
Khan, Khyber 171
Khanan, Barry 174
Kharabsheh, Mahmoud 54, 76–7, 79
Khattak, Ajmal 109
Khayri (killer) 148, 149
Khouri, Norma 90–100
Khuloe law 77–9
Kifaya (1, victim) 1, 2–7, 15–18
Kifaya (2, victim) 19–23
Kilani, Ibrahim Zeid 78
Knox, Malcolm 96–7
Koch, Tony 97
Al-Kohali, Abdullah Saleh (killer)
136
Al-Kohali, Belal Qassim (victim)
136

Kumar, Rajesh (victim) 209
Kurdistan:
and honour killings 121, 122–4,
167–8, 192
need for extradition treaty 180
and women's rights 116, 123–4
Kurds, Turkish 144–5, 146
Kuwait, honour crimes in 143–4
Kvinnoforum 186, 188, 191

law, Jordanian *see* Article 98; Article
340
Lebanese Council to Resist Violence
against Women (LCRVW)
140
Lebanese Women's Council 139
Lebanon:
honour crimes in 137–41
Penal Code 138–40

Mahaddin, Muwafaq 58–9
Mahmood, Bahman 164
Mahmood, Banaz (victim) 162–6,
178, 180
Mahmood, Behkal 163–6
Mahmood, Mahmod (killer) 163–5
Mahmoud, Houzan 120
Mai, Mukhtar (victim) 113–14
Majali, Abdul Hadi 51, 56–7, 64
Malhas, Abdul Rahim 79
Al-Maliki, Ali 141
Manal 48
marriage, arranged 143, 165, 174,
179
marriage, forced
in Afghanistan 115–16
in Bangladesh 175
and children 215
in Iran 133
in Jordan 24–5

marriage, forced (*cont.*):
  in Kurdistan 193
  in Pakistan 211
  in Palestine 150
  in Turkey 145, 197
  in UK 158, 164, 167, 173, 175–6,
    181
Matta, Susan 201–2
media 9, 14, 35, 65, 103, 220–1
  Australian 192
  British 141, 158, 161
  censorship xi
  Egyptian 147, 150
  Pakistani 111–13
  Palestinian 152
  Swedish 187
  US 209
  see also The Jordan Times
Meeke, Martin 202
mental illness 212
Middle East Times 143–4
Midik, Huseyin 198
Million Signatures Campaign (Iran)
  132–3
minors, involved in honour crimes
  26, 146, 185
mobile phones 118, 123, 127, 167–8
Mohammad, Azeem 166
Mohammad, Faqir (killer) 179
Mohammad (1, killer) 19–23
Mohammad (2, killer) 45–7, 49–50
Mohammad (rapist) 1, 4, 17–18
Mohammad, Waheed Allah
  (attempted killer) 211–12
Morabito, Giovanni (killer) 201
Morocco, honour crimes in 104,
  116
Mouvement Ni Putes Ni Soumises
  196–7
Ms magazine 136, 201

Al-Mualimchi, Amaal 126
Muhammad, Amin 213
Muhannad 117, 121, 122
murder:
  dowry-related 156
  honour as excuse for xiii, 19–30,
    71
  premeditated 12, 33, 68, 135–6,
    140, 149, 167, 212–13
Musharraf, Pervez 104, 109
Mushiji, Ali Jasib (killer) 125
Muslim Brotherhood 52, 65

Nadia (victim) 20–3
Naffa, Randa 61
Nammi, Diana 165, 175–6, 178
Narula, Smita 209–10
Nasir, Sari 39
National Centre for Social and
  Criminal Research (Egypt)
  147–8
National Council for Family Affairs
  (Jordan) 69–80
National Institute for Forensic
  Medicine (Jordan) 82–5
National Iranian American Council
  (NIAC) 133
Nawaz Khan, Haq (killer) 171
Naz, Rukhsana (victim) 157
Naz, Shazad (killer) 157
Nazir, Samaira (victim) 168
Nejati, Fereshteh (victim) 133–4
Netherlands:
  honour crimes in 195–6
  and Jordan 73
New York Times 146, 148, 205, 218
Noor, Queen of Jordan 39–40

Obeidi, Ahmad (killer) 199
Obeidi, Morsal (victim) 199

O'Brien, Mike 161
Orfali, Ani 36
Organization of Women's Freedom
  (Iraq) 120

Pakistan:
  and forced marriage 211
  honour crimes in 103–4, 105–14,
    218
  need for extradition treaty 180
Pakistan Human Rights
  Commission 110, 111, 112
Pakistan People's Party 109
Palestine, honour crimes in 104,
    150–4
Pandjiarjian, Valéria 155
Parliament, Jordanian:
  and Article 340 31, 54–8, 69–71,
    74–9
  and campaign against honour
    crimes 31–2, 37–8, 40, 52–3, 87
  and royal march for justice 60–7
  and Sharia law 71–2
  women members 52, 74, 79
Parsi, Trita 133
patriarchy 101, 141, 155, 167,
    172–4, 187–8, 190–1, 201
Peacock, Kenneth (killer) 208
Peacock, Sandra (victim) 208
Peltek, Ismail (killer) 212
Pepper, Sarah 179
Pervizat, Leylâ 145
petition against honour crimes
    32–8, 41–4, 51, 53–4, 56–8, 75
Phillips, Nicholas Addison, Lord
    Chief Justice 182
Pimentel, Sylvia 155
police:
  and campaign against honour
    crimes 34, 82

failure to intervene 119–20,
    165–6, 168, 185, 206, 211, 213
  investigation of honour crimes
    xiv, 1, 21, 24, 42, 108, 128, 137,
    160–3, 178, 186
  and virginity testing 83, 85
Prentice, Bridget 177
punishment xiv, 36
  for adultery 33, 37, 51, 57, 112,
    131, 139, 149, 154
  increase in severity 77, 85–6,
    200
  lenient
    in Afghanistan 115
    in Brazil 154
    in Egypt 149–50
    in Iraq 116–17, 126
    in Jordan xiii, 8, 11–13, 15, 23,
      26, 35, 49, 64, 68
    in Lebanon 139
    in Palestine and Israel 153
    in Syria 134–5, 136
    in Turkey 145
    in USA 208
  of minors 126, 185
  for rape 112, 150
  as right of ruler 37, 70

Qatan, Iyad 34

Rafat, Mohammad 57
Rahan, Uzma (victim) 174–5
Raheema (victim) 110–11
Rai, Chiman (killer) 212–13
Al Rai (newspaper) 42, 56, 71
Rai, Rajeev 212
Rai, Sparkle Michelle (victim)
    212–13
Al Raida (magazine) 137–8
Rajabi, Atefeh Sahaaleh (victim) 132

Rami (killer) 26
Rani, Monika (victim) 209
Rania, Queen of Jordan 38–9
Rania (victim) 23–6
rape:
    and honour killing 1, 2–4, 10–15,
        45–7, 125–6, 138, 144, 145,
        151–2, 156
    as punishment 113–14, 163
    punishment for 112, 150
Rasa, Dad Mohammad 115
Rashdan, Na'eyla 76
Rashdi, Hussain Shah 109
Rashid, Chaudry (killer) 211
Rashid, Ismail (victim) 166
Rashid, Kanwal (victim) 211
Rawabdeh, Abdir-Ra'uf S. 38, 54,
        64–7
Reebok Human Rights Award 31
Rehman, Habibur 106–7
Rehman, Imran 167
Riaz, Adam 172–3
Riaz, Caneze (victim) 172–4
Riaz, Mohammad 172–4
Rifai, Zeid 63–4
rights of women 37–8, 52–4, 76, 86,
        115–17, 132
Royal Commission on Human
        Rights 77
rumour, and honour xiii, 51, 64, 76,
        78, 102, 153, 220
runaways 24–6, 28, 105, 121, 142,
        144, 158–60, 162–4, 175–9,
        210, 221
Rus, Carla 196

Sabbagh, Amal 97
Al-Sabeel newspaper 72–3
Saddam Hussein 116–17, 124–5
Saeed Ali, Tahsin 120

Sahindal, Fadime (victim) 184–7
Said, Amina Yaser (victim) 210–11
Said, Islam 210
Said, Patricia 210–11
Said, Sarah Yaser (victim) 210
Said, Yaser Abdel (killer) 210–11
Saifi-Husseini, Randa 43–4
Salem, Soraia 206
Salma (sister of victim) 49, 123
Samander, Rahimullah 115
Samera (victim) 150
Sana (sister of victim) 45–7
Sanghera, Jasvinder 168
Sarhan (killer) 9–15, 85, 217
Sarwar, Malulvi Ghulam 114
Sarwar, Samia (victim) 105, 106–10
Sarwar, Yunus 106–7
Saudi Arabia, honour crimes in
        141–3
Seale, Margaret 97
Shaheen, Mohammad 171
Shahroudi, Ayatollah Seyed
        Mahmoud Hashemi 131
Shakoor, Abdul 113
Shalbak, Ihab 96, 99
Shamroukh, Nadia 51, 55
Sharaf Heroes (Sweden) 190–1, 215
Sharaf, Leila 57, 87
Sharia:
    and divorce 78–9
    and honour killing 16, 35, 52, 64,
        68–70, 73, 127–8, 190
    and politics 71–2
Singh, Jagdeesh 169–70
Sisters Arab Forum for Human
        Rights 137
society, and honour killing 5, 10,
        13–16, 29, 36, 58, 64
Somayeh (victim) 132
Spain, honour crimes in 197

Steffens, Volker 197
stoning 106, 112, 118–21, 131–2,
    145
Straw, Jack 170
suicide:
    forced 151, 199
    and honour 117, 125–6, 156, 159,
        196
    killing disguised as xi, 102, 127,
        137, 146, 150, 175, 199
Suleimani, Rahmat 162–4, 165–6
Sürücü, Ayhan (killer) 197
Sürücü, Hatin (victim) 197
Sweden:
    honour crimes in 104, 184–7,
        191–2
    immigrant communities 188–91,
        195
Sydney Morning Herald 96–7, 99,
    152–3
Syed, Mushahid Hussain 109
Syria:
    honour crimes in 134–6
    Penal Code 135
Syrian General Union of Women
    135–6
Syrian Women Observatory 135

Al-Tahrir Party (Liberation Party)
    53
Al-Tamimi, Sheikh Izzedin
    Al-Khatib 51–2
Tangelder, Bernard 73
Tantawi, Sheikh Mohammad Said
    69–70
Tarawneh, Fayez 58, 70, 87
Tarazi, Nasri 41
Tawalbeh, Israa 85
teenagers, and honour-based
    violence 179–80

Thornberg, Richard 205
Thornton, Sarah 181, 182
Al-Timani, Fatima (victim) 142–3
Time magazine 106, 109–10
The Times 168
Touma-Sliman, Aida 151–2
tourism, in Jordan 59, 90, 95
tradition:
    in immigrant communities 157,
        214
    in Iraq 119–20, 123, 128
    in Jordan 5, 10, 13–16, 36, 58,
        64–7
    in Pakistan 108–9, 111
Turkey:
    honour crimes in 104, 144–7,
        217, 219
    Penal Code 145–6
Turkish Islamic Cultural Federation
    (TICF) 196

Uganda, honour crimes in 104
UK:
    and crimes of passion xiii,
        181–2
    and forced marriages 176–7
    and government action 176–82
    and honour crimes xii, xiv, 59,
        104, 157–82
    Kurdish immigrants 145
Um Kalthoum 135
Um Mohammad 45–7, 49–50
UN Assistance Mission for Iraq
    (UNAMI) 122–3, 127
UN Commission on Human Rights
    104, 108, 183–4
UN Development Fund for Women
    (UNIFEM) 40, 207
UN Special Report on Violence
    against Women 124

United Nations:
  and number of honour killings
    xi, 102
  Resolution 57/179 103
Universal Declaration of Human
    Rights x, 140
USA:
  and campaign against honour
    killings 53, 73, 78
  honour crimes in xii, xiii–xiv,
    104, 156, 203–13
  Violence Policy Center 207–8
USA Today 90, 93
Usman, Zilla Huma 114

Van Gogh, Theo 195
veil 114, 166
violence against women:
  in Afghanistan 114–16
  in Iran 131–4
  in Iraq 117–24
  in Jordan ix–x, 40–1, 81–3, 86–7
  in Lebanon 140
  mobile-phone related 123
  in Pakistan 105–6, 110, 112–13
  in Syria 134–6
  in UK 158
  as worldwide issue 102–4
  in Yemen 136–7
Violence against Women network
    184
virginity:
  in China 217–18
  and honour 83–5, 143–4, 148–9,
    185
  loss seen as crime 10–13
  tests 83–5, 126

Wakim, Joseph 99
Wardam, Batir 56

Whittaker, Paul 97
Winkler, Theodor 102–3
witnesses, intimidation 166
women:
  acceptance of honour crimes
    46–8
  in Afghan Parliament 115
  blamed for adultery 41, 51, 52, 58
  committing honour crimes 48–9,
    138
  and divorce 77–9, 82
  and genital mutilation 117, 215
  in Jordanian Parliament 52, 74,
    79
  as property x, 101–2, 174, 208–9
  in protective custody 27–30, 221
  and suicide 125–6
  see also discrimination, gender;
    virginity

Yasmin (victim) 10–15
Yazidism, in Iraq 117–21
Yemen, honour crimes in 104,
    136–7
Yildiz, Ahmet (victim) 146–7
Yones, Abdullah (killer) 158–61
Yones, Heshu (victim) 158–60, 184,
  • 221

Zaki, Akram 109
Zaki, Zakia (victim) 114–15
Zamzeh, Zeid 56
Zarife (victim) 195
Zehri, Israrullah 109, 111
Zia, Mussuut 174
Zia ul-Haq, Mohammad 111
Zima, Suzanne 151
Zuby, Ghaleb 79
Zuhd, Abdul Latif 41
Zuhur, Sherifa 137